OUT IN L.A.

OUT IN L.A.

THE RED HOT CHILI PEPPERS 1983

HAMISH DUNCAN

Published by Chicago Review Press Incorporated
814 North Franklin Street
Chicago, Illinois 60610
ISBN 978-1-64160-801-5

Library of Congress Control Number: 2022945609

Interior design: Nord Compo

Printed in the United States of America
5 4 3 2 1

In memory of

Hillel Slovak
1962–1988

Jack Sherman
1956–2020

For Rosa
the light I see the world by

"The facts and figures aren't important to me,
the colors and the shapes that make up my world are;
they are who I am, right or wrong."

—Flea, *Acid for the Children*, 2019

CONTENTS

PROLOGUE

AUGUST 23, 2003

Slane Castle, County Meath, Ireland

WE FADE IN from darkness. At first, all that's visible are the bare branches of a tree, but this tree soon begins to overhang tens of thousands of people, their breath bated, their bellies full of hard cider, their legs sore and the backs of their necks red after hours of waiting in the Irish sun. Music has been playing, but it's just the preshow selection, quietly blasted out over wildly powerful speakers that reach all corners of the packed field. Anticipation is in the air, so thick you can sense it through the screen.

Something changes somewhere. It's not that the lights go down; there is no descent into darkness that usually accompanies moments like these. We're outside; it's only dusk, and in this late Irish summer, the sky won't go black for at least another hour. But the audience realizes the moment is here. As one, they *scream*.

The camera glides across the front row of a crowd that is packed with young faces, a crush of people who have stood at the hard metal barricade all day. They're a mess of body parts, arms sticking up from nowhere, anxious clapping, sweaty heads. Most of them are wearing shirts with band logos on them; most of them are for the band they're here to see.

Onstage, and out from behind a stack of car-sized Marshall amplifiers, come guitarist John Frusciante and bassist Flea, grins on their faces. Frusciante, long-haired and skittish, has his 1962 sunburst Fender Stratocaster slung over his shoulder, and he mutters something to himself as he sees the crowd properly for the first time.

It looks like "holy fuck."

Shocked or not, he starts to play a piece in the key of D—an improvised melodic wail, emotional and comforting at the same time. An introduction to something bigger. Flea—dressed in a skeleton suit as a nod to bass hero John Entwistle—joins in, playing bass his own way, not just sticking to root notes but crafting an individual melodic piece. Soon their drummer, Chad Smith, sitting on the riser behind them, picks up the beat and guides them to a finely tuned crescendo as the lights sparkle all around. It's something they've done thousands of times before, but in different permutations, each composition made up on the fly and unique to the performance. These are world-class musicians. When they're done—the moment decided upon seemingly via telepathy—their singer Anthony Kiedis bounds onstage to a further rapturous cheer, and like that, they've begun.

On August 23, 2003, the annual Slane Concert was headlined by the Los Angeles–based rock band the Red Hot Chili Peppers. Held on the grounds of Slane Castle, an eighteenth-century manor in County Meath, Ireland, the day also featured performances from rock legends PJ Harvey, Queens of the Stone Age, and Foo Fighters.

The show was an enormous affair. Eighty-five thousand adoring fans lay sprawled and screaming across the expansive castle grounds, with a fireworks display capping off the long day of music and festivities. It was a special day when all had gone right. A professional film crew captured the ninety-minute-long performance by the headliners, and it was released soon after as a bestselling DVD, whose audience has only grown thanks to online streaming.*

In August 2003, the Red Hot Chili Peppers were on top of the world. Arguably, they were the biggest band in the world at the time. Their latest album, 2002's dream-pop inspired *By the Way*, was already well on its way to selling an eventual nine million copies worldwide, and the songs performed during the Slane Castle show included many of their beloved worldwide hits, like "Can't Stop," "Scar Tissue," and "Under the Bridge." That month, the band were in the middle of an enormously successful world tour that took them to virtually every continent. In the years to come, they would release a Greatest Hits collection that rarely left the charts, and three more blockbuster albums. In 2012 they undertook a victory lap induction into the Rock and Roll Hall of Fame, all the while constantly writing new music and flexing their creative muscles.

Way up in the top rungs of the music industry, the Chili Peppers could have quit at any point over the last two decades and still remained an all-time legendary act. They are big enough that they can disappear for half a decade—which has happened on several occasions—and still make the news upon their reemergence. They can headline any festival the world over, whenever they wish. They are big enough that their sound is easily reproduced and satirized, yet never bettered. Each individual member is a celebrity in his own right, especially the two founding members, singer Anthony Kiedis and bass player Michael "Flea" Balzary. Longtime guitarist John Frusciante is frequently labeled one of the best guitarists of his generation, if not of all time, and Flea and Chad Smith have received similar accolades. Anthony Kiedis, while perhaps no virtuoso, is irreplaceable to the band, and has perhaps grown the most in his role out of any of them.

* The most viewed version of the concert on YouTube has, at writing, approximately eighteen million views.

One may wonder where these four individuals came from. How they got to that stage in Ireland on that late summer's day in 2003. What journey had they been on, and what odds had they beaten to get there? Like all great groups, they were shaped and molded by their own histories; nothing great ever emerged from a vacuum, and the Red Hot Chili Peppers are no exception.

Does one look to John Frusciante's triumphant return in 1998, and the band's subsequent world domination with the release of *Californication* the next year? Or maybe the pivotal moment was earlier, when Frusciante first joined the band a decade previous, replacing original guitarist Hillel Slovak after his tragic heroin overdose, setting them on an entirely different course? Is it one of the many times—1992, 2009—when they've been left without a key member, and yet decided to move forward as a band anyway?

What explains their longevity, their uniqueness, and their unbreakable spirit?

To answer that question, one certainly won't go amiss looking as far back as possible to compare the Red Hot Chili Peppers of 2003 with their original incarnation in 1983. Twenty years is a long time. It is longer than most bands are together, after all.

In August 2003 the band were superstar behemoths, an autonomous industry with hundreds of employees and a fleet of trucks, playing on this particular day to so many people that, for safety reasons, the band had to helicopter into the show.

In August 1983 the very-different looking and sounding quartet was only about eight months old. They had, if one is being generous, ten songs in their repertoire. And of those ten, two were over in under a minute, one was a quick-fire Jimi Hendrix cover, and three were simple campfire-style a capella jokes.

They were almost a joke themselves. The early Red Hot Chili Peppers didn't take themselves seriously, and neither did the crowds they played to. It was not a career yet. Most of the members played in different, more serious bands: bands that had real potential, bands that had been built from the ground up and amassed actual fan bases outside their own circle of friends. This new thing was just a side project, something that had taken them three live performances to even think of a real name for.

But by the end of 1983, things were in motion in a way that nobody, especially the band, ever expected. Maybe they weren't such a joke after all; maybe there was something *real* happening there. They had developed their act onstage, playing live approximately thirty times, and had worked out most of the kinks in their live show. They had recorded a blistering demo, a perfect representation of their repertoire as it stood at that moment, with an energy and economy that they would spend the rest of their careers trying to re-create.

They had also suffered the first setbacks of their careers, the first in a long line of setbacks that would have destroyed any other band. They had lost their guitarist and drummer—key members and close, childhood friends—who wrote music and partied and bled and loved and danced with those that had remained.

They would lose a guitarist nine more times in the next three decades, and a few drummers on top of that for good measure. This first parting was merely a warm-up. The decision to continue the band at the end of 1983 by Anthony Kiedis and Flea was a decision made many times again.

As their stage time at Slane Castle finishes, and the band (half of them shirtless, all of them sweaty and exhilarated) wave to their adoring crowd, the Red Hot Chili Peppers head backstage to catch their breath and prepare for their next move. More stops on the traveling behemoth beckon: one more show in Scotland, and then another leg of an endless US arena tour. A far cry from the miniscule world they inhabited in their formative year, in which all but one show was performed in their beloved native state of California.

Everything that made the Red Hot Chili Peppers the superstars of modern rock that they are today was only able to happen because of the events of 1983. Each step made in that chaotic year planted the seeds for the rest of their illustrious career. There were moments of chance, moments of chaos, moments of lunacy. But there were common threads: a love of music—more specifically, a love of a certain kind of music—and a love for each other, whether it was all four band members or just the core two, Flea and Anthony. This band could have broken up countless times since they came together; because of 1983, they never have. Without 1983, there's no Slane Castle, no story beforehand, and no story afterward.

What follows is the story of how the young men who became the Red Hot Chili Peppers met, how they formed their band at the tail end of 1982, and how they decided to turn a one-off show into much more than that. It is the story of *where* they played, *what* they played, and *who* they played with. This is also a story about the punk scene in Los Angeles in the early 1980s. Unique, vibrant, and as wholesome as it was seedy, these often sparsely populated shows took place in wildly different venues across the city. Converted restaurants, country-and-western bars, and strip clubs all feature.

Most important, it is the story of Anthony, Michael, Hillel, and Jack, four kids who got lucky and tapped into something unexpected that to this day still endures.

BEFORE THE BEGINNING: 1982

MICHAEL BALZARY WAS nineteen years old and technically homeless when he moved into the Contemporary Artists Space of Hollywood (CASH) at the end of 1981. Run by Janet Cunningham and located at 1953 Cahuenga Boulevard, CASH opened in June of that year and was immediately home to a variety of punks and street kids, including Laurence Fishburne, star of the recently released Francis Ford Coppola film *Apocalypse Now*.

CASH was Cunningham's ploy to get grant money from the federal government. Having already been involved in similar spaces in her native New Orleans, she decided to incorporate her own after moving to Los Angeles: "Get grant money, open up a performance space, put on shows, theatre, live music, readings." A calendar from the period shows a typical week of performances on Monday, video and film screenings on Tuesday and Wednesday, and new music nights on Thursday.

An extremely informal enterprise, over time CASH evolved from a gallery and artists space into a crash pad for a few locals. Frequently, those that hung out there were invited to stay the night, as long as they helped out. Though he never lived there, Fishburne would provide free security for shows, and Balzary's ongoing residence was dependent on his sweeping skills. Early ads for the space listed the opening times as "9 p.m. until whenever people decide to leave. Bring your own refreshments."

Cunningham, "a no-nonsense woman who took shit from no one," also kept her scrappy guests fed with generous meals of New Orleans–style beans and rice while they slept off hangovers, created art, and formed countless bands; some one-off, others a little more serious.

Michael Balzary wasn't yet the internationally famous rock bassist better known as Flea. Born in Melbourne on October 16, 1962, his customs officer father moved the family to New York from Australia when Michael was seven. His parents broke up shortly afterward, and his father, Michael Sr., moved back home on his own permanently, not wishing to disrupt his children's education. His mother, Patricia, subsequently moved the family into the home of jazz double bassist Walter Urban Jr., a teacher at the Manhattan School of Music, where she was learning guitar. They soon married.

The Balzary family was uprooted again to Los Angeles, arriving in the city on November 14, 1972, and ten-year-old Michael was soon torn from a pleasant but dull suburbia and quickly surrounded by music, violence, and illegal drugs on the West Coast. Despite the hardships, an important connection to music, specifically jazz, was sparked during this time. Walter Urban would hold jam sessions at home with local musicians, and Michael would watch, mesmerized at what he was seeing: "These guys would pick up these things and start blowing and sucking and hitting and plucking, and it made me so happy I'd roll around on the floor laughing."

But his stepfather and his friends were rarely employed and often in trouble with the police, causing family friction and driving Michael to start roaming the streets in order to escape the trouble at home. Eventually, he developed drinking and marijuana habits. "These guys couldn't really catch a break," he remembered years later. "They had shitty jobs. My stepdad would fix cars in a backyard. He was a great bass player, man. God bless him, it was very difficult." When Walter Urban *was* working, it was with greats such as Dizzy Gillespie, Roy Gaines, and Joe Greene, but those gigs were few and far between.

Unsurprisingly, Michael also picked up a musical instrument. Urban played double bass, but his son-in-law strayed slightly and started playing the trumpet at eleven. A scholarship student, Michael was soon highly proficient, even playing with the Jr. Philharmonic Orchestra and the Los Angeles City College Jazz Band for a spell, in addition to his school marching band, choir, and orchestra.* But by the time he had moved into the CASH club in 1981, he was, more or less, a full-time electric bass player, and in a rock band, to boot.

The band Michael played in formed at Fairfax High School, on Melrose Avenue, on the border of West Hollywood. They first played as a three-piece, without a bass player, under the name Raven, which was changed to Chain Reaction, and again to Anthem. Once they discovered that another band from the San Fernando Valley already had that name, they switched up the spelling and started calling themselves Anthym. By mid-1981† they had moved on again to something more arty, and more permanent, and by the autumn of that year the foursome were playing local clubs and developing the beginnings of a following under the name What Is This.‡

---

* A 1973 photoshoot shows a young Michael, with a curly afro and freckled cheeks, playing in master trumpet maker Dominick Calicchio's studio.

† The latest available concert listing for an Anthym show is June 21, 1981; the earliest listing for a What Is This show is August 16, meaning the band must have changed their name at some point over the summer of 1981. They supported local legends Oingo Boingo on July 24 of that year, but what name they went under at that show is unknown.

‡ No question mark. The name might be phrased like a question, but it's presented as a blunt assertion.

Michael was drafted into the band (back when they were still known as Anthym) by his school friend Hillel Slovak toward the end of 1979, as a replacement for their original bass player, Todd Strassman, who joined around the time they changed their name to Anthem. Hillel and the band's vocalist Alain Johannes saw potential in their friend, who by then was only a trumpet player, but who had grown up with a double bass-playing stepfather. "We needed a bass player," Johannes recalled, "and we thought it would be really good to take somebody who didn't play and mould them to our own style."

In later years Alain Johannes mentioned that Strassman left amicably to focus on his plans to go to law school. But in 1994 the incoming bassist remembered the situation a little differently: "Hillel said, 'Our bass player's a jerk, why don't you learn to play bass?'"*

He recalled the moment he was asked in a televised conversation with longtime producer Rick Rubin in 2019:

> He [Slovak] said to me, "Why don't you join our rock band, and we'll get rid of the bass player we have 'cause he's not willing to give his life to it." And that was, you know, and I'll never forget that moment. Like sitting in his car, pulled over to the side of the road, it was raining outside. And the DJ, Kim Ladd on KMET, was playing "Riders on the Storm,"† and it was raining. I don't know if I ever felt that loved in my life, ever. Like in that moment, you know what I mean, join our band?

A few months after picking up a bass guitar for the first time, Michael and Anthym were performing live at the legendary club

* Strassman is now a lawyer in Los Angeles.

† A 1971 song by the Doors.

Gazzarri's in a Battle of the Bands competition. Soon afterward, the new member involved himself deeper by becoming the band's booking agent. Anthym came in second at the competition at Gazarri's, but only because the winning band carted a busload of their friends in to cheer for them. Michael didn't drop the horn entirely; he still played it from time to time, including onstage with his new rock band, but the bass became his musical focus going forward.

Hillel Slovak was born in Haifa, a coastal town in northern Israel, on April 13, 1962. His parents were Holocaust survivors, and the family, which by then included a younger brother James, moved (like the Balzary family) first to New York and then to Los Angeles in 1967. Hillel received his first guitar as a Bar Mitzvah present from his uncle Aron and went to music lessons on Fairfax Avenue with his schoolmate Jack Irons, a Los Angeles native, also of Jewish heritage.*

As a child, Jack had seen a drum set in the window of a music store and had known immediately that drums were his future, once he was able to convince his father to buy him a set. "He didn't think I

The poodle-haired boys of Anthym. Alain, Michael, Hillel, and Jack just before a show at the Troubadour, their biggest show yet. Circa 1980.

* As they had started their lessons at exactly the same time and were good friends beforehand, Jack Irons and Hillel Slovak had the longest and perhaps strongest relationship out of all of the members of the Red Hot Chili Peppers when they came together.

was ready to take it on seriously," he remembered. The drums would come with his thirteenth birthday, but in the meantime, bashing away on pots and pans with cutlery would do the trick. Around the same time, Jack and Hillel started a KISS cover band,* miming to album cuts in front of their homeroom classmates at Halloween in Junior High, one of whom was their future bandmate.

The lead vocalist and rhythm guitarist in What Is This was Alain Johannes Mociulski. He was born in Santiago, Chile, on May 2, 1962, but had moved to Los Angeles (by way of Switzerland and Mexico) with his parents as a twelve-year-old. After watching Hillel and Jack mime KISS tracks on that day in homeroom, Alain, for reasons still unclear to him many years later—"I was very shy, I spoke very little English"—decided to test the structural integrity of Jack's flimsy homemade codpiece, which was actually just a tennis ball cut in half and spray-painted silver. He quickly discovered it had very little. After a frenzied apology, the trio began to jam, and Raven was formed, with the band rehearsing in a variety of bedrooms and garages across Los Angeles. Alain (whose father was a musician, and whose uncle, Peter Rock, was a star back in Chile) had been playing the guitar since he was four years old, and so was the most experienced musician in the group as well as its de facto leader.†

What Is This comprised these four members, but their circle of school friends was extensive; some of these friends were musicians, like Keith Barry, who played viola and whose father sold Michael his first bass, and Patrick English, who played trumpet. Some were not musicians, or at least not yet. One of these latter friends was Anthony Kiedis.

---

* Hillel was guitarist Paul Stanley, but Jack was the bass-playing Gene Simmons; his choice of KISS member didn't line up with the instrument he wound up playing.

† That there was so much musicality in the hallways of Fairfax High was no surprise; by the late 1970s, Fairfax alumni already included Warren Zevon, legendary producer Phil Spector, Tin Pan Alley legend Jerry Leiber, and jazz trumpeter Herb Alpert. Likewise, Robert Wolin, the guitar teacher who provided lessons to Alain and Hillel, also tutored Guns N' Roses lead guitarist Slash.

Anthony was born in Grand Rapids, Michigan, on November 1, 1962. As a child, his family moved to Los Angeles to follow his father, John Kiedis, in his dreams of becoming an actor. But fame did not come as quickly as all had hoped, and the family fell apart soon after; Anthony moved back to Michigan with his newly single mother, while his father stayed in Los Angeles. In the intervening years, John Kiedis graduated with honors from UCLA and studied at the Lee Strasberg Institute, known for its method acting techniques. He played bit parts in *Starsky & Hutch* and *Charlie's Angels* in the late seventies, but most of his income in these early days came from publicity work and drug dealing.

John was a mythical figure to Anthony. Aside from the odd visit during summer holidays or an impromptu visit east to run drugs, Anthony would only ever hear from his father through letters and care packages that showed a vastly different life to the one he was living in the snowy, freezing, boring Midwest. But in 1974 they reconnected, as the younger Kiedis got his wish and finally moved back to California, and right into a life of movie auditions, close proximity with rock legends, and free and easy drug use. Eventually the elder Kiedis rebranded himself as Blackie Dammett, a stage name inspired in part by pulp crime author Dashiel Hammett.

Michael and Anthony met when they were both fifteen years old. At first, Anthony had tried to attend University High upon his graduation from Emerson Junior High but had been prevented by the school from enrolling once the administration discovered that he had been lying about his address.* He was sent to Fairfax High, seven miles to the east, instead.

This was a disappointing shock at first, but it changed his life in many ways. About a month into the school year, Anthony was confronted with the image of his friend Tony Shurr being held in

* The false address belonged to entertainer Sonny Bono, a family friend.

a headlock by a runty kid with a puffy afro and a gap tooth; to add further insult to injury, this suddenly present bully was in the process of administering a noogie. Pulling the kid off Shurr, Anthony came face to face with Michael Balzary for the first time and threatened him with violence if he ever lay another hand on Tony. The altercation was quickly defused, but later that day the two were sat next to each other in driver's education class. Their teacher had a pet peeve about students writing on school property; when Anthony left his seat, Michael wrote "Anthony Kiedis Was Here" on his vacant desk, which Anthony could only find funny upon his return.* The next day, they sat together in the gym bleachers as rain interrupted a physical education lesson, starting a conversation that, as Michael said, "continues forty-odd years later."

"Even though we were starting off on this 'I'll kick your ass aggressiveness,'" Anthony remembered, "I felt an instant connection to the remarkable little weirdo." They were quickly inseparable, even if they were polar opposites in many ways. This was perhaps a result of Anthony's admitted attempts to befriend "all the loneliest and most unwanted kids in school."

More consequential friendships were to be made. One day shortly after meeting Michael, Anthony watched a strange band full of poodle-haired boys called Anthym perform during a lunch break in the Fairfax High quad and took one of the band's pins that were being passed around. He happened to be wearing this pin shortly afterward when he ran into Hillel Slovak, who invited him over for a snack after school. They bonded over egg salad sandwiches and immediately became close friends as well. Anthony, Michael, and Hillel became their own little group inside the larger friendship circle that blossomed after they graduated from Fairfax in July of 1980.† More into outrageous

* This event was also immortalized, like many adventures in their early years, in the spoken-word intro lyrics to "Deep Kick," off the band's 1995 album *One Hot Minute*.

† Decades later, Anthony paid tribute to these early years with Hillel in a stream of consciousness–style verse on the Red Hot Chili Peppers track "Open/Close."

antics and illicit substances than, say, Alain Johannes or Jack Irons were, the three of them were Los Faces, a joke gang in which they all had their own Cheech & Chong–inspired Mexican alter egos. Michael was "Poco," Hillel was "Paco" or "Slim" or the "Israeli Cowboy," and Anthony was "Swan" or "Fuerte."*

Anthony was a natural showman who had already taken acting classes, was in the Theatre Club at Fairfax, and won several parts in commercials and Hollywood films as a child under the stage name of Cole Dammett, inspired by his father. The most prominent of these early roles was opposite Sylvester Stallone in 1978's *F.I.S.T.*, a crime drama directed by Norman Jewison. Cole Dammett, playing Stallone's son, only has one line, but it was a line that millions saw.

Capitalizing on this element of his personality and perhaps craving time in the spotlight, Anthony began to open for Anthym (and later What Is This) as emcee, around the time Michael joined the band.† Just before the band played, Anthony would bound onstage and rip off some of his father's moves: he'd tell jokes, scat mostly nonsense rhymes, and warm up the crowd (who were often there to see someone else). Anthony's material would fluctuate naturally, but there was one frequent passage that he returned to when the time came to introduce the band: "Cal Worthington calls them the hottest rockers in Los Angeles. Their parents call them crazy, and the girls call them all the time. But I call them like I see them, and I call them . . . Anthym!"

After his minute-long set was finished, he would join the crowd and jump around as wildly as possible, influencing the crowd now from within. That he ever considered himself a full-time member of Anthym or What Is This is unlikely, but in the future, homework-avoiding

* In his handwritten liner notes for the band's 1994 odds-and-ends compilation *Out in L.A.*, Flea also listed the following names: Fire Man, Earth Man, Wind Man, Clem Phlegm, and Huey Spitoon. Anyone's guess as to which name belongs to whom, though some educated guesses can be made.

† Anthony also roadied for the band occasionally but was not known for his reliability.

journalists would frequently give him membership, though sometimes only as a "ringleader and agent provocateur."

Anthony was perhaps the least musical of his friends, but he did still have experience being in a band. In 1980 he, Michael, and their friends Dondi Bastone and Patrick English were in a "jam band" named Spigot Blister and the Chest Pimps. They were a short-lived affair, and Anthony may have been merely screaming into a mic while the other three wailed on their instruments behind him, but this combination of unashamed stage presence and experience with a microphone would prove useful in the near future.*

Like Michael, by 1982, Anthony was also in a state of semi-homelessness. He had been living with his friend Bill Stobaugh, a filmmaker and musician, but that arrangement had ended when Stobaugh accused his boarder of stealing his prized collection of guitars.† Before that, he and Michael lived with a third friend, John Karson, in a house near the Formosa Cafe off Santa Monica Boulevard. But the pair were evicted after a particularly raucous party that was so bad that the less adventurous Karson snitched to their landlord and had them kicked out, leading Michael to move into CASH.

Anthony, like Michael, was also no stranger to drugs. Always a free spirit and living out the effects of his fairly undisciplined childhood,

---

* In the Chili Peppers' photo book *Fandemonium*, Anthony calls the band "Chest Pumps," but in *Scar Tissue* he refers to them as "Chest Pimps." As they were (according to Anthony) named after Michael's acne problem, one would assume that "Pimps" is the correct name. Further, in *Fandemonium*, Anthony doesn't mention Michael being in the band; in *Scar Tissue*, the band is *named* after Michael, so it's fair to assume he was a member. He also says that Dondi Bastone played bass in one telling, and guitar in another: bass is unlikely if Michael was around, but perhaps the point was that everyone switched instruments. Dondi Bastone and Patrick English had been in the school orchestra with Michael at Bancroft Junior High.

† Stobaugh, who would play guitar with Thelonious Monster for a time, ended up directing the music videos for the Red Hot Chili Peppers tracks "Higher Ground" and "Show Me Your Soul," so he and Anthony evidently patched things up a few years down the line. He also directed Flea in the music video for "Who Was in My Room Last Night?" by Butthole Surfers. Stobaugh passed away in 1996.

by 1982 he was off the rails and likely addicted to cocaine, dropping out of a political science degree at UCLA and barely sustaining himself as a driver for Mid-Ocean Motion Pictures, a Los Angeles–based computer animation company.* From time to time he would crash in the Mid-Ocean offices overnight, sleeping in a storage loft, but also stayed with Hillel's family, Keith Barry, and at the CASH club.

Unsurprisingly for teenagers growing up in California in the 1970s, the main entry point for their recreational drug use was cannabis. Thanks to his father, Anthony had his first joint at twelve, and Michael had his at roughly the same age, although in his case at the introduction of his sister Karyn. Throughout their teens and their early twenties, the pair experimented with different substances, often moving into dangerous intravenous territory.

Michael and Anthony lay at the opposite ends of a spectrum in a number of ways, and their relationship with drugs is one example of this division between the two. In his autobiography, Michael noted the difference between himself and his closest friend. "I liked to smoke weed," he wrote. "But when I started to hang with Anthony, it was a different vibe. We had to get it every day, it was a mission to make it happen the second we walked off campus. The inner engine that drove him to get high was relentless." At the risk of oversimplifying, this early insight might help explain the differences between the two men further down the line; Anthony Kiedis would struggle with addiction until he was almost forty, while Flea quit all hard drugs in the early 1990s. "I didn't have that hard-core addict gene."

It was during these first few years of the eighties that heroin entered their lives in a serious way. Some took to it more intensely

* Anthony mentions in his autobiography that Mid-Ocean did "all the animation for *Blade Runner*," though none of the credits in the film correspond with that claim. He appears to have worked for a time at Entertainment Effects Group, run by Douglas Trumbull out of a warehouse in Marina del Ray. EEG did, in fact, do all of the special photographic effects for *Blade Runner*.

than others. Michael steered relatively clear, only dabbling in it occasionally, but Anthony and Hillel became consistent users of the drug, beginning the addictions that would haunt them in the years to come. They'd had experience shooting cocaine intravenously, and it wasn't a large shift to the more serious of the two narcotics. Anthony, in particular, had first experimented with heroin as early as fourteen, also thanks to his father, albeit without the use of a needle at this early stage.

In the meantime, CASH was burning too brightly, and was frequently targeted by the Los Angeles Police Department. In early 1981 the space was raided after a noise complaint, and Janet Cunningham was arrested for "disturbing the peace," a strange charge considering all the raiding police found was a beat poet accompanied by a bongo player. Nevertheless, she was forced to implement an acoustic-only policy for the live acts that played at the venue. But after one too many visits and some rent payment issues, the club was shut down in mid-1982, and the folks that were staying there were forced to leave.*

Scrounging together some money, Michael moved to an apartment at 1857 North Wilton Place in Hollywood with his friend, French-Caribbean percussionist Joel Virgel-Vierset, whom he had met at CASH and with whom he intended to start a band. When the pair needed a third tenant to offset rent and to help pay for the installation of a phone line, they asked photographer and artist Fabrice Drouet. Drouet was also French; he had met Virgel-Vierset in Paris and followed him to Los Angeles, and what started as a one-month tourist trip turned into nearly ten years.

For a short while, Drouet had been living with Gary Allen, an Arkansas native whose band, Neighbor's Voices (which included Joel

* There is evidence that the club was open in May 1982, but no later. Janet Cunningham passed away in 2017. Her connection to the men who became the Red Hot Chili Peppers is nothing compared to the countless connections she forged with many, many other people in those early years in the 1980s.

Where it all started. In late 1982 Flea moved into an apartment in this building at 1857 North Wilton Place, Hollywood, with two French friends, Fabrice Drouet and Joel Virgel-Vierset. A few months later, a new band held their first a capella rehearsal in the living room. *Gary Allen*

Virgel-Vierset, among others), had recently broken up. Allen, whom Hillel Slovak once called "a great human being," was also a man of many talents: a former dancer on *Soul Train*, a personal chef (to Elton John, no less), and a fashion designer who would wind up working closely with Billy Idol in the years afterward. Michael, Anthony, Jack, and Hillel had first seen Neighbor's Voices, and subsequently met Gary Allen and Joel Virgel-Vierset, at a club called Brave Dog in downtown Los Angeles. Held on weekend nights in an empty storefront at 418 East 1st Street, the club used a clever postcard system to keep the parties underground, invitation-only, and private—for about eighteen months, until the Los Angeles Police Department caught wind of it and shut them down.

Anthym played the club at least once, on June 21, 1981; Neighbor's Voices played the following weekend. The clubs were more than a space to drink and dance, they were *events*, whose "festivities," Michael remembered, "bled out into the parking lot and alley behind, where on those hot summer nights the unexpected always happened." During this period, Michael was working at Miller Animal Hospital on Melrose Avenue. Dr. Miller himself was an "amazing man, a cloud of gray hair and a bulbous face of spirals." It was a gig that gave the swindling Michael occasional access to protected, potentially hallucinatory medicines, but which also had its downsides, as he was subjected to countless scarring dog and cat autopsies.*

The apartment on North Wilton Place, just a block away from both the bustle of Hollywood Boulevard and the winding quiet mazes of the Hollywood Dell, was quickly dubbed by its new tenants the "Wilton Hilton." The building was home to many a musician and artist, and even an elderly landlady who eventually committed suicide by leaping off the roof many years later. Memories from these

---

* In a blog post from 2003 for the Red Hot Chili Peppers website, Flea wrote about ripping the hospital off to buy drugs, but also made note of his efforts to make up for these transgressions years later, once he was in a better place financially.

days are hazy, but all involved recall extensive partying, and little in the way of serious thinking about the future. Hillel, too, would become a tenant; he had lived with his mother and younger brother nearby but moved into the building to be closer to his friends and bandmates, and would be there the rest of the year as What Is This, with new manager Kevin Staton on board, continued to gig around Los Angeles.*

Initially, the members of What Is This were inspired by classic rock staples like Led Zeppelin, Jimi Hendrix, and KISS, and their early live performances in the latter half of the 1970s (when they were still known as Chain Reaction) heavily featured covers of acts from that era. One centerpiece was Queen's "Ogre Battle," off their sophomore album, *Queen II*. But like any band looking to really make it, they eventually started to write their own material, and during that period the band were influenced more by progressive rock acts such as Rush and King Crimson. Not many recollections of the band's repertoire as they morphed into Anthym remain, aside from a select few: "The Answer," "One Way Woman" with Hillel on vocals,† and "White Knight Part I and II," which featured dueling guitar solos. Another heavily prog-inspired song that featured Hillel and Alain battling each other was "Paradox," a slow and sluggish epic that combined the low-end doom of Black Sabbath with the frenetic changes of Rush. The band recorded a demo of this song in 1979 and most likely recorded their entire repertoire in the same sessions.‡

* In the liner notes to the band's 1994 compilation *Out in L.A.*, Flea writes that Anthony lived at the Wilton Hilton. Anthony only mentions *staying* there frequently in *Scar Tissue*. Whether he was a permanent tenant there is unknown, but it's safe to say he was a fairly constant presence in the apartment.

† A snippet of which was sung by Flea in a 2019 interview with Malcolm Gladwell: "Hey there, baby, have you heard the news?"

‡ After surfacing in 2021, this 8-track recording now has the honor of being the earliest available recording associated with the Red Hot Chili Peppers. Another in-studio recording of the Anthym song "Clocks" is also known to exist, and was even played on local station KWEST's regular demo night.

Growing up in the 1960s, it's a given that the boys grew up listening to classic rock staples, and the broad variety of Los Angeles radio stations would have provided them with a steady diet of everything and anything under the sun. "I loved the radio back then," Jack remembered as an adult. "There was a lot of Motown and great R&B." Anthony also wrote of listening to the radio with his father after moving to Los Angeles in 1974 and proclaiming that he would one day be a singer. While Michael began his musical life focused heavily on jazz, once his mind was opened to the world of popular music, there was ample opportunity for him to catch up. His favorite radio station was KJLH, owned by Stevie Wonder, and there were many willing friends ready to offer other suggestions.

As they left high school at the beginning of a new decade, Anthym started to lean toward more experimental sounds, digging deeper into progressive rock but also into new wave. Hillel and Alain Johannes went to every L.A. show of a King Crimson tour in November 1981, studying Robert Fripp's guitar theatrics with specific intent. It was a far cry from their KISS dress-ups, or their stalking of the hotel that Gene Simmons and company were staying at only a few years previous. But in essence, they simply replaced one outfit with another: "We cut our hair and started wearing suits," Alain recalled, but it was still a band heavily inspired by another act.

It was not just progressive rock that caught their ears: Michael would write that after hearing the English postpunk outfit Gang of Four for the first time in 1979, "I knew at that moment what I wanted my music to sound like. . . . It completely changed the way I looked at rock music." The sounds of Gang of Four feature heavily in a recording of an Anthym show at Flipper's Roller Boogie Palace from that same year.* The band may be playing at a roller-skating rink in Santa

* The undated recording, which leaked to the internet sometime in the mid 2010s, runs approximately forty minutes long; probably the entire Anthym repertoire at that point. The exact date the band performed can't be pinpointed.

Monica, but the sound is mostly Leeds; angular, choppy guitars from Hillel and Alain (with matching false accent from the lead singer to boot) and complex, bouncing basslines from Michael.* That said, some of the band's earlier material, like the prog rock–inspired "Paradox," still survived, even if it had started to seem out of place in the band's repertoire.

But while they may have expanded their interests, some artists were perennial. In an interview held in Miami Beach in December 1987, Hillel said his two favorite guitarists were Andy Gill, of Gang of Four, and Jimi Hendrix. Where even KISS had eventually gone by the wayside, Hendrix was the permanent fixture.

What Is This got off to a slow start in 1982, and their attempts so far at procuring a recording contract had been mostly unsuccessful. They were a difficult band in many ways: Their name, for one, was an inside joke and descriptively arty, but may have turned off would-be fans and labels, who persistently and mistakenly turned the name into a question. They were also hard to pin down musically and didn't exactly fit to one genre. This is not necessarily a negative thing, of course, but selling the act could be tricky in a city full of bands that announced themselves in clearer ways and were simpler to market. It wasn't all bad: the band's name, perhaps by design, lent itself to clever ads. "An audience watching a modern group that mixes an eclectic brew of jazz, post-punk and funky rhythmic textures might ask What Is This" begins one concert listing in May 1983.

During 1982 What Is This only played a handful of gigs, with nine documented, though the true number is possibly double that. They played at the Hollywood club Cathay de Grande on April 7 and May 22, at the Chinatown venue (and favorite haunt of punks everywhere) Madame Wong's on September 24; there they opened for

* Sadly, no recordings have surfaced of What Is This from Michael's tenure with the band, though a photo from a 1981 concert is reproduced in his autobiography, *Acid for the Children*.

Burning Sensations, who are best known now for their 1984 appearance on the *Repo Man* soundtrack. Sadly, the band's repertoire from this period is unknown, and no recordings of their live act have surfaced, but it's unlikely that a set from 1982 resembled the performance recorded back in 1979 in any way.

It was during this slower period that Michael's musical tastes began to stray from those of his bandmates in What Is This. Throughout his time staying at CASH and beyond, he frequently played impromptu concerts and jammed with local musicians, most frequently with drummer Joel Virgel-Vierset, and quite often attempted to form more permanent projects, with varying success.

One player Michael spent considerable time with was Rick Cox, an experimental musician who played guitar, saxophone, and clarinet, among many other instruments. Cox was a noted improviser who had spent the turn of the decade in various bands with drummer Read Miller in New York City, recording for the ambient music label Cold Blue. The two returned to Los Angeles in early 1982 looking for their next move. "When I got back, I was just really hungry to meet other players," he remembers. Cox answered a personal ad for a musician in a Los Angeles newspaper that caught his eye, a young woman seeking other musicians and listing influences that interested him. When he showed up to the rehearsal hall, he met someone else who had answered the ad: Michael. "We just kind of hit it off. At the time I was playing alto saxophone and guitar, both, and we would just get together." This musical project, developed in apartments and loft spaces across Los Angeles, turned into something serious enough that it actually made its way to the stage a few times throughout 1982, at least once at the Anti Club, a concert venue run out of a rowdy tavern on Melrose Avenue. These performances were improvised and without a name, and so they would go by without much notice and left no public record. But they, along with the jam sessions at CASH, were an important step in Michael realizing that there was a musical world outside his immediate friendship circle.

Above all, the thing drawing Michael's attention away from What Is This was punk. Though for some it had already peaked and was on its way out, hardcore punk was relatively new on the L.A. scene, and was still remarkably active in clubs in Hollywood.

Punk music had exploded in the late 1970s, and by the early years of the next decade, Los Angeles was a hotbed for its own special brand of outrageous, often-violent, DIY punk shows. It was an uncomplicated genre on the surface, but exceedingly difficult to do *right.* More important, it was an emotional and physical outlet for Michael, who found the music freeing and welcoming. He was one of thousands in Hollywood, and one of millions across the world, who always considered himself an outcast.

"Punk rock changed my life," he recalled. "I was always the kid you called a fag in high school. Punk rock gave me a home." It was a physical sensation, this music, but more important, it also attacked the status quo; gone were the lofty pop gods, and the affected posturing, and the irritating clichés: "Punk deflated the whole bloated rock-star thing." It was a vehicle for a "vicious, animal energy."

It would be impossible to list every important band from the early period of punk. Many have an overinflated image today; many have been lost to time; many existed for a single show only. This was an era of hand-copied fliers for basement shows and enforced impermanence. But there are some that can be held up as important waypoints in the career of the Red Hot Chili Peppers.

Like the more rudimentary rock music from decades earlier, punk came in waves and generations. There are the early bands that made inroads and influenced the generation that followed, like the Sex Pistols and the Ramones, who were already established icons detached from their edgy, vanguard roots by the 1980s.* Then there are the second-

* The Ramones crossed paths with the Red Hot Chili Peppers many times. Beyond a notable shared stage in 1988, the Chili Peppers recorded a cover of "Havana Affair"

wave legends that have persisted, such as Black Flag, and their offshoot, the just-as-influential Circle Jerks. From Washington, DC, Bad Brains combined musical virtuosity with unbeatable speed. All three bands would cross paths with the Red Hot Chili Peppers before long.

By 1982 there were also bands that made their mark and then fell apart, because of personality implosions or the all-too-prevalent drug and alcohol problem. One such band that suffered from the latter was the Germs, whose singer, Darby Crash, overdosed on heroin and whose death was immediately overshadowed, as it occurred the day before John Lennon's murder. Michael tried to attend their last-ever show, on December 3, 1980, but couldn't gain entry into the packed club.

Anthony remembered a 1977 show with Devo and the Germs at the Hollywood Palladium as his first punk concert. While the two bands had diverging sounds, they were of the same wildly unique scene, and this show is a prime example of the kind of variety available to fans in one night. At first, he kept a distance from the proceedings: "I was standing at the back, just fascinated." But that show offered him a number of firsts. "There was this girl with some fucked-up punk-rock haircut, and she was taking giant safety pins and piercing her cheek with them, one after the other. That was new to me." He might not have immediately understood it, but after that show, he was undeniably hooked.

In interviews over the years, Michael would highlight two different performances that introduced him to the punk scene. The first was a Black Flag show at the Starwood in West Hollywood on November 18, 1980.* His initial impressions weren't entirely positive: "I just thought it was disgusting," he remembered. "People were getting the shit kicked out of them for having long hair." But the band's music was enthralling. Later, Anthony was careful to separate the good from

in 2001. John Frusciante became a dear friend of Johnny Ramone and was by his side when he passed away.

* A live recording of this show is available on YouTube.

the bad: "Whatever we thought about a small segment of Black Flag's audience was no reflection on how we felt about their sound and what they were doing as performers." Despite the initial concerns about the scene surrounding it, a love for the music took root quickly.

The other show that Michael held aloft was one he saw at Hollywood's Club Lingerie on May 8, 1982, by a band that were cheekily calling themselves the North Central Van Nuys Gay Young Men's String Quartet. In reality, their name was FEAR.*

Formed in 1977 and fronted by Lee Ving (born Lee Capallero), FEAR had risen to national attention after a chaotic turn on *Saturday Night Live* in 1981 that had culminated in a trashed set and "$20,000 in damages."† A key song of theirs, 1978's "I Love Livin' in the City," was an ironic love-hate ode to their hometown, highlighting and celebrating all the negative aspects of a modern, downtrodden Los Angeles life in true punk fashion.‡ While they were at it they contributed to the East-West "feud" then present in the punk scene, with "New York's Alright If You Like Saxophones." The inverse of "I Love Livin' in the City," "New York's Alright" was pure controversy fodder, and the one that seemed to get them in the most "trouble" with a pearl-clutching press.

Like many other bands on the scene, FEAR were no strangers to internal turmoil. Shortly after the May 1982 release of their debut album, *The Record*, they filmed a small role in *Get Crazy*, a musical comedy starring Malcolm McDowell and Lou Reed.** When filming ended in early September, founding bassist Fred "Derf Scratch" Milner was fired.

---

* At this show, to keep up appearances, the band did actually hire a string quartet to open for them.

† That figure was tossed around at the time as a joke; the real figure was, according to the June 13, 1982 edition of the *Los Angeles Times*, closer to $40.

‡ "My house smells just like a zoo / It's chock-full of shit and puke!"

** The film, incidentally, helped kickstart Janet Cunningham's career as an extras casting agent, giving her a role in the punk community after the closure of the CASH club.

The official reasons for the personnel change varied; years later, drummer Tim "Spit Stix" Leitch would state it was because Derf wasn't "pulling his weight" and was a few steps behind the rest of the band. But Derf himself would counter this, saying he had gotten on the wrong side of Lee Ving's hard-to-handle jealousy, and that he had witnessed the singer taking money from a promoter meant for the rest of the band.

After being fired, temporarily replaced by Dickies bassist Laurie "Lorenzo" Buhne, then called back and persuaded to play a tour that ended in late September, Derf left the band for good. Because they had studio time already booked, they were joined for a short time by Eric Feldman, roommate of drummer Spit Stix. Feldman played on "Fuck Christmas," their festive yuletide single, but wasn't able to continue in the band. Enter Michael Balzary.

It was no secret that Derf had left FEAR, and after hearing about the opening in a local newspaper, perhaps the September 16, 1982, edition of the *LA Weekly,* Michael got in touch with Lee Ving directly and cockily told him that he was their next bass player. He was given the opportunity to audition shortly thereafter at their Reseda rehearsal space, a "crazy-looking dingy storage shed," in early October 1982. The audition got off to a rough start; Michael neglected to bring his bass amp into the maze of storage units, and when asked where his "gear" was, he mistook the term to mean a syringe, for shooting up. "I think he thought we were junkies or something," Spit Stix recalled, an assessment that Michael agreed with. "Man, were my reference points in life askew or what."

Michael's bass amp retrieved, the foursome, including guitarist Philo Cramer, played together for the first time. The young man, having already learned the majority of FEAR's back catalog over the previous years as a fan, nailed the audition. Lee Ving offered him a spot in the band that night; that he was related to a friend of Spit Stix may have helped his case.

While overjoyed at the offer, Michael expressed concerns about merely being someone's sideman sticking to a typical bass player role. But these circumstances were somewhat different. In FEAR he would still be a sideman, but it was his first experience being in a band outside his circle of friends, and the need to toe the company line would be expected of him. There was no mistaking that Michael was a perfect fit for the band; FEAR was different from many other punk acts at the time in that they were all actually quite proficient at their instruments, in a scene in which any evidence of practice and professionalism—of caring too much—was a cardinal sin. Lee Ving was a great singer when he wanted to be, and the rest of the band were practically classically trained musicians. FEAR's songs were more rhythmically and harmonically complex than their goofy, intentionally offensive lyrics might have suggested. FEAR "blew my mind," Michael said. "They were all really good players playing their butts off. Awesomely tight musicians." In FEAR, he would not only be playing with a band he adored, but he would also be using a different part of his brain; the music was not any less demanding than what he was playing in What Is This, it was just faster and more intense, and it felt a whole lot more natural to him. Michael would later write about the internal conflict between the two bands in his memoir:

> What Is This got some good deep grooves going and were clever and interesting, but we weren't robbing people's hearts and making their bodies move. No one in the audience did anything physical at a What Is This show. They just nicely appreciated the art. As cartoonish as FEAR could be, they moved people. I was tired of being clever, I wanted to fuck the music, fuck with people's heads, and go crazy.

What really set FEAR apart from the rest was an ironic detachment, evident in that strange disconnect between the goofy lyrics and its complex backing music. They were metapunk; the outrageousness was intentional, the insulting lyrics the entire point.* They were snotty punks, sure, but they were only *acting* like snotty punks, and they knew exactly how to draw attention to themselves by amping things up at just the right time. The key was being in on the joke. It was all an act, something Michael and Anthony understood keenly the first time they saw them: "FEAR was no kiddie punk rock band," Anthony remembered. "It was a cartoon of what some heavyweight musician dudes thought the most ridiculous punk rock band could be." And Michael fit right in. In an undated letter to the band's fan club written during his time with them, his contribution is short and sweet: "I want to have a 3-way with your mother and your sargeant [*sic*]."

While he may have been riding high from the offer, there was the tricky question of breaking the news to the rest of his bandmates in What Is This. Using Anthony as a sounding board, Michael had decided that if he had to choose between any particular type of music to hitch his wagon to, punk was it. Now it was time for him to act on this belief. "He was confiding to friends, 'I dunno what the fuck to do. Do I leave my blood brothers?'"

There was another factor, aside from his flailing interest in the music, that required him to reconsider his place in What Is This. Lee Ving required total loyalty; he did not allow his underlings to perform with other bands.† If he was going to be in FEAR, he'd have to leave What Is This anyway. In this sense, a decision about his future in each band may have been made for him.

Eventually, Michael—nervous enough that he threw up beforehand—sat Hillel down to tell him he was leaving. It didn't go well. "Hillel turned ashen, stared at me for a painfully long moment with a disgusted, angry, and disappointed look, and wordlessly left the

---

* Guitarist Philo Cramer held a degree in physics from UCLA—not exactly punk.

† This problem would resurface over the next year.

room. . . . Hillel saw it as careerist, selfish, disloyal bullshit." He was so upset, in fact, that he didn't speak to Michael for several weeks.

That angry reaction makes a great deal of sense. For one, it came seemingly out of nowhere; Michael appears to have auditioned without telling anyone in What Is This what he was doing, only going to Anthony for guidance. Second, Hillel and Alain were the very reason he had started playing the instrument and joined a rock band in the first place. They dragged him away from the trumpet and slung a bass guitar over his shoulders, and he was key to their rock star dreams. And now he was abandoning them for these older, more established players?

Hillel would forgive his friend in the end. It was only a matter of when, not if; the departing member would write that within a few weeks "Hillel softened his resentment, letting forgiveness in." But at the time it was a serious conflict between the two old friends that might not have been repairable.

Michael pressed on; his first performance with FEAR took place on October 22, 1982, at the community center in Goleta, a college town about a hundred miles up the Pacific Coast from Los Angeles. His arrival on the scene was understated, but he did attract the smallest of mentions in the UC Santa Barbara *Daily Nexus:* "The rhythm section was neatly polished off by their new bassist," they wrote, before quickly clarifying that he was "not Derf Scratch." Photos taken on the day show Michael grinning behind the wheel of a truck (his ride to the show) in a bright yellow Fairfax High School Marching Band T-shirt. It was just days after his twentieth birthday.

But that one show in Goleta was just about it for the time being. FEAR's next confirmed date took place on December 6 when they opened for art-rock heavyweights Oingo Boingo at the Long Beach Veterans Memorial Stadium. This show was part of a Toys for Tots charity drive for radio station KROQ, held under an enormous circus tent on a blustery fifty-degree night. The US Marine Corps runs the

A twenty-year-old bass prodigy calling himself Mike B the Flea, moments before his first show with his new band, FEAR, in Goleta, California. October 22, 1982. *Jennifer McLellan*

charity, which provides toys for underprivileged children; a ticket to the show cost $5.50, and a new toy, which was to be donated upon entry. Marines in their dress blues were stationed at each entrance to collect, but the punk crowd acted true to form and brought in dismembered, deformed dolls of their own design.

The rest of the night was pure chaos. After FEAR's quick set, the power went out, thanks to the salty seawater air shorting out the generators, and the rowdy crowd almost rushed the stage. Some of the braver members of the audience climbed the support ropes that held the tent together, swinging over their friends like primates. Intermittent blackouts sent the tent completely black, then fully lit, then black again. After Oingo Boingo cut the electrical feed to their gear, punks started to tear chairs from the ground and hurl them at the stage in protest. The fear of electrocution was evidently uncool.

The marines left, and the police arrived, parking at each entrance to the tent and shining spotlights into the darkness. A riot seemed likely, but Oingo Boingo leader Danny Elfman refused to cancel the performance and persuaded the Long Beach Police Department to let the night continue, connecting the makeshift stage to the stadium's main power grid and assuaging the rowdy crowd.

After that tense performance, the band didn't play again until December 29 in San Francisco. There may have been dates in between, but no record of them has survived.

Why the large gap between October and December? It may have made sense for FEAR to perform live far more frequently than they did in the later months of that year, especially with a recent album out and even accounting for the loss of a member. But there was another, more pressing issue for Lee Ving: his acting career. He had just scored a role as strip club owner Johnny C. in Adrian Lyne's *Flashdance*, which filmed from October to December in Pittsburgh, Pennsylvania. And it wasn't just *Flashdance*; he also had a role in Joseph Sargent's *Nightmares*, which likewise filmed in the later months of the year. Ving wouldn't have been on set the whole time, of course, but rehearsals and the need to be available to filmmakers would have taken up most of his time. Perhaps Ving's Hollywood commitments explains the lack of FEAR performances in late 1982; he had swapped one acting gig for another.

In the meantime, What Is This replaced Michael with German-born Hans Reumschüssel and continued on without their star bass player.* But Michael's leaving put a further dampener on an already

* Most references to What Is This mention Chris Hutchinson as Michael's replacement, but Hutchinson didn't join the band until late 1983.

struggling band; their last performance for 1982 appears to have been on the night of October 4, when they played once more at Chinatown venue Madame Wong's, which was ostensibly Michael's last show with the band. It took a while for What Is This to recover; whenever the new lineup managed to rehearse, Hillel and new bassist Reumschüssel clashed, musically and personality-wise, and it was a long time before they could get themselves back in playing shape. While Flea was off rehearsing with his heroes and having the thrill of a lifetime, Jack, Hillel, Hans, and Alain put their heads down and tried to get back on their feet.

They were four different people, prone to arguments and jealousies, and the connections between them were as fragile as those in any other social group.* But it was not all was gloom and doom during this period. Michael, Anthony, Hillel, and Jack played their music when they could, and hung out together when they could (even if things were tense between Michael and Hillel for a month or two). They likely never stopped seeing each other, even if the band that connected them was ripped apart by the realities of real life. They visited clubs and bars and restaurants; one favorite was Canter's Deli on Fairfax Avenue, though before long they had run out on their bill one too many times to return. They spent the endless currency of youth and soaked up as much of Los Angeles as possible. This was a city that spoiled them.

They moved out of the city as well: the band's 1999 VH1 *Behind the Music* documentary displays photos of Anthony and Hillel on a camping trip that likely dates to the later months of 1982, and there was always the so-called Errol Flynn estate to escape to closer to home, a 160-acre North Hollywood park filled with decrepit buildings and an empty swimming pool, mistakenly believed to have once been owned

* Anthony and Jack, in particular, were never very close; it's apparent from Anthony's biography that the first real time he spent with Jack was after they started a band together. Jack is also the only band member not mentioned by Anthony in "Out in L.A."

by the swashbuckling actor. After years of neglect, it became a punk hideout; WELCOME TO HELL was spray-painted on the tennis court floor, and mischievous drunken hands smashed or broke anything within arm's reach. Away from the prying eyes of police (unless they were raiding the place), it became somewhere to go if you weren't old enough to drink legally.

At one point in early autumn, Anthony and Michael gave each other Mohawks and hitchhiked to San Francisco for a drug-fueled weekend.* The gang, especially the trio of Anthony, Hillel, and Michael, was tight; they were still Los Faces, still the same silly kids who did voices and clowned around. But there were some undeniably large changes taking place: as Michael joined FEAR, there became a shift in his life that was more than just a change in the style of music he played. While there have been differing recounts of how it happened, the generally accepted story is that his nickname Flea arrived during a camping trip in the Californian wilderness with Keith Barry, who was given the less parasitic nickname Tree, still in use today, and John Karson, who was given the less-permanent Squeak. It's not exactly clear when the trip took place; in his autobiography, Anthony implies it was in 1982, which is most likely correct, but other sources have dated it much earlier, even at some point during the late 1970s. Flea himself suggested that it was Anthony who gave him the name, in a 2014 fan interview on Reddit.

Regardless, in those earlier years, it was merely a nickname. Now, it had morphed into an entire persona. The exact point that Michael Balzary "became" Flea is hard to pinpoint, but it seems to have been around the time that he joined FEAR. Another factor was most of the other members of his new band all had nicknames already. Flea was simply doing what needed to be done to fit in. "I'd been called Flea

* Even for a young man, Michael's hair grew freakishly quickly. In photos from September, he has a fresh mohawk; by late October the rest of his hair has completely grown back.

here and there before, amongst other nicknames," he remembered, after being asked his name at his FEAR audition, "but without thinking, and wanting to appear like a punk rocker, I blurted out, 'I'm Flea.'"

The new name wasn't exactly popular at first. Gary Allen asked him, "Why you wanna call yourself something that gets under the skin and sucks blood?" And as Janet Cunningham remembered it, she thought it was "dumb," but her comment is helpful with a timeline: "He was Michael when I met him, and he was Flea by the time he moved out [of CASH]." The name also went through some changes before it crystallized: a Slash Records promo shot of FEAR refers to him as "the Flea," and in other appearances from around that time, his name is given as "Mike B the Flea." It most likely started out as "Mike B the Flea," a sort of rhyming couplet, before it was shortened.

Flea is more than just a nickname for Michael Peter Balzary, the little blond boy from Australia with the spirally hair and the gap tooth. A shy kid who has said that he only felt comfortable when he was around his friends, this new persona allowed him to open up and act the way he wished he had been able to all that time. As a person, Michael was a quiet and sensitive boy, introverted to a fault; if Anthony ever failed to show up for a day of school, he would instead wander around all day, scared that people would see he was by himself, alone, friendless.

As Flea, he could be different. He could be a pest, a provocateur. He could be the type of person that might not have come naturally but that he felt was the real him.

But it wasn't just a new name that helped him make this change; upon that meeting in high school, Anthony had changed his entire worldview, and the nickname seems to be merely the culmination of years of personal change. "[Meeting Anthony] had a lot to do with how I ended up as a musician," he would later reflect. "He was the first kid I met who didn't give a shit about being like anybody else. The way he talked, the way he dressed, and the way he acted had a big influence on me. He was so anti; he thought anyone who tried to be like anyone else was lame." Friends, girls, and even bands came and went, but Flea and Anthony were inseparable. *Mostly* inseparable; the dynamic did lead to the odd fight and occasional resentment, as is the case in any closely knit relationship. As Anthony would remember, "I was kind of a bastard and a mean-spirited bully at times." But these were not unusual spats, and were never irreparable.

Joining FEAR, Flea had risen immediately to a sort of scene-wide fame, with a cachet that could only come from an established band. "It created a profound shift," Anthony, who benefitted second hand from said shift, remembered. "We were movin' on up from gawkers in the pit to where one of our own was now up there in one of the greatest L.A. bands." But this fame hit another level when he met Penelope Spheeris, the director of *The Decline of Western Civilization*, a legendary documentary about punk and the punk scene in Los Angeles that featured a pre-Flea FEAR show as one of its chaotic centerpieces. Filmed throughout 1979 and 1980, it also showed off

Philo Cramer, Mike B the Flea, Spit Stix, and Lee Ving of FEAR. Early 1983. *Jennifer McLellan*

Black Flag, Circle Jerks, Germs, and X to the world, striking a nerve when it was released in July of 1981, and cementing Spheeris's punk credentials in the process.

Born in New Orleans, Spheeris spent a large portion of her childhood traveling with her father's carnival. After he was shot and killed in Troy, Alabama, she was sent to live with her mother and a constant procession of new husbands in California, and eventually majored in film at UCLA. Here, too, was another *Saturday Night Live* connection: Spheeris directed many shorts that were shown on the show's first season, as part of a close partnership with comedian and filmmaker Albert Brooks.

Spheeris kept in touch with the bands she had filmed for *Decline*. While visiting Lee Ving one afternoon in the later weeks of 1982, she met Flea, who was there for Ving's weekly Sunday dinner of hearty home-cooked Italian food.* There was an instant connection. "The moment I set eyes on him," Spheeris said, "I was like, that kid's a star."

"Lee introduced me as his new bass player," Flea remembered. "She's like, Oh whoa, there's this movie I'm making, and I soon got in that, too." That's a condensed version of events. In reality, he auditioned for Spheeris the next day a little worse for wear, coming down off a large dose of MDA, the unpredictable and semihallucinogenic parent drug of the more common MDMA, or ecstasy. He originally auditioned for a bigger role and didn't get that part, but Spheeris couldn't resist the energy he was giving off:

> I was fucked up on MDA and Penelope's face was getting into all sorts of distorted figures and her nose was dripping down to her chin and the words she was saying were separated apart and it was real weird, and I told her about it.

* Owing to his transitory lifestyle, Flea may have actually been temporarily living with Lee and his wife at this point.

> I said, "I'm fucked up on MDA right now and I'm sort of having a hard time." And she understood and she gave me the part.

Spheeris was unhappy with how difficult it had been to get *The Decline of Western Civilization* released—documentaries just weren't salable, she was told—and decided that her next film would be a drama. That would get more butts in theater seats and make future projects easier to fund. The ensuing film, *Suburbia*, is a narrative based on her experiences in the punk scene. It's a movie about punks and punk music, but it's also about the failings of Reagan-era capitalism on the family unit. It's part concert film and part Peter Pan fantasy, where entire blocks of abandoned California suburbia have been taken over by rowdy punk teens, a gang named The Rejected, or TR, who live according to their own rules away from the eyes of their parents and of The State, each with their own little story within the whole.

Suburbia was filmed throughout the winter of 1982 and early months of 1983, meaning Flea was free to film his parts when required during a quiet period for FEAR. Credited under the earlier version of his nickname Mike B. the Flea, he plays a TR kid named Razzle. He and his pet rat are only in a handful of scenes, but they steal the show, and there's a chaotic, raw vitality to his performance that suggest most of it came from real life. But, true to punk fashion, the film's creation was marred with financial and distribution problems, and it would take some time for it to finally be released.

Syndee Coleman played one of the TR kids and spent time with Flea on set in those winter months. "I was 20 when we were filming. I read lines for the main female character and was told I'd have the part except I wasn't able to come back the day they wanted. Flea and I would sit in the trailer between shots. We'd play gin rummy for hours and talk," she remembers. "Shooting a movie is very dull at times. It's all 'hurry up and wait,' the exact term Penelope used."

Elsewhere, Anthony's time as a driver for Mid-Ocean Motion Pictures came to an end in August, around the same time the company filed for bankruptcy. What he did to sustain himself after this hasn't ever been disclosed, but during those days he had spent in their delivery truck, with the windows down and the radio blaring, a seed had been planted that would change his life going forward. It was all thanks to a new track that had dropped that summer, "The Message," by a hip-hop group named Grandmaster Flash and the Furious Five.

Rapping and hip hop had only emerged at the tail end of the 1970s and were still brand-new to the general public, with only the rare track making it into weekly charts still dominated by rock and pop. But by 1982, Grandmaster Flash—born Joseph Saddler—and his Furious Five had already conquered the streets of New York City and were quickly sweeping the rest of the country. As a young man, Saddler had invented and perfected a method of switching between two records playing on a turntable at the same time to create unique mixes and was soon at parties and get-togethers joined by rappers and dancers. After playing local New York clubs and making a name for themselves, Flash and his backing group* released a few early singles, and 1980's "Freedom" in particular had made waves. But "The Message," which was released on the first day of July 1982, and accompanied by an album of the same name that October, was one of the first hip-hop tracks to move away from what was the norm at the time.†

Where before, early hip-hop was for the most part filled with rhymes centered around big-headed braggadocio and displays of dancing skills, "The Message" was a political commentary that told a story

* Flash, while the "frontman," actually spent most of his time behind the decks. The majority of the rapping was done by the others in the group.

† "The Message" was heavily inspired by "Rapper's Delight," a 1979 track by the Sugarhill Gang that is considered to be the prototypical hip hop song, and was, along with Kurtis Blow's "The Breaks," the first commercially successful single in the genre's history. It features braggadocio lyrics over a prominent bassline, a vein that the Chili Peppers would mine heavily in their early years.

and made a real point. It was more than just something to throw on during a party. "The Message" was about the poverty, the threats, and the pressure that came with life in the urban jungle, expertly rapped by the group's main emcee, Melle Mel. But it was damn catchy as well; it peaked at no. 62 on the Billboard Hot 100 in November 1982, was named the best single of the year by the *Los Angeles Times*, and made a huge impression on Anthony when he heard it on the radio throughout that summer.

But seeing the group live, at Reseda Country Club on October 18, 1982—a few days before Flea's first performance with FEAR—made an even bigger impression. Watching the Furious Five rap onstage with Grandmaster Flash's backing opened up something deep inside the young man, still a few weeks away from his twentieth birthday. The group told their story and moved the audience both emotionally and physically, and all without relying on traditional musical talents. They were talking about a familiar subject matter but doing it in an unfamiliar way. "It was mind-blowing," Anthony remembered, "I subconsciously vowed I would somehow create that type of energy to entertain others. I didn't have a clue how to write a song or sing, but I thought I could probably figure out how to tell a story in rhythm."

He would return to this show time and time again when discussing his career as a singer and lyricist, even referencing the moment in the track "Aquatic Mouth Dance," recorded almost forty years later. "It started dawning on me that you don't have to be Al Green or have an incredible Freddie Mercury voice to have a place in the world of music," he wrote. "Rhyming and developing a character were another way to do it." Even Flea was aware of the effect it had on his friend: "He'd never been in a band before, but he had gone to see Grandmaster Flash and the Furious Five and fell in love with hip-hop and said 'Wow, I could do that.'"

While not previously connecting it with music, Anthony had always been interested in writing, and the wordplay that he displayed when "opening" for Anthym and What Is This showed that he had no qualms about mixing this form of creativity with a presence onstage, and in the live music scene. He had also written bursts of poetry over the years, and had been praised for it, but hadn't developed it past an occasional hobby that remained hidden in the odd journal or school exercise book. But now he had the urge to do something with the words he had written, and the explosion of rap had proven that he didn't need to be a soulful (or even particularly talented) singer to make a musical contribution. His voice could be the key. He knew plenty of musicians; he had even shared stages with some before, but music wasn't something he had seemed interested in: "I had never noticed musical aspiration, he'd never mentioned a desire to focus on music," Flea recalled.

The day after the Grandmaster Flash concert, he "came into the kitchen at the Wilton Hilton bursting with excitement" and "sat right the fuck down in the kitchen and starting writing lyrics." But if it wasn't for Gary Allen, he may never have had the opportunity to act on these new desires. Indeed, if it wasn't for Gary Allen, this whole story would have gone a lot differently. But 1982 was a year of change for these four, and it was all leading to this one moment.

SHOW #1

DECEMBER 16, 1982

The Rhythm Lounge at the Grandia Room,
5657 Melrose Avenue, Los Angeles, CA

AFTER HIS BAND Neighbor's Voices split up, Gary Allen kicked off a solo career with an EP under his own name in the latter half of 1982, entitled *In White America: This Hollow Valley Broken Jaw of Our Lost Kingdom.* Self-released on his own label, it's a piece of work ahead of its time: where Neighbor's Voices were upbeat, kinetic and energetic, *In White America* is for the most part sparse and synth driven, laden with drum machine beats and industrial sounds.* A music video was put together for the track "Oops It's an Accident," and it's part *Blade Runner*, part home movie, a heartbreak song soundtracked by a blistering, propulsive beat.† It's available on streaming services but has become sought

* That said, one song on the EP, "Mogul at Home," is actually just a repackaged Neighbor's Voices track.

† The song itself bears a striking similarity to New Order's "Blue Monday," which came out a full year later.

after in recent years, and secondhand copies of the original vinyl release sell for upwards of seventy dollars online.*

Allen had plans to throw a release party for the EP at a club in Hollywood. Located at 5657 Melrose Avenue, the venue had been many things in the past—a grocery store, a meat market, a cocktail lounge, the Sonny Haines Talent Center—but in the late 1960s restaurateur Peter Sargologos took over and renamed it the Grandia Room. Sargologos had transformed the building into part nightclub and part Greek restaurant, with a tiny stage in one corner, and fake trees and grape clusters hanging from the roof.

It was considered a dive, at least to the snobbier elements of Hollywood, but the Grandia Room was popular with a gamut of scenes, thanks to its ability to take on a completely different persona virtually every night of the week, starting in March 1981. One night it held a punk show, the next a dance club; other nights, DJs would spin their favorite tracks while pop-lockers did their thing onstage. These nights quite often evolved (or devolved) into dance "battles" between rival crews. And all the while it remained a restaurant and nightclub, with its own regulars shouting drink orders over the cacophony.

The type of music performed in the club might have been new, but performances themselves were not. For much of the previous decade various enterprising promoters had held shows there, including Sandra Lane and her Hollywood Showcase, which presented a "no-strings-attached evening of free entertainment" and provided many new acts with their first bit of stage time.

On Thursday, at around 9:30 PM, the Grandia Room became the Rhythm Lounge. It was a night hosted by Frenchman Salomon Emquies, who had already been spinning tracks and holding film

* A close inspection will reveal Michael Balzary being thanked in the liner notes, and Laurence Fishburne providing vocals on one track.

nights at the club and had taken over when the previous promoter left. Emquies—who directed the "Oops It's an Accident" video—gave the night a new name, slapped a five-dollar cover charge on the door, and made the enterprise his own. Matt Dike was another DJ and constant presence. While working at the lounge that year, Dike would meet Mike Ross, and the two would eventually form the *Delicious Vinyl* record label, home to Tone Loc's smash hit "Wild Thing," and Young MC's "Bust a Move," which featured Flea on instantly recognizable bass. Later in the 1980s, Dike helped produce *Paul's Boutique* by the Beastie Boys.*

The first Rhythm Lounge session was the night of September 9, 1982, and was held every week thereafter, until the early months of 1985. It was a beloved place for the gang. "We'd hang out at the Rhythm Lounge every Thursday," Flea recalled. "Get fucked up and hit on chicks." Gary Allen, always sartorially concerned, considered it "fashion-influenced, as much as it was about the music." Photos from the era show many a young, glamorous thing mugging for the camera, including a prefame Ice T, who was house rapper. In these photos, the surroundings are curious; kitsch wood paneling and cheap dining sets are placed right up against turntables and microphones. It looked like the group had taken over a small, family-run restaurant—in essence, they had—but in those trying times the crowd had to party where they could, and some clubs would be run out of the most unusual of places. Artist Jean-Michel Basquiat was a regular at the club and would later film a music video with Emquies and hip-hop and graffiti pioneer Rammellzee at a Rhythm Lounge session in early 1983.

Held on the night of Thursday, December 16, 1982, Gary Allen's release show was to be an all-star affair—a "very special set" to introduce his EP to the world. He would be not only be playing tracks

* Matt Dike passed away in January 2018 from salivary gland cancer.

L.A. polymath Gary Allen released his solo EP at the end of 1982 and needed an opening act for his December 16 release show. Enter Flea, Anthony, Hillel, and Jack. *Salomon Emquies*

from the new release with a backing band, but also incorporating an extravagant, over-the-top theatrical element to proceedings. Joining the star of the show onstage were Russell Jessum on synthesizer, Keith "Tree" Barry on violin, Rodney "Wizard" Turner on drums, Tequila Mockingbird on backup vocals,* and Michael "Flea" Balzary on bass.†

* Tequila Mockingbird, actress, singer (including a stint performing backup vocals for Nina Hagen), and club booker, decided on that name upon being introduced to X singer Exene Cervenka by Germs singer Darby Crash. To this day, she has not publicly revealed her real name. Mockingbird also worked as a music supervisor on *New Wave Theater*.

† This lineup is sourced from a flier for Allen's show at the Rhythm Lounge in December 1982. Elsewhere, Allen has spoken of fronting a band that featured Hillel Slovak, Jack Irons, and Flea behind him, but it's unclear if those performances were the same night as this Rhythm Lounge show; Hillel and Jack are not mentioned on the December 16 flier.

This was a close-knit group of musicians; Turner and Allen were friends in high school, Tequila Mockingbird and Allen were too, and of course Flea and Keith Barry had known each other since junior high as well. Jessum had played on much of Allen's EP, and this was not the first time that the rest of the band had played together in some form. But they wouldn't be the only act playing that night.

This is the way the story is normally told in band biographies, autobiographies, and magazine articles over the years: after seeing him warm the crowd up before What Is This gigs and in the crowds around the clubs of Los Angeles, Gary Allen—sensing some hidden, unexplored talent—suggested that Anthony be the front man of a one-off band, backed by Flea, Jack, and Hillel, three of the musicians in the original (and favorite) What Is This lineup. Anthony, at first gobsmacked at the outlandish suggestion, but at the same time flattered, turned out to be the perfect candidate; he had experience onstage, was a natural leader of a crowd, and was possessed with a newfound passion for rhyming and rapping that was burning a hole in his brain. In his induction speech at the Rock and Roll Hall of Fame in 2012, Anthony repeated this version of the story, telling the crowd that "a chap named Gary Allen suggested, 'You know, why don't you give that guy Anthony a crack on the mic?'"

Memories are tricky things, of course, and thirty-plus years is a long time, but Gary Allen himself remembers this process differently. In fact, he says, it happened in reverse; it was Anthony who approached *him*:

> Flea and Hillel were living in an apartment off Hollywood Boulevard [the Wilton Hilton]. Anthony moved in for a while. During this time, he started rapping and they worked out a couple of songs. Anthony called me and told me that I should come over and hear what they were doing. I did go right over to

> listen, I was impressed. When they finished playing, Anthony said I should let them open up for me. I agreed, and they did.

No members of the band have ever described its formation in this way before, and so Allen may be misremembering events, or is remembering a last-minute rehearsal session he saw just before the show. But if this is how it really happened, it presents a fairly different version from the official story. One piece of evidence in its favor is the two-month gap between Anthony seeing Grandmaster Flash live in October and this performance being arranged in mid-December. If, like he said, Anthony was immediately inspired by the concert and, according to Flea, the very next day started writing his own raps, what was happening in that two-month period?

Perhaps the band had already come together, at least in a very early form, in idea only, and it just required Gary's nudging along for it to become something real. If this is the case, then Anthony shouldn't have been too surprised that he was approached to be a singer; it may have been his idea in the first place.

Nevertheless, whether it was Gary Allen's idea or Anthony's idea, the decision was made to perform something—a song, some kind of performance, it didn't matter. The exact specifics could be worked out later—at the forthcoming show at the Rhythm Lounge on December 16. Anthony Kiedis on vocals, Flea on bass, Hillel Slovak on guitar, and Jack Irons on drums.*

There are two main reasons why this combination of musicians made so much sense. First, it was inevitable that Anthony and Flea would team up musically; so much of their friendship was based around music, whether listening to it while at home at the Wilton

* Writing on his official website in 2005, Jack Irons said that Anthony and Flea asked Jack and Hillel to play with them after the show had already been booked, suggesting, perhaps, that the guitarist and drummer weren't immediately included in the initial plans. A small but important detail that would be pertinent as the next year unfolded.

Hilton, going to punk gigs at Club Lingerie or Al's Bar, or dancing to new hip-hop records at the RadioTron in MacArthur Park. To transform their friendship into a musical partnership was to push it into unexplored, but still very familiar-feeling, territory.

There was also the fact Flea would have certainly missed playing with his old bandmates from What Is This, and vice versa. Hillel was one of the two musicians who had taught Flea how to play bass, after all, and the trio, including Jack Irons, had a keen unspoken musical bond, the kind of connection that can only be formed after years and years of playing together, playing hours of music that nobody would ever hear while they were cooped up together in a cheap and dirty rehearsal studio—or sometimes only a bedroom. FEAR may have been an exciting new experience for the newly minted Mike B the Flea, but he didn't possess the kind of relationship with his new bandmates that he did with his *old* ones. And as exciting as punk was, it was a fairly one-track type of music—quick, hard, and fast, with little space for freedom to express anything besides *fuck you.* There were still other avenues they had yet to explore.

Likewise, Hillel and Jack weren't getting the results they were hoping for with their new bass player, Hans Reumschüssel, and would have leapt at the chance to play with their old friend once more, once they—Hillel in particular—had forgiven Flea for leaving in the first place. Add the potential of the charm and stage presence of Anthony to this already-burgeoning desire for the three to reconnect as musicians, and the perfect scenario presented itself. One wonders why they hadn't thought of it before, but now the stars had aligned and "the unplanned, unexpected, and organic series of events" had transpired.

Flea approached Salomon Emquies to make sure the promoter approved, and he was more than happy to accommodate them. It was a one-off, something designed to self-destruct after one performance, the kind of thing the scene had seen done a hundred times before.

You blinked, you missed it; that was the point. "We had no idea what to expect," Anthony remembered a decade and a half later. "It was just for the hell of it."

Now, the only decision left that needed to be made was: what would they play?

The band have been more than happy over the years to wear their influences right on their sleeve (in Flea's case, right on his shoulder), and when it comes to the track "Out in L.A." they've been even more forthright than normal about the source of its creation.* The major musical inspiration for their first song was the band Defunkt, and in particular, their titular song, "Defunkt."

Formed in 1978 in New York City, the band were a particular favorite of Anthony and Flea's to dance to at house parties and at clubs. Flea had even made a nuisance of himself one night in 1982 at the Cathay de Grande, by jumping up into the booth and insisting the DJ flip the Defunkt record that was currently playing ("In the Good Times," a loose cover of Chic's 1979 hit "Good Times") to the song on the other side (the slower, groovier "Strangling Me with Your Love"). The DJ, Bob Forrest, was upset with the way the young man went about broadcasting his request, but he was impressed with his gusto, and couldn't deny his taste.

"Defunkt" begins with the multilayered voice of lead singer Joseph Bowie, which rises and builds from each speaker to a crescendo before the drums and bass emerge with a crack. The song hits a hypnotic groove and stays there for the remainder, save for a breakdown and mini drum solo as it comes to its end. Though it seems on its surface a song about partying—"I wanna dance, I wanna party-hearty, I wanna get down tonight, with the Defunkt"—the song hits a sourer note, even if the instrumental backing stays upbeat and happy. "I live for

* Elsewhere, track down John Frusciante describing the writing (or "ripping off") process for the 1991 track "Under the Bridge" during a solo performance in Amsterdam, in February 2001.

you, but you want me to drop dead," Bowie deadpans, over crunchy bass and scratchy guitars.

Flea and Anthony had been introduced to Defunkt (and many other acts) by Dondi Bastone, Anthony's former roommate. Anthony and Bastone had even met the band's guitarist, Kelvyn Bell, in New York in 1980. That interaction with Bell was one of the catalysts for the feeling, later cemented by his exposure to Grandmaster Flash, that Anthony wanted to "make people feel the way this music was making me feel."

Unlike punk's relative freshness, funk was not a new phenomenon; in fact, by the early '80s its heyday was already over. Where punk sped rock music up, funk tended to slow it down, or at least make it far more danceable, syncopated, and sparse. Funk could give a band time to breathe, even if it drove an audience wild. Evolving out of the R&B and New Orleans blues scenes, it put a focus on the downbeat, the drum and bass, and often a short, sharp, accentuating stab from a horn section. In the mid-1960s, artists like James Brown brought it to a worldwide audience, but by the next decade, elements of funk had incorporated themselves back into rock music, and the lines became blurred; what constituted funk, exactly, become harder to pinpoint. Funk, with its reliance on drums and bass, became one of the key early development points for hip-hop's emergence a few years on. All music—rock, funk, punk, hip-hop—began to share the same DNA.

The writing process for this new song has been told a few different ways. In his autobiography, Anthony states it was entirely made up in the few days they had to prepare for the show, and that Flea came up with the bassline during that period. Elsewhere, in the band's *Oral/Visual History*, Jack said that it "was just a guitar riff that Hillel and I had jammed on for hours for fun." There's the possibility that Anthony already had the lyrics handy, having drafted them originally as a poem ("[he] was translating poems he had written into rap songs"), resulting in a eureka moment when he heard the bassline that Flea had been toying with casually in the months before the show. Most likely, it was a combination of all these possibilities, and of course, Gary Allen remembers the four of them already having written it before *they* approached *him*. Exactly when the song was conceived isn't known, and it most likely floated around in several separate forms before it was refined in that final week or two before December 16.

In various interviews over the years, Flea has implied that he devised the bassline as a direct attempt to mimic "Defunkt" in both sound and style; in a 2006 blog post he went one better and stated that "the very first song that we ever wrote . . . was born from me doing my best to copy the groove [of 'Defunkt']." Listening back with the knowledge that Flea cribbed his bassline from the song, the similarities are there and the inspiration is obvious, but there's enough changed that it isn't a direct one-for-one lift.

The merging of punk and funk was something that Flea had been toying with for some time toward the end of 1982. According to Syndee Coleman, his *Suburbia* costar, "He was still in Fear at the time, but was excited about a new music project he was working on. . . . At the time I thought it sounded interesting, but I remember thinking I wasn't sure how well that would go over. I was so wrong!"

Rehearsal was a quick and casual affair. Fabrice Drouet remembers the band running through the song in the apartment that they shared the day of the performance, and Flea repeated the same in his autobiography. This may have been the only time they actually rehearsed it; in an interview in May 1984, Flea states it was *never* rehearsed, but this was mostly likely simple punk rock posturing. In an interview a year later, he admitted that at the very least they "hummed it to each other." Anthony also recalls a quick a cappella run-through in his autobiography.

Darkness fell on Thursday, December 16, 1982, and Gary Allen's show started at the Grandia Room. It can't be known for sure how many people were there that night, but according to Anthony, there were thirty people in the club at the beginning of their performance. Flea had invited many of his costars and friends from the then-filming *Suburbia*, such as Chris Pedersen, Christina Beck, and Maggie Ehrig, whom he was dating at the time.* Also present was the house DJ for the night, Nuala, who also worked at local radio station KXLU, Fabrice Drouet, and, of course, everyone who was there for Gary Allen's performance, unaware of the moment they were about to witness. Anthony's estimate of thirty attendees is probably on the mark, if a little low, whereas Flea quips with the specific figure of twenty-seven. There also would have been people in the periphery; outside on Melrose Avenue, smoking in the fifty-degree weather, or at the other end of the club, there to have fun, drink, and listen to the records put on between sets.

Besides their short-and-sweet song, the new group had one other idea to make a mark; a choreographed dance routine to the Jonzun Crew track "Pack Jam (Look Out for the OVC)." This was another space-age hip-hop track only a few months old, and was probably something Anthony heard one night while at the RadioTron. Entering the Grandia Room through the main entrance off Melrose Avenue, they held their boom box aloft, and danced and mimed all the way to the stage. Once there, the rest of the routine supposedly fell apart thanks to Jack's inability to get the moves right, but by that time they were ready to start their performance proper.

As is often the case in the band's early history, existing accounts leave some lingering questions. There's confusion about the exact point this dance routine happened. In his autobiography, Anthony states that it was at the second show, and that on this particular night—the first show—the band went unnoticed until they were onstage and

* Maggie Ehrig was a former member of Twisted Roots, a short-lived band featuring Pat Smear and keyboardist Paul Roessler. In 1998, Flea planned on covering a Twisted Roots song on a (cancelled) solo album.

plugging in their instruments. Gary Allen agrees, remembering the dance, "the boom box up on one shoulder, old school hip-hop style, no shirt," and thinking it was more likely to have been the second show. But Flea and Salomon Emquies insist otherwise; Flea mentions the dance at the opening show in the *Oral/Visual History* and in his autobiography, and Emquies remembered the boombox routine happening both at their first show *and* at a later show in his *Oral/Visual History* interview.)

Regardless, what's certain is that the foursome wasn't credited on any fliers for the night, nor were they mentioned in any newspaper ads, but it has been oft repeated that they performed under the name Tony Flow and the Miraculously Majestic Masters of Mayhem. Apart from being a funny story to tell when they were world-famous, the name—if mentioned at all on this night—may have merely been something silly they told the crowd and the promoters in jest when they were setting up, or repeated later that night when asked what the act was called; the words didn't appear anywhere in print until 1991. They may have also played under the name the Flow, which they would play the next two shows as.* Flea recalled it being something Anthony had specifically made up to be farcically alliterative, and one can discern the influence of Grandmaster Flash and the Furious Five.

Whatever the name, when they were ready on the tiny stage in Grandia Room's southwest corner, Jack counted them off, and Anthony, stone-cold sober on a night out for a change, and in a paisley robe and orange hunting cap, did an impromptu flip on the tiny stage. When he landed, it was time to go.

Assuming that the version they played that night closely resembled the demo recorded six months later, "Out in L.A." was a prototypical

* If any fliers did exist with that full name, none have survived, and the band never mentioned the name in the first few years of their career, despite plenty of chances to do so.

punk-funk piece, based, essentially, in the key of E.* There isn't much in the way of a verse-chorus-verse structure, but it does follow a pattern of sorts: Anthony ends the song the way he begins it, and along the way there's room for a bass solo, a hip-hop inspired drum-and-dance break, a guitar solo, and a vocal breakdown lifted directly from the Ohio Players' 1975 track "Fopp."

Anthony and Hillel were huge fans of "Fopp," and it would have particularly amused them to give the song such a knowing nod. To some, this might seem like a blatant bit of plagiarism, but it was closer to a sample; hip-hop artists often lifted a drum break or a hook from an existing track and repurposed it, and this was in the same spirit (even if it appears that Anthony never acknowledged the lift). Almost two decades into the career that this song would launch, Anthony spoke of "Fopp" in the midst of the *Californication* tour:

> There was a time when Hillel and I used to go out dancing, and we'd get our mind in just the right place to go free-styling on the floor. And we'd kind of be at opposite ends of the dance floor, if you will, in a Hollywood nightclub environment in the early '80s, which was a very stimulating environment, and this song would come on. . . . And we would slowly but surely make our way, like fish swimming upstream towards each other, until we found each other in the middle of the floor, and we'd just freak out.

In the way that punk took the concept of a regular three-chord rock song and sped it up to the point of attractive abrasiveness, stripping everything but the basics and yet increasing its intensity at the same time, "Out in L.A." took "regular" funk and added the

* However, the version played on this night *may* have been a wildly different one that hadn't been refined yet, and which only barely resembles the demo version recorded in May 1983.

speed and intensity of punk rock to it. But instead of the music being cut down to the essentials, it retained an element of complexity; Flea's slap bass solo is not something you'd have heard at a FEAR or Circle Jerks show. Traversing the entire length of the neck of his instrument, it was much more aligned with a funk solo. This was his rare talent, and he wasn't afraid to show it off. Hillel's guitar solo is utterly blistering—Hendrix on acid *and* amphetamines. Aside from his uncredited lift, lyrically Anthony takes a lot from early hip-hop; in a staccato rap, he tells the world about himself and his friends in rhyming 4/4, and isn't shy—one could never accuse him of being shy—to move into straight braggadocio. He even manages a FEAR namedrop.

The performance would have lasted for a maximum of five minutes (it was probably only about three) and when it was over, Gary Allen took center stage, and the rest of the night was his. No recording of the performance was made, no photos from the night have surfaced, and under fifty people would have witnessed it. But those few minutes certainly made their mark. After the seemingly impromptu performance by this (potentially unnamed) band, the crowd were stunned, and each of the band members knew they had unleashed something special, something that was "so much fun" and gave them a high that lasted for "days and days." "As we performed," Anthony remembered, "everybody who was in that room who hadn't been paying attention zombied all the way up to the stage." Flea said it was "BAM! From the first note," and Gary Allen said, "They were so good, everyone knew they were witnessing history in the making."

Salomon Emquies approached Anthony and Flea shortly after the performance, handed them their fifty-dollar fee, and asked them to come back two weeks later, but with a few more songs. The performance was amazing, but it could have been longer; he was stunned and thought they should have been the stars of the night.

They had no plans, no other songs, and no expectations. But there was no question; they agreed, and in that agreement, something special was born.*

As expected, in the years since, much has been written about this special night, and virtually every retelling of it features conflicting, incorrect details. Dave Thompson's 2004 biography *By the Way* gets the date wrong, saying the show was in April of 1983; Jeff Apter's *Fornication*, also released in 2004, makes the same mistake. Thompson's earlier, 1993 version of his biography states it was spring of 1983: less specific, but still inaccurate.

Even the band members themselves are prone to misremembering certain facts. Anthony wrote in his 2004 autobiography that the band's inaugural performance was in February 1983, and that the show was a regular Neighbor's Voices performance. But Neighbor's Voices had broken up in 1981, years before this night. In fact, it was Gary Allen's solo debut release that was the impetus for this show. Flea's 2019 memoir repeats the date of February 1983, probably lifted from other inaccurate sources, such as Anthony's book. In a 2003 interview, Anthony stated, "It's hard to actually remember the exact date that we became a band, but we guesstimate between Flea and I, who have little, or no memory left at all, that it was February 13." This isn't possible, as February 13 was a Sunday and the Rhythm Lounge was only held on Thursday nights. In a September 1990 interview with the Dutch television station VPRO, Flea—standing in front of the Grandia Room itself, the very site of the performance, only a few months before it shut—is already entirely unsure of when it was: "Way, way back in, I think it was, February, or it might not have been February, it might have been March . . ." The month of February was mentioned as early as June 1984, in an interview with LA

* And for an intended one-off, "Out in L.A." certainly had legs. It would go on to be performed at virtually every show the band ever played going forward, only exiting regular rotation in 1992, almost ten years after its debut.

street mag *BAM*, and repeated that August in the press kit for the band's debut album. Flea, Anthony, and the other biographers were only two months off, and clearly close enough for their own comfort; they've used the date of February 13 as an anniversary for the band in the years since, including for a period on a time line on their official website. This is especially ironic, considering they didn't play in the month of February 1983 at all. The later January 6, 1983, show under the name the Flow is listed in the time line at the back of the band's *Oral/Visual History* book as the earliest entry in the band's career. While not the first show—it is, in fact, their third—it's the closest the band have ever come to getting it right.

Thankfully, there are primary sources, in the form of fliers for Gary Allen's show on December 16, 1982, provided to the author by Salomon Emquies, who ran the Rhythm Lounge during the period the band played there, and newspaper advertisements for the same date in the *Los Angeles Reader*. This, of course, adds a curious asterisk to the band's formation; for four decades they have been an act that began in 1983, and that date accompanies the band's biographies, their online presence, their merchandise, and appearances in reference books. But the fact is, the band's inaugural performance was actually at the tail end of 1982.

SHOW #2

DECEMBER 30, 1982

The Rhythm Lounge at the Grandia Room, 5657 Melrose Avenue, Los Angeles, CA

A WEEK AFTER the newly forged act opened for Gary Allen, there was another What Is This reunion of sorts, when Flea, Hillel, and Alain Johannes played a cabaret night at the Lhasa Club on December 23, only a few blocks away from the Grandia Room. "The Flea" duetted with high school friend Patrick English on trumpet,* while Slovak and Johannes played acoustic guitar together on the same night, at the arts space that doubled as a gallery, café, and cinema. No recollections of this particular night remain, but it was one of a million little interesting performances held up and down the strip, and one of a million that have been lost to time.

On December 29 Flea headed north to San Francisco, playing what was perhaps only his third-ever show with FEAR, at the Old Waldorf nightclub, as they opened for English punk band UK Subs. The day after, Thursday, December 30, 1982, Flea, Anthony, Hillel, and Jack played a

* The source for the slang word "Spigot" (i.e., a penis) used in the short-lived Spigot Blister and the Chest Pimps.

return engagement at the Rhythm Lounge. This second show was the first time the foursome appeared in print, and perhaps the first time they were ever given a name. They were booked as the Flow—no Tony, and no Majestic Masters of Mayhem—and this time they weren't opening for Gary Allen. They had the tiny stage of the Grandia Room to themselves.

The *LA Weekly* listing advertising the Rhythm Lounge's weekly takeover refers to "performances by *The Flow*, featuring Anthony Kiedis and members of Fear and What Is This." As far as names go, the Flow closely aligns the band with rap and hip-hop; a "flow" refers to a rapper's technique. Anthony, being new to the scene and a White boy, to boot, still had a lot to prove, and the first step to proving one's worth was to act the part even if the chops might not have been developed yet. But using this name suggests they thought of themselves as a rap or hip-hop oriented act rather than one in the punk or rock scene, and their playing the Rhythm Lounge, with its focus on rap and hip-hop, only solidified this early direction.

That they found time to write another song during this busy week is impressive; that they had the time to rehearse, even more so. But their promise to Salomon Emquies was kept, and they returned with more than one song in their repertoire, and a stage show that lasted for more than three minutes. After "Out in L.A."—another ninety seconds of kinetic bliss—came "Get Up and Jump," a quick, jagged song based around a complex and intertwined slap bassline from Flea, with Hillel's syncopated chicken-scratch accompaniment, and a smooth and funky introduction and coda. It starts off quite reasonable, then devolves into chaos.

In a way, Anthony's lyrics resemble the music: they're a frenzied call for a ready crowd to start dancing and jumping, containing faster and trickier wordplay than "Out in L.A.," and when it's put together, the whole thing is a frantic jumble. And instead of rapping strictly about himself, in this track he also acts as a wingman of sorts, making reference to Ronit Frumkin, a young local lady that Hillel had his sights on.* Much like "Out in L.A.," "Get Up and Jump" is another track that came to mean a great deal to the band; it would be the song issued to radio stations as a promotional single for their debut album and played live at virtually every show until October 1991, with a variety of loving teases performed from time to time thereafter. Not bad for something hastily thrown together in a week.

This show would have lasted only a few minutes longer than their first, and it may have also been the site of the aforementioned "Pac Jam" dance routine that fell apart shortly after it began. Much remains unknown and untold about this show and the performance that followed it a week later, as most of the focus in retellings over the years is on the previous, first-ever show. All that is known is that they played their two songs, and then they were off, into the night again, while Rhythm Lounge DJs bookended the insanity.

One show was a fun curio that could have been a one-off, but two shows was maybe the beginning of something real. This could have been the end of the experiment; two fun nights for the guys, two nights away from their regular bands playing a different type of music, and for Anthony a dipping of his toes into something that he had never done before. When Salomon Emquies quickly asked them back for a third engagement, they could have said no. After all, they had other things to think about: other bands, other engagements, other plans. In Anthony's case, perhaps other careers.

But it was too much fun to stop, and the rich vein that they had tapped seemed to have so much more to give. They told Salomon they'd be back again. Two shows had quickly become three.

---

* According to Anthony's retelling in *Scar Tissue*, this technique worked wonders.

SHOW #3

JANUARY 6, 1983

The Rhythm Lounge at the Grandia Room, 5657 Melrose Avenue, Los Angeles, CA

THE NEW YEAR, 1983, dawned on the streets and valleys of Los Angeles, and the Flow played the Rhythm Lounge's Thursday night spot for a third time. This show was perhaps the most heavily advertised yet, and the first sign that the band was taking this new and interesting undertaking quite seriously; fliers were distributed, and further dedicated ads were placed in the *Los Angeles Reader* and in the listings section of the *LA Weekly*.

One flier, created by Salomon Emquies, was a chaotic collage of the type that would have been on display on the walls at the CASH club, with a mix of typed captions and hand-scrawled titles. To one side of the flier, a top-hat-clad man wearing a defaced smile and a hand-drawn THE FLOW shirt stands in front of a chandelier-style balloon arrangement. "P-Funk Rap by The Flow," the typed-and-pasted text advertised, introducing the "coolest, the badest [*sic*]":

M.C. Rapper Master Anthony K.
Rhythm Maker Jack I.
String Bender Hillel S.
and Big String Bender Michael B.

An extensive effort was made to advertise these shows, which is interesting in that most acts listed alongside them in newspapers and on flier walls were established acts that would have played for at least thirty minutes, not the five or ten that the Flow did. One possibility is that they would have drawn a crowd for the rest of the night at the Rhythm Lounge, whose managers would have taken a cut on drinks and food sales. This is supported by looking at the flier; it's an ad for the Rhythm Lounge ("the party machine that will make you screammm") as much as it is for the Flow. Another reason is that they advertised because they could; they were not the type to turn down any publicity, especially with this exciting new endeavor thrust upon them. At the end of the day, the more people that attended the show, the bigger their cut of the night's takings—which would have only been about fifty bucks anyway.

These two performances as the Flow have mostly been condensed into one night in the array of Chili Peppers histories and biographies over the years, but primary sources reveal that there were in fact two shows over two weeks in addition to the first December 16 performance. Yet sadly, once again, there are no surviving photos or audio recordings circulating to definitively document what was said, what was played, and how they played it; only imperfect remembrances ravaged by time and liberal use of narcotics throughout the rest of the decade.

And after the show, there was a strange sense of stillness. The band did not continue on an immediately upward trajectory as has been suggested. In fact, the Flow underwent a period of hibernation following these three initial performances. The rest of January

After a red-hot first performance, the new act decided to keep the good times going under the short-lived name the Flow. This flier was distributed ahead of their January 6, 1983, headlining performance at the Rhythm Lounge. *Salomon Emquies*

and all of February was dedicated to the main acts for Hillel, Jack, and Flea; What Is This played all across Los Angeles, including two shows at the Club Lingerie, and one at the O.N. Klub, Music Machine, and Madame Wong's West. What Is This also recorded a series of demos with producer Neville Johnson, a few of which have surfaced unofficially online.

Flea continued to record off and on his parts in *Suburbia,* and FEAR played two shows about a week apart in late January and early February.* The second of these shows was at Devonshire Downs, a former horse racing track in Northridge that had become part of California State University. FEAR, playing with Angry Samoans and Vandals, were filmed onstage and backstage that night, February 4,

* The band also entered a recording studio at some point in February, most likely to record the track "Brainwashed." To date, that recording—the only one with the band featuring Flea—has not surfaced.

as part of a multinight look at the punk scene by KTTV, a Los Angeles TV station. As Chris Harris, the mustachioed host puts it, punk was "indeed fast and hard, the lyrics often dealing with violence and destruction, with raw sexual overtones," and KTTV were on the scene to stoke the concerns of the parents of Los Angeles (and by extension, parents across the entire country). The multinight exposé on punk is at moments a classic moral panic hit piece and fairly clueless, managing not only to miss the joke of FEAR but also to fall right into its trap. But it provides us with some invaluable on-the-ground reporting of the scene as it stood in 1983 (and it does, to its credit, offer many different viewpoints, giving punks of the day substantial airtime).

After some onstage footage of the band playing their tracks "Let's Have a War" and "I Love Livin' in the City," they cut backstage, where Spit Stix and Lee Ving are interviewed, being surprisingly frank about the band's tongue-in-cheek philosophy, which somehow didn't manage to cut through to the show's producers. A young, silent Mike B. the Flea sits to their right and offers no words throughout, but he's there, and aside from his scenes in *Suburbia,* it's perhaps the earliest footage available of him. It's an interesting period for the young man; the seeds have been planted for his eventual worldwide fame—the band, the movies, his place in the scene as a whole—but they have yet to take root. A few more weeks, and that quiet young man's life is about to become a whole lot louder.

SHOW #4

MARCH 4, 1983

Cathay de Grande, 1600 Argyle Avenue, Los Angeles, CA

IN THE WEEKS AFTER the three performances at the Rhythm Lounge, Anthony, Flea, and Hillel pooled their resources and left the Wilton Hilton for their own place. Their new three-bedroom home was on Leland Way, a cul-de-sac just off Sunset Boulevard colloquially known by locals as Pot Alley. They weren't made welcome; the existing residents, wary of newcomers, threw bottles and rocks at them on the day they moved in, but it wasn't enough to deter them from sticking around.

There was more than just a change of address. After three shows performing as the Flow, it was also time for a change of name. The exact timing of the change is impossible to pin down, and the exact reasons for changing it can only be speculated on, but it happened shortly before this show at the Cathay de Grande in early March. The Flow were no longer. Now, they were the Red Hot Chili Peppers.

Like much related to the band in these early days, there's not much in the way of concrete information about who came up with the name for the band or where it was sourced from. High school friend Keith Barry takes credit for it in the band's *Oral/Visual History* book, and Matt Dike recalls the uncertainty about whether they should stick with the Flow or change to the Red Hot Chili Peppers in the same publication. In his autobiography, Anthony writes about actively drawing upon jazz groups who had similar names in the past: Louis Armstrong and the Hot Five being one example, Jelly Roll Morton's Red Hot Peppers being another offered up by others as a possible influence. In an early interview, Anthony also drew upon the Biblical story of Moses and his burning bush as the source for the name, but this genesis was obviously in jest. Others have speculated that that the Robert Johnson song "They're Red Hot" served as inspiration for the band's name, which explains why the band would then wind up covering the track in 1991, but this is a claim without much merit. Gary Allen recalled sitting in a car with Hillel the night of a show—either this March 4 show or perhaps an earlier performance—and suggesting the name the Red Hots, and then being surprised when he heard the very similar final name shortly afterward. Whether this was a pure coincidence or part of the actual provenance of the name will likely never be known.

Regardless of who actually came up with the Red Hot Chili Peppers, it was agreed upon during the quiet month of February and unleashed at the Cathay de Grande nightclub, right in the middle of Hollywood, on this night in early March of 1983. Opened in its current form in December of 1973, the long, flat rectangle of a building at 1600 Argyle Avenue had long been a restaurant called the Nickodell, with a sister location on Melrose Avenue, but this was the lesser, quickly closed location of the two; by the time the Red Hot Chili Peppers played here, it had been a Chinese restaurant for about a decade.

While drinks were served up on street level, the club and stage were in the basement, and as you descended the stairs to the dance floor you would be confronted with a torrent of scrawled names over the white walls; some of these names were legends in the scene and now legends worldwide, some anonymous fans, but everyone was given equal footing in the subterranean stairwell. The room itself was in rough shape. Photos and videos from the era show a collapsing patchwork of a roof, with tiles missing and the wiring exposed. It was a serious fire risk that could never operate legally in the twenty-first century. Bands stood to one side as they played on the same level as the crowd—meaning those at the back of the room would have a hard time seeing the action—but it was a small enough space that you were never very far away anyway. It was the kind of place where the walls would be wet after a particularly raucous show, and as little existed in the way of ventilation, they would remain that way for some time.

This night was another theme; the "Rap-Beat-Funk-Off," a hip-hop and DJ night held by Wayzata de Camerone. Originally, the nights were supposed to be held at two other L.A. clubs and suffered a few false starts, but by late February they had moved to Friday nights at the Cathay de Grande.

Born Mark Cameron Boyd in Jonesboro, Arkansas, de Camerone was a member of the Brainiacs, a short-lived punk and funk band in the late 1970s and early '80s. But he was better known as the proprietor of the Zero Zero, an infamous Hollywood speakeasy club whose first iteration was only doors down from CASH and was well known for being the only place in town someone could get a real drink after hours. Shortly after opening, it was being visited by the likes of John Belushi, Bill Murray, and other hip Hollywood stars. Much like CASH, the Zero Zero also doubled as an art gallery, and many L.A.-based photographers and artists, such as local legend Gary Leonard, exhibited their work there until it petered out of existence in late 1981.

Also appearing between bands that night were two DJs—John Callahan and David Hughes—who would have been more known to the crowd for their band, Age of Consent. The duo met in early 1981 at a presentation given by Hughes about contemporary music, in the course of which Hughes had dismissed disco as a lesser genre. This incensed Callahan; he stuck around afterward, and the two struck up a conversation that blossomed into a friendship, and then into a band. Forming much in the way the Chili Peppers had, as an intended one-off performance of a single rap song, Age of Consent quickly started performing around Los Angeles, developing into a more established live act that would later include Parliament-Funkadelic guitarist DeWayne "Blackbyrd" McKnight, short-lived member of the Red Hot Chili Peppers in 1988.

But Age of Consent did not actually perform this night; instead, they let their record collection do the work for them. A look at their record collection at the time suggests some of their possible selections, blasted over the PA system while audience members danced, flirted with one another, and did whatever secret maneuvers in the bathrooms that they needed to while the bands set up their instruments; "Nasty Rock" by the P Crew (1983), "The Bottom Line" by South Bronx (1982), and "Shake It Off" by November Group (1982). There was even "Pack Jam" by the Jonzun Crew, a track very familiar to certain members of the audience. They were varied and full of deep cuts, in a world where this music was less readily available than it is today, with little presence on the radio.

The month away from the stage didn't mean the Chili Peppers weren't busy; this show doubled their repertoire again, with two more songs, and a couple of extra additions padding out the set. Where the band's original two songs adapted certain elements from hip-hop, with their silly storytelling and chest-pumping braggadocio, this first new one took certain influences further, touching on the real-life social issues suggested in tracks like "The Message." The first new track,

"Police Helicopter," was about the omnipresent lights shining through Anthony's new bedroom window on Leland Way from the police circling above, trying in vain to uncover and disperse the constant stream of drug deals happening in the streets below.

Much of Los Angeles was a rough place to live in 1983, and Hollywood and its surroundings, South Central LA in particular, were the epicenter of a rising drug and gang problem.* Crack cocaine had just arrived on the streets; this had been done by business savvy dealers to combat the oversaturation of the powder version of cocaine, and with that came wider distribution, lower prices, and more crime. The response from state and federal governments steeped in Reagan's tough-on-crime policies, which were as popular with suburban America as they were damaging to its urban counterpart, was to flood the city with police officers and insist on tougher penalties for those caught with drugs. This is despite the fact that much of that crack cocaine is alleged to have been funneled into Los Angeles through Nicaraguan cartels backed by the CIA in the first place. Leland Avenue itself was the site of a drug bust in July 1983 that netted eight pounds of cannabis and fifty-eight arrests, mostly of illegal immigrants. While this increased police presence may have resulted in more arrests, it also led to palpable tension between ordinary citizens and those enlisted to protect and serve them. As drug users, even casual ones, if Anthony, Flea, and Hillel weren't in constant fear of the police, they were at least wary of them, and their relationship with the police was never particularly harmonious (even if, as straight White men, they had it relatively easy). It wasn't just drug related, either; police were constantly shutting down shows in the punk community and moving whatever crowds they deemed unruly along. And, like many police forces around the world, they were unfairly targeting minorities over

* But to be fair, according to statistic compilers the Disaster Center, crime rates in California as a whole fell during the year. (Disaster Center. "California Crime Rates 1960–2019." Accessed July 18, 2022. https://www.disastercenter.com/crime/cacrime.htm)

White people. It was a decade before Rodney King and the L.A. riots, but the problems were obviously very much already there.

"Police Helicopter" is a beat poem of sorts, one that laments the state of Los Angeles as it stood in the early 1980s, with a constant police presence and persistent waves of paranoia clouding most, if not all, social interaction. It was inevitable that these remote-surveillance instruments would turn up in the band's music. As Anthony would state in an interview six years later, quoting the song in question, "Growing up in Hollywood gives you a lot of tension, aggression and frustration because there's so much sensory input. . . . The people, the traffic, the lights, the movies, the palm trees, the ocean, the breeze, the hills—the police helicopters landing on your eyeballs. They're all there barking down your face day and night. What can you do but regurgitate it in your music?"

Much like "Out in L.A.," "Police Helicopter" is more of an extended play on a riff than a typical verse-chorus-verse piece. Anthony raps, and the band responds, and they all repeat their parts until it comes to a screeching halt. It's a short track—especially when the band was in a manic and uplifted state—running only about eighty seconds in most performances. By design, the song sounded like an attack from its titular subject. To extend it at all would reduce its impact.

The other track premiered that night wasn't much longer than "Police Helicopter," and it wasn't dealing with quite as grown-up themes. "Nevermind" is a claim of sorts that the band, only a few weeks old and with a few scrappy tracks to their name, were actually more worthy of time, respect, and adoration than many of the "in" chart-topping artists of the time.

It's all very tongue in cheek—at least, partly. In his a capella opening lines, Anthony scoffs at the Pac Jam, but they were the soundtrack to a dance piece that opened one of the band's first shows; he rejects the Gap Band and the Zapp Band, two different funk pioneers he adored, and who had just hosted Grandmaster Flash in concert a few months previous. Funk was a scam, he said, but never fear, because the Red Hot Chili Peppers were there to make things right. In the next verse he focuses on some more obvious targets, like Wham, Duran Duran, Men at Work, and Hall & Oates ("Those guys are a couple of goats!"), all acts that were charting high in the early months of 1983. They might have been worthy of some scorn, but of course, some of these acts would be joining the Red Hot Chili Peppers in the Rock and Roll Hall of Fame in the distant future. Perhaps the lyrics don't hold up to much scrutiny, but the inherent message was key here, and it became the band's version of a big-headed hip-hop track and a chest-pump football chant rolled into one.

In recordings from later that year, and for every performance thereafter, including the album version, "Nevermind" is introduced by a spoken word piece from Anthony, a tongue-twisting story about pool hustling lifted from "Sport," a 1973 track by the poet and rap frontiersman Lightnin' Rod, but with Anthony's name inserted into all the relevant areas.*

Both these new tracks also revolved around Flea's slap bass, an ingredient that along with Slovak's punk-influenced jazzy scratching, was becoming a signature touch. Bass slapping had been around since the 1920s and was a constant in jazz when it was performed on a standing double bass, but Sly and the Family Stone bassist Larry Graham (among others) had refined the technique for the electric, and had turned it into a funk mainstay—especially when Graham formed his own band, Graham Central Station, in 1973.† But where Graham, and later funk bassists like Bootsy Collins of Parliament-Funkadelic, kept the bpm relatively low, steady, and groovy, Flea—inspired by the

* "Well, now they called me Sport 'cause I pushed a boss short, and loved all the women to death" became "Well, now they call me the Swan, 'cause I wave my magic wand," but the rest of the piece is basically unchanged.

† The band's track "Hair," off their 1974 self-titled album, is just one example of a bass sound that eerily resembles what Flea would later be known for.

bass player for Star, the *other* established band at Fairfax High during the Anthym days—added a punk element to slap, turning it into a thrashing, percussive instrument that wound up driving the band a large amount of the time, as opposed to it being the less present support system that bassists trended toward. Instead of hitting root notes and letting Hillel lead the show, a slap bassline from Flea is a complex, octave-stretching exercise in dexterity. Slap would treat Flea well, and he would return to the technique on virtually every original Chili Peppers track over the next few years. Soon the name Flea would be synonymous with slap bass, for better or worse.

Aside from "Police Helicopter" and "Nevermind," the band filled time at the show by entertaining the crowd with the occasional a capella campfire song. One was "Stranded," a song about being stuck on the toilet without any toilet paper, adapted from the theme song for the short-lived TV Western *Branded*, which aired on NBC between 1965 and 1966. Virtually immediately, the theme song had been transformed into a schoolyard joke, and almost twenty years later was still being gleefully performed by immature young men, backed up by Jack Irons and a snare pattern from his marching band days. Jack himself would look back on the a cappella tunes with a laugh, remembering that "they went down really well, because everybody else knew them as well. Gigs turned into these enormous singsongs!" Judging from the recording of the song done in May of 1983, it would appear that Slovak took the vocal lead in this song; Anthony later stated that it was Hillel who introduced the song to the rest of the band.

"Oom Chucka Willie" was another a cappella track that may have been sung on this night, a dirty limerick from the gang's childhood that Anthony had already partially cribbed for a verse on "Out in L.A." According to one biography written around the band, another traditional campfire song also said to have been performed that night was a play on "She'll Be Coming 'Round the Mountain." These were all useful techniques to flesh out too-short sets, or fill time while guitars were tuned or restrung, which was a common occurrence.

This historic March 4 show was sparsely attended, with only about thirty people in attendance, but that didn't stop Anthony from diving into the crowd, spinning like a top and spraying the crowd with his beer as if it was a chock-full club. "So fun, no thought involved," Flea remembered. "Wild expression only." Everybody who was there loved the show, but the low turnout would cause problems when Anthony went to collect the band's earnings. After promising $200, Camerone had only been able to come up with $40, and so Anthony pushed him into a urinal in the men's room until he came up with some more cash. "I couldn't conceive of someone breaking a deal and then trying to weasel out of it," he would later say. Already, he was taking certain aspects of this endeavor quite seriously.

This show also provided the band's first mention under their permanent name in the *LA Weekly*, the first of millions of inches of worldwide newspaper coverage they would enjoy in the years to come. In the March 11, 1983, edition of L.A.-Dee-Da, the ear-on-the-street gossip section, one of the roving reporters raves about the show the previous Friday:

> A four piece funk combo consisting of Flea from Fear and members of What Is This, the Chili Peppers were a wild, hot thang featuring Flea rolling through somersaults (with his, ahem, instrument on) and the whole ensemble singing perverse jump rope songs acapella in between tunes.

L.A.-Dee-Da was presented with four bylines, but there's a good chance this specific part was written by Pleasant Gehman, a young writer who had started the column in 1980, and whose gaze would remain fixed upon the Chili Peppers as they soared through their formative years. There was one other connection; Gehman was the booker for the Cathay de Grande, and so in a sense she was advertising her own shows through the column. Perhaps slightly iffy in the ethics department, but a clever way to spread the word. Looking back, Flea seemed aware of the new attention, but took it all in stride. "Hollywood scenesters are there—just these people who hung around."

They were making waves, and making them pretty much instantly.

SHOW #5

MARCH 25, 1983

Cathay de Grande, 1600 Argyle Avenue, Los Angeles, CA

DESPITE THE DISAGREEMENT with de Camerone (or perhaps thanks to the influence of Pleasant Gehman), the band were invited back to the Cathay de Grande three weeks later for another show alongside Restless Natives, a flash-in-the-pan band whose name doesn't appear anywhere outside this show's listings, and de Camerone's own Wayzata Band. There's no word on what the Red Hot Chili Peppers played, but the set list probably closely matched the previous show; What Is This played three shows around Los Angeles during the latter half of March, including one at 321 Club with Martini Ranch, actor Bill Paxton's band, and so the band most likely didn't have the time to write any new songs.

A flier for this show, with FUNK TO DEATH scrawled up top and Flea's recognizable (even by then) gap-tooth below, is reproduced in the band's official photo book. Most interesting, in this flier the band are considered the headliners for this show, even though Wayzata was running the night, but perhaps that's just because the band themselves made the flier; in these wild-and-free times you could make yourself the headliner if you wanted to be. Anthony explained their promotional methods in these early days three decades later: "There was absolutely no shame in our game and we didn't care that we were self-promoting with the most grandiose and kind of arrogantly egomaniacal, obnoxious attitude, because A) we were twenty and B) we were nothing. So it was okay to promote nothing like it was the greatest."

Anthony's father, John "Blackie Dammett" Kiedis, appeared backstage this night as well, and would begin to show up fairly frequently at Chili Peppers gigs, bringing dates and friends and starting the unofficial precursor to the official fan club he would one day run. One of the friends he brought to these early shows was James Granville Brown, known professionally as Jay Brown. Dammett had met Brown in 1977 after scoring a bit part in the crime drama *Final Chapter: Walking Tall*, and the two had been drinking and skirt-chasing buddies ever since. Brown was impressed with the band, and an idea started percolating that night about where they could head—under his guidance.

Also backstage at the show was Nina Hagen, a musician originally from East Berlin who by then had already lived a wild life on both sides of the Iron Curtain, and had achieved some success in Europe in the late seventies before being thrown out of East Germany. But having dissolved her eponymous Nina Hagen Band, she was now performing as a solo artist; in June 1982 she had released *NunSexMonkRock*, which had peaked just inside the Billboard 200, her first charting in the United States. Anthony met up with Hagen and her two-year-old daughter, Cosma Shiva, either the day after the show or shortly thereafter, and the two quickly developed their relationship from simple flirtations into something physical that would ebb and flow over the course of the year.

Photos taken backstage at this performance by scene legend Gary Leonard give an insight into the wild scenes of an early Red Hot Chili Peppers show; Anthony in his stage costume of paisley coat and fluorescent-orange hunting cap, Flea and Jack in similarly manic shirts, Hillel with his own backward cap and what looks like a dinner suit, all of them up against the Cathay de Grande's dirty wall like four perps in a police lineup that are inappropriately happy to be there. It seems almost bizarre to see them in so many clothes, but the energy is palpable, even through these gritty black-and-white snaps.*

* Because these two shows happened at the same place in the same month, there's a chance many of these stories—the argument with de Camerone over payment, the Leonard photos, Anthony meeting Nina Hagen—have been misremembered and misdated, and actually took place at the other show that month.

SHOW #6

MARCH 31, 1983

Club Lingerie, 6507 Sunset Boulevard, Los Angeles, CA

WHAT IS THIS played the Roxy on March 29, opening for the Plugz, an early Latino punk group and DIY pioneers who would perform as Bob Dylan's backing band on *Late Night with David Letterman* the following year. A few days later, the Chili Peppers, in a stroke of insane luck, played the Club Lingerie.

For a band playing their sixth-ever show, with only a handful of songs and a set that would last about fifteen minutes max, an upgrade to the Club Lingerie opening for an act as big as the much-revered Minutemen was something truly special. In fact, it's such a meteoric catapult in their fortunes that it's strange that the band have never acknowledged it in the years since—typically reserving, in memoirs and retellings, their "big break" story for another show at the Club Lingerie three months later, opening for another legendary act. Their good fortune in booking the show may have come from being a last-minute addition. Early fliers don't mention the band, and they only finally appear in an *LA Weekly* newspaper ad circulated on the morning of the show. If they *were* only a fill-in for another band, or the only band free at such short notice on the night, this might be why they were given such a great opportunity at such an early stage; there was simply no one else available, and they were in the right place at the right time.

This shift to a more legitimate venue meant that the band came up against the issue of their fresh ages. By this point in March, none of the band members were over the age of twenty-one; Hillel would be the first to come of age, but not for another two weeks. Because of this, Brendan Mullen, who booked and ran the Club Lingerie, had the band wait outside before and after they played, lest the authorities shut down another one of his clubs. Linda Kite, a friend of the Minutemen and D. Boon's next-door neighbor growing up, was in the audience and witnessed this awkward maneuvering: "My friend Kevin that I went with went backstage to go talk to them and had to go find them in the alley."

Mullen was born in 1949 in Paisley, a tiny town in the Lowlands of Scotland, and was a journalist and part-time drummer in his homeland before he moved to the United States in 1973. In January 1979 he founded the Masque, a club on Cherokee Avenue, just off Hollywood Boulevard. A ten-thousand-square-foot basement behind the X-rated Pussycat theater, the Masque was intended as a rehearsal space at first, but within a few months Mullen was supplementing the income derived from that by also putting on shows in the room, hosting the likes of the Weirdos, and the Germs, and Chili Peppers favorites, X. "Local rock bands that couldn't get bookings at more formal clubs because of their looks and behavior found a home in the seedy cellar," wrote Cindy Jourdan in the *LA Weekly.* "Punk enthusiasts poured in."

Flea was a big fan of the venue himself, writing in 2010 that "when Brendan started the Masque, it was a pure act, creating a place for people he liked to do their thing, have fun and get wild, no salesmen allowed. It became a nucleus for a thrilling new music environment that gave birth to the Southern California punk rock music scene."

Like many other clubs at the time, it was shut down a number of times for licensing, permit, and noise issues, having to open in alternate locations from time to time, and by 1979 it closed for good after one last raid by the LAPD and a serious fire code infringement. Mullen quickly opened another club, the King's Palace, but this, too, was short-lived, and he soon moved on to more permanent digs at the Club Lingerie.

The Lingerie had been open under various names since the 1940s—Whisling's Hawaii, the Sundown Club, and the Summit, where it was host to jazz greats like Dizzy Gillespie—but had changed its name to the Lingerie in mid-1981. Mullen had originally been asked to DJ a Latin music night but offered his booking services instead, and within a year of him taking over, the Lingerie stage had been honored with the presence of jazz oracle Sun Ra, R&B singer Big Mama Thornton, and FEAR, the first time Flea ever saw them play live. What Is This had even played there, on January 10 of that year; to Hillel and Jack, this big break was their second go-around.

But here were the Chili Peppers on this Thursday night, as part of an "evening of mayhem funk" sponsored by Long Beach's SST Records, which had just released the Minutemen's second album, *What Makes a Man Start Fires?*, and were about to release a follow-up EP, *Buzz or Howl Under the Influence of Heat*. On the ad posted in the *LA Weekly*, a quote attributed to Parliament-Funkadelic bandleader and funk legend George Clinton is listed alongside the Chili Peppers' name: "Funk not only moves, it re-moves."

Cribbed from the 1975 Parliament song "P-Funk (Wants to Get Funked Up)," it's notable that such an overt Clinton reference appears so early in their career. In later years, band members would admit to an initial level of naivete when it came to George Clinton's work. Anthony states in his autobiography that he only discovered the work of Clinton, his bands, and his solo work after *The Red Hot Chili Peppers* had come out in August of 1984. "After our first record, people came up to us and said 'You must be students of the P Funk,'" he recalled. They were admitting as much as early as 1985; in an interview with street mag *BAM*, Anthony said that, after being told about Clinton's work, "we checked him out. We bought all his records, listened to them all, and really liked them all." Flea later concurred, stating that he "didn't know very much about that stuff yet" until well into 1984; Bob Forrest also takes credit for introducing the duo to Funkadelic after they moved in with him later in the year. But this reference (and the other early reference to "P-funk rap" in the flier for the January 6 show as the Flow) might imply that, early on, they knew more about his work than they were perhaps letting on, for whatever reason.*

Formed in 1980, the Minutemen were fronted by Dennes "D." Boon, who would die in a tragic car wreck in 1985, bringing the band to an early and abrupt end just as they were on the cusp of attracting a much wider audience. Their bass player and occasional singer, Mike Watt, would continue to live in the Chili Peppers orbit for many years; his post-Minutemen band, fIREHOSE, would support the band on a 1988 tour and be name-checked on 1989's "Good Time Boys," and his solo act would support the band on tours in 2003 and 2006. The Chili Peppers would even dedicate their multimillion selling 1991 record *Blood Sugar Sex Magik* to Watt, and to this day, a sticker of D. Boon adorns Flea's $35,000 1961 Fender bass.

This show took place on the eve of Boon's twenty-fifth birthday, and as such the night was replete with celebration. A dance contest

---

* If it was their doing at all; the ad could have been placed by a third party who assumed the Chili Peppers were already the disciples of Clinton that they would later become. There is also the (slimmer) possibility that the quote is meant to accompany the entire listing, not just the Chili Peppers' name, but this doesn't make much sense when considering the music of the Minutemen, which doesn't exactly align with George Clinton's work.

took place, and the prize was a large pizza. Unfortunately, for the talented audience member who ended up winning, Boon ate the entire thing before it could be given out. But then again, it was his special night.

Their ages aside, the Chili Peppers probably didn't see the dance competition. In addition to having to wait outside before and after their set, they had other places to be that night.

SHOW #7

MARCH 31, 1983

The Rhythm Lounge at the Grandia Room, 5657 Melrose Avenue, Los Angeles, CA

THE RED HOT CHILI PEPPERS returned to the Grandia Room on March 31 for one final midnight session at the Rhythm Lounge, an hour or so after opening for the Minutemen across town. While it was only a few months after their last appearance at the club, they were a changed band this time around, with a new name, twice as many songs, and an already somewhat-established crowd of fans to follow them in.

Salomon Emquies put another advertisement in the *Los Angeles Reader* anticipating the show, reproduced in the band's *Oral/Visual History*. This time, there's more of a dancing (or breakdancing) spirit to the ad, as each member of the band is given their own corner, represented by a cartoon man pulling some interesting moves. There are echoes of the previous flier, in which each member is introduced separately, but there's more of a New York graffiti or Keith Haring–style effect* instead of the wild, hand-drawn scribbles of the first flier from December 1982.

Also of note is the *M* to represent Flea; to some he was still known simply as Michael or Mike, but with every passing day and every Chili Peppers or FEAR performance, that name was receding into his past.

It's unknown what else happened at this show; a thousand different things took place, of course, but no stories have surfaced, and the specifics relating to it have been lost to time. There's also the very firm possibility that, owing to the show with the Minutemen being booked for the same night, this booking was canceled at the last minute. There was nothing to stop the band from making the one-mile trip from the Club Lingerie to the Rhythm Lounge in order to make their midnight show, but then again, they might not have considered such a trip necessary after playing their first-ever club show earlier that night.

* Keith Haring's work featured in a number of Rhythm Lounge ads placed in the *LA Weekly* and *Los Angeles Reader* throughout the year.

SHOW #8

APRIL 13, 1983

Anti Club at Helen's Place, 4658 Melrose Avenue, Los Angeles, CA

A NEW VENUE FOR THE CHILI PEPPERS, though they didn't have to travel too far, the Anti Club was only a mile east of the Grandia Room, still well inside that L.A. bubble of theirs, which was yet to be pierced. First held in 1979, one of the club's bookers was Russell Jessum, who played synthesizer at Gary Allen's EP release show, and that connection perhaps explains the band's appearance here in the second week of April, on Hillel Slovak's twenty-first birthday.

Jessum's reasons for starting the club were, by now, quite a familiar story. It was a "place for me and my friends to play," he told the *Los Angeles Times* a few months before the Chili Peppers played there. It was "an alternative for people who can't play the Troubadour or the Roxy. If someone doesn't have the standard bass, guitar and drums then I'm usually pretty excited by it."

The Anti Club was another night held at an existing venue. This time it was Helen's Place, a tavern owned by Helen Guttman on Melrose Avenue. The relationship between Guttman and Jessum and his cobookers, Jack Marquette and Jim Van Tyne, was fractious on a good day; it would devolve even further as the years went on. Guttman barely tolerated the bands that performed at her place, and frequently shut shows down herself when she considered them to be getting out of hand or just too plain weird. Jessum embraced the weirdness: "If someone said they wanted to play the same note for 45 minutes and they thought it was a really important piece," he said, "then I'd probably let them do it."

With punks and freaks (and even the relatively tame same-note-for-forty-five-minutes arty types) gracing Helen's stage on a nightly basis, those shutdowns were happening more and more frequently, and the combatants were frequently canceling booking arrangements on each other. In 1986 there would even be a public and messy divorce between Guttman and Jessum and his cobooking crew, with a multimillion-dollar lawsuit over the use of the club's name spilling out into the letters section of the *LA Weekly*. Jessum and company eventually moved their night elsewhere, but Guttman, clearly deciding that she could tolerate the punks and freaks after all, kept the Anti Club name. Years later, writer Pleasant Gehman, thinking back on Helen, recalled that "she's the only one that could ever get away with charging a performer who wasn't even getting paid twenty-five cents for a cup of water."

Despite the possibility of it, this show went ahead without any lasting drama. A flier was circulated and survives, hand-drawn (probably by Anthony) and advertising "funk from the holy land," alluding to Hillel's Israeli heritage, and his special day.* Underneath is a threat, of sorts, to "be there, or we'll pull out your pubic hair."

Two other acts played on the night. Tucson-based Green on Red were first. Formed in 1979, they were originally known as the Serfers

* A similar nod to Hillel's Israeli heritage would appear in the 1987 track "Organic Anti-Beatbox Band."

but had changed their name at the suggestion of a member of the Germs upon moving to Los Angeles, and soon released a self-titled EP. A few weeks away from recording their debut album, entitled *Gravity Talks*, Green on Red were quite a different sound to the Chili Peppers; the *LA Weekly* referred to them as "working class psychedelia" in a mention later that year, and they were lumped in with the "paisley underground" fad that reached its apex in the mid-1980s. A world away from the frenetic punk-funk of the early Chili Peppers.

Also playing were the Leaving Trains, a band closer in sound to Green on Red (in a sense the Chili Peppers were the odd one out at this show). They were fronted by James Moreland, who would wind up briefly marrying Courtney Love in 1989.

Green on Red vocalist and guitarist Dan Stuart has no memory of playing this show. However, he recalled being in a student film with Anthony that would have been shot around the same time, perhaps in the year beforehand. Directed by a film student from UCLA, which Anthony attended for a short period, it was unfortunately never released, despite some preliminary screenings. Stuart was hard pressed to recall any details but remembered spray-painting Anthony's face for a scene filmed by the Los Angeles River. An interesting curio that has yet to see the light of day, though it may yet survive in an unofficial archive somewhere.

A series of photos from this night have surfaced, taken by the ever-present and future-thinking Fabrice Drouet. Anthony's look is unique—decked out in a backward cap, leather vest, and short-sleeve muscle shirt, his choices are questionable, but one can't question his commitment to individuality. Flea and Hillel are topless and wear matching bowler hats, and it's obvious even through these still images that the band are a chaotic and thrilling sight to behold up on the little stage at the back of Helen's main room. If these photos do date from this night (there's a slim chance they could have also been taken at either of the band's two engagements at the Anti Club in June),

After taking February off, the band—now named the Red Hot Chili Peppers—play the Anti Club on Melrose Avenue. This is the earliest circulating photograph of the band onstage. April 13, 1983—Hillel's twenty-first birthday. *fabulosfab*

they have the honor of being the earliest images of a Red Hot Chili Peppers show. Of the over 1,800 and counting they've played, here in crisp black and white is the earliest look available.

FEAR finally played for the first time since February shortly after this show, with an April 16 performance at the On Broadway club in San Francisco with fellow punk acts Toxic Reasons and Minus One. Spirits were high: on the way back from the trip, Spit Stix recalled Flea laughing so hard the "peanuts and beer he was consuming came out of his nose."

SHOW #9

APRIL 29, 1983

The Plant, 12446 Ventura Boulevard, Studio City, CA

FINALLY LEAVING THE CONFINES OF HOLLYWOOD, the band headed north for this show, across the hills and into Studio City for the first of several performances at the Plant on Ventura Boulevard. The building was a health and beauty spot throughout the 1950s and '60s, offering massages, "figure diagnosis," and "supervised exercise" to the ladies (and strictly the ladies) of Hollywood, but by mid-1977 the Bla Bla Café had moved in.

Originally located about two miles east of this new location, the original Bla Bla nightclub was where many comedy and music behemoths put in their practice hours, with the likes of Peter Allen and Jay Leno making a name for the place amid many a late night and early morning. But seeking larger quarters, they headed west, and it was here that the Bla Bla stayed until it shut for good in mid-1982. By March the location had opened once again as the Plant, and was predominately a restaurant, serving omelets, burgers, and the house sandwich: cream cheese and spaghetti sauce on a sesame egg bun. The first show held there was headlined by the Plugz, who had played with What Is This the previous month.

While in these days, bands would play in all kinds of rooms, from bare basements to converted theaters, the Plant had a particularly interesting interior. Most of the floor was a fairly elegant dining room, with striking industrial lamps and metal ventilation tubing on the roof giving the place a kind of factory or spaceship vibe. But instead of a traditional stage, or even just a raised platform in the corner, the talent (not just musicians; comedians still played on Monday nights) performed from a boxed-out area revealed by a roll-up garage door that doubled as the stage curtain. This is where the Red Hot Chili Peppers played on this Friday night in April.

It's at this show that the band most likely debuted their next composition, something that they had been working hard on between parties at the house on Leland Way. If "Police Helicopter" spoke directly about Anthony's displeasure with the state, "Green Heaven" casts a wider net, comparing the pristine natural world with the manufactured one, contrasting the pollution-filled life above the ocean with that underneath. It's another dark funk track based around an E7 chord, with a driving, snarling riff that switches halfway through to something more serene, as Anthony takes a break from rapping about police brutality and institutional xenophobia to take a carefree swim with the dolphins instead. It sounds silly on paper, and toes the line on tape, but it's an intense song that shows off its contrasts beautifully.*

Flea, in particular, was a big fan of "Green Heaven," and upon hearing Anthony's lyrics for the first time, called multiple people

* With its aquatic themes, it's not clear why the song is called "Green Heaven" and not "Blue Heaven," but that's perhaps a question only Anthony can answer.

Flea and Jack during a Red Hot Chili Peppers show at the Plant on Ventura Boulevard. April 29, 1983. *fabulosfab*

(including his mother) and read out the whole set of lyrics.* The band were proud of it, and spent twenty-four straight hours working on its early arrangement. If there was ever an ideal time to debut the song, it would be on this night.

The band opened for a duo of art-punkers. First up were the Party Boys, who were considered "industrial," but in a different sense from the way we might recognize today; they weren't quite Throbbing Gristle or Nine Inch Nails, but they had propulsive beats and came

* A copy of Anthony's handwritten lyrics for the song (seemingly written in 1983) appear in the liner notes of the 2003 reissue of the band's debut album.

from the swaths of Los Angeles that held factories and warehouses, with a sound that was primitive dance.

Alongside the Party Boys was the Minutemen, whom the band had played with a few weeks previously at Club Lingerie. The Chili Peppers loved the Minutemen and would have been keen to impress them; "Green Heaven," with its social bent and irresistible, intertwining groove, may have been just the thing to bring out to achieve that, if they hadn't already played it at their March 31 show. "Green Heaven" sounded nothing like a Minutemen track, but it shared similar themes to many of them, and the bands were more alike than one might assume.

Fabrice Drouet also attended this show, and once again brought his camera with him. It's from his vantage point that we have one of our clearest looks at the early Red Hot Chili Peppers onstage. It's a chaotic set of photographs, full of backscatter ghosts that make it seem like the band were playing in the middle of a bonfire, but the energy is unmissable. Flea and Hillel are topless, performing somersaults in between riffs, and while Anthony is wearing a shirt, it's only for a brief portion, as he quickly removes it even while keeping his ever-present fluorescent hunting cap on. The band look crazed and young and like deer in the headlights.

It's also notable that they've virtually immediately ditched the layers of clothing that they had worn at earlier shows. Gone is Anthony's paisley jacket. While the immense heat of performing might have explained their initial move away from wearing clothes onstage, there was another reason, as Anthony remembered many years later. "Everyone else was kind of dressing up in these very sort of pompous, arrogant costumes, and we thought, *Let's just strip it down.*"

Before this show, Jay Brown, friend of Anthony's father, Blackie, told *his* friend Mark Richardson about the band. Richardson, an Atlanta-born musician and recording engineer, had spent time in

Anthony and Hillel during a Red Hot Chili Peppers show at the Plant on Ventura Boulevard. April 29, 1983. *fabulosfab*

recording studios in New York and London, and knew Jay Brown thanks to some television work they had done together. Richardson remembered that he first saw the band in a "strange bar in LA, not at all the sort of place you'd expect" that had "rarely, if ever, staged live music before," and was enamored with their "dangerous energy and sexual bravado," deciding on the spot that he had to become involved with them. Richardson, Brown, and the senior Kiedis planned a meeting with the band shortly afterward, with the intention that Richardson, who "knew a thing or two about management," would quickly take over the reins.

The band were a no-show, which perhaps was a result of poor communication, or just indicative of the kinds of antiauthoritarians they were at this period. But Richardson didn't give up, keeping the band in the back of his mind, waiting for his moment. In the meantime, the band had some plans of their own.

RECORDING SESSION

EARLY MAY, 1983

Studio 9 Sound Labs,
5504 Hollywood Boulevard, Los Angeles, CA

IN EARLY MAY 1983 the Red Hot Chili Peppers, a rough-and-raw group barely six months old that had played fewer than ten shows and had only a few real songs to their name, found themselves in a recording studio to track their first batch of demos.

There were many reasons why the Chili Peppers needed to get their sound on tape, aside from the simple and understandable desire to hear what they sounded like at full fidelity. Demos were an important tool for bands, not just to attract record company attention but also to book shows; many club promoters around Los Angeles (and the rest of the country) required an example of a band's sound before they would allow them on their hallowed stages, especially if they were unsigned. Usually, this took the form of a cassette, mailed in after a solicitation from somewhere like the *LA Weekly*. The Chili Peppers had already played a number of fairly high-profile gigs, but they were about to reach the ceiling of what was possible without recording a demo, and so time was booked.

Reminiscing about the session in later years, the band spoke of it as a natural progression, something that felt like the right thing to do at this stage. "For me, this whole process was a two-part thing," Anthony wrote. "You wrote and practiced the songs, and then you played shows. And we wanted to play bigger and bigger shows." This was also one of the first inklings that this Chili Peppers project was more than just something fun to do a few nights a month. Here there was some forward thinking. Bands who don't make plans certainly don't record demos.

They had no record company backing yet, but luckily, they had friends with connections who could get them cheap studio time. Tim "Spit Stix" Leitch, Flea's drummer bandmate in FEAR, was working at Studio 9 Sound Labs in the Hollywood & Western Building during this period. At Flea's request, he pulled some strings and managed to book them a few hours of cheap studio time, for probably around twenty dollars an hour, which would have also included equipment hire and dubbing services. As for Stix, he worked for free. "I was just happy to be recording and mixing."

Hollywood & Western, named as one might expect after its location on the corner of Hollywood Boulevard and Western Avenue, was an Art Deco masterpiece opened in the late 1920s that had a long history in the film industry. Containing the offices of the Motion Picture Association of America and its Central Casting division, it was here in the golden era of Hollywood that many a deal was made, many a career was started, and many motion pictures had their content dictated to them by Will Hays and his morally puritanical Motion Picture Production Code.*

The three-hour long session was bankrolled by Anthony, who said he was the only one with any real money that week, but Flea

* Of course, like many other places in Hollywood, the building and, indeed, the entire neighborhood devolved into squalor, and by the mid-1970s the building was used to film pornography. A far cry from Hays's days.

also recalls Fabrice Drouet chipping in. Drouet attended the session and a few days later was given one of the many cassette dubs that were inscribed by Anthony, a prized object that he still has in his possession today.

Stix, who was also working on a reggae record at Studio 9 at the time, engineered the recordings. He was free, of course; FEAR hadn't played live since April 16, and wouldn't play again until July, and so he had to busy himself with other projects. Stix engineered as well, utilizing some of the tricks he had picked up in his time at the studio. For instance, while setting the sound levels, he had the band specifically play music that they *wouldn't* be recording—a jam, or a cover they all knew—so that once recording started he could capture takes that were truly first takes. In the end, he only ended up recording one take of each song.

The tracks recorded were a typical set by the band: ten different pieces coming to about sixteen minutes, highlighting that without their stage banter they really struggled to fill time during performances. It's unclear what the recording order was, and there may have been no real reason to record them in any specific order; this was a raw demo for an unsigned band, not an artists' audition or an attempt at cutting a specific single. A dubbed cassette runs as follows: "Get Up and Jump," "Out in L.A.," "Green Heaven," "Police Helicopter," "Nevermind," "Sex Rap," and "You Always Sing the Same." This order was retained when the tracks were released on the 1994 compilation *Out in L.A.*, and so perhaps this was the recording order; no documentation seems to have survived to suggest otherwise.

That wasn't all. The band were so productive that day that they had time to include their campfire tracks as well, recording a take of "Stranded," "Oom Chucka Willie," and "Flea Fly," endeavors which weren't a part of the original plan. These extra songs were hardly something to start a bidding war over, but they were a fun bonus for the other side of the cassette.

Where "Stranded" and "Oom Chucka Willie" were adaptations (or straight rips) of existing songs gleaned from camps and school grounds, "Flea Fly" was ostensibly an original. However, it was a mostly nonsensical call-and-response tune; maybe about Flea, maybe not, and less than a minute long, that served no real purpose except to show off the friendly dynamics between the band members.* It shares some similarities with one of the first songs Flea and Anthony ever wrote, entitled "Himi Limi" and written on a backpacking trip during their teenage years. This older song was pure nonsense, but it was sung in such a way that it seemed like a secret language existed between the two boys, and decades later they could still recite it effortlessly; it was a muscle memory, like the ESP that twins report.

It's unknown what date the recording session took place. The month of May has generally been agreed upon, and the chronology of the band's schedule that year requires it to fall generally into the early days of this month. In his memoir, Blackie Dammett claims Thursday, May 5, although this may not be particularly reliable, as he gets several other details about the sessions wrong, and other dates in the book are inaccurate. Anthony says in his own memoir that it was "a couple of months after" the band formed, which matches loosely. Thinking back thirty-six years later, Spit Stix said May "sounds about right." It may have been as late as Tuesday, May 10.

Except for Anthony, this wasn't the first time the members of the band had been in a recording studio,† but this recording remains our earliest chance to hear the Red Hot Chili Peppers in full flight, and they don't disappoint; it's a blistering set of performances, one that

* The band are only confirmed to have performed "Flea Fly" in concert once, a few weeks after this recording, but it most likely appeared at a fair amount of their early shows when they were short of other material. They teased it several times in the years afterward, including once in 1994, when they were perhaps reminded of its existence by the preparation for its release on the *Out in L.A* compilation.

† Anthym had already recorded several sets of demos in the late 1970s, and What Is This had their own session at some point in early 1983; these tracks have surfaced online. Flea had also recorded with FEAR earlier in the year.

the band still considers among their best even today, with decades of recording experience behind them. As Anthony remembered, the results of the day were "by far the most productive and inspired recording that we've ever done. . . . Everything was perfect."

These were economical recordings, lacking maybe in fidelity (the tape hiss is especially noticeable in quieter moments), but in no way to their detriment. The impact of just the four of them in a room is immense: Hillel's Stratocaster through his humming Marshall amplifier, Flea's StingRay bass fighting for the lead, a closely mic'd drum kit manned by Jack, and Anthony's live vocals were all they needed. Mixing was rudimentary and overdubs were minimal, if any were undertaken at all. Except for perhaps a track or two, these recordings are also vastly superior to their album counterparts, recorded eleven months later with a different guitarist and drummer, and all the auditory trickery that major label backing and a fully kitted-out studio could give them.

"Get Up and Jump" kicks off the proceedings. Slower than they would probably play it in a live setting, it's perhaps the weakest performance of the bunch, with the band sounding slightly nervous and a little too self-aware. They go through the changes well, but when it comes time for Anthony to scat and lead the show, he sounds lost, and it results in an uneven, stodgy mess. This is maybe the one instance in the sessions where a second take would have resulted in a better performance, but it's all forgiven when the next song starts.

Conversely, "Out in L.A." is perhaps the best performance of the band's entire career, from any of their lineups, live or in studio, from any type of song. In under two minutes, the band announce themselves, irresistibly excite the listener, and wrap things up. Other bands would kill to have this kind of ace up their sleeve. If their first performance was anything like this recording, it makes sense that the band made such an impact at the Rhythm Lounge the previous December. Everyone is at the top of their game, and the band are an entirely cohesive whole. Even Anthony, who in the future would struggle getting through the complex and wordy verses when playing the song live, has perfect diction in this recording.

"Green Heaven" begins with a talk-box solo by Hillel, a special intro that is perhaps unique to this performance.* The technique, also known as a "singing guitar," is achieved by a player modulating the sound from a guitar (or another instrument) with a speaker and tube combo that enters a mouth. The guitarist would play, and the signal from their playing would then be shaped by their mouth, a kind of hands-on wah pedal. Talk-box solos might have sounded like fun, a way to get real live words of a guitar, but in 1983 it was mostly a kitsch novelty that would have been synonymous with Peter Frampton's indulgent 1976 track "Do You Feel Like We Do." But Hillel adds a bit of grunt and sass to it, speaking to some unknown person, or perhaps to the entire world: *Why don't you fuck with me?*† A nice entrée, if a little bitter, to the rest of the song, which the band performs perfectly; Jack's drum work, in particular, is a standout.

"Police Helicopter" is next, and it's a tight performance, with palpable tension in between each break. Hillel counts back in each measure with a frenetic pluck behind the nut of his fret, a trick he picked up from (among other places) Robert Fripp, during the King Crimson residency at the Roxy with Alain Johannes.

"Nevermind" features Anthony's rapped intro, a performance the band regarded so highly that they used it on the final version of the

---

* In his autobiography, Anthony states that Hillel's talk-box solo would be the centerpiece of every early show the band played. However, recordings of "Green Heaven" from May and July don't feature the talk box, and photos of the band on stage throughout the year don't feature the required setup on stage with the band. There's a chance he may have only done it this one time as a special studio performance. Of course, there were many shows played this year, and very few recordings made, or photos taken.

† Or is it, "Why *do* you fuck with me"? Hard to tell, but Hillel might be doing a satirical Frampton impression.

song they recorded with George Clinton in Detroit two years later. It's curious why they did so; there's no reason why Anthony couldn't have rerecorded it, so maybe they just wanted to reference these sessions slyly. As for the song itself, it's an entirely serviceable take, featuring interesting, alternating drum patterns from Jack, and harsh, whistle-like guitar from Hillel that adds a kind of tense discordance to the whole thing. But the final version, which features a break for a guitar solo, and a complementary horn session, arguably captures the intended spirit of the song more faithfully.

The two final songs from this session were most likely the newest songs in the band's repertoire. "Sex Rap" is an ode to the female form (and what the male form can do to it) that borders on pornographic. Again, the irony of it being performed in what was once the conservative headquarters of Hollywood is palpable, and while the music is rollicking and thrashable, another song that hinges around a Hillel Slovak E7 chord, it's perhaps a little too immature for its own good.

Anthony wasn't shy about broadcasting his (exuberant) love of sex and sexuality in general; "Out in L.A." already featured an oath to sleep (in less delicate terms) with a multitude of women, "Get Up and Jump" was centered around an attempt to get his friend laid, and the intro to "Nevermind" features a line about his sexual prowess that he didn't even write. The very act of sex—though in this case in a public sense—would also get him in trouble in the months to come, and even in the local news. And what was an immature distraction in this early period would grow more serious as the years went on. In 1990 Anthony was convicted of sexual battery and indecent exposure, after an encounter with a university student at an April 1989 Virginia concert—an incident that he always denied happened. (More recently, Anthony's relationships with young women, women that quite often stayed young even as he grew older, has become a cause for concern among fans.)

But here it's a raw and awesome performance; the vocals are impressive, even if the lyrics might not have been something to write home (or in Flea's case, call home) about, Hillel's feedback-laden harmonic screech to kick things off shows the band already with a telepathic connection, and Jack's drumming to bring the track to a close is so good it's a wonder it hasn't been sampled for a hip-hop track somewhere. Comparing it to its finished counterpart, it's a little undercooked; there's no real chorus, and the whole thing comes to an end in about ninety seconds, but its impact is undeniable.

The other new track was, technically, a cover, though the band would treat it as an original: "You Always Sing"* was originally composed by Joel Virgel-Vierset and had been sung in French during its earlier performances at the CASH club, sometimes accompanied by Flea. It's a sarcastic song; their shortest by far, and its genesis probably lies somewhere in the same vicinity as "Nevermind"; it teases, but the source of the teasing hardly has a leg to stand on. It's all braggadocio, but where "Nevermind" was a wallop of irony, here it's a subtle dig. And you could hardly be bored by the track—it's hardly a track at all: ten seconds long and five words total, and then it's over.

There's a good chance the band may have already played "Sex Rap" and/or "You Always Sing" live, but there's no real evidence to suggest that this was the case. These may be their earliest performances outside of a rehearsal session, but they don't sound *under*-rehearsed.

As the band only recorded one take of each song and were so productive that when they finished their main set and had recorded the schoolyard / campfire /a cappella tracks as a bonus, they still would have had about an hour in recording time left over. But the

* The name of this track differs from appearance to appearance; on the demo tape from May 1983 and the band's debut album a year later, it's simply "You Always Sing." On the 2003 reissue of the album and on 1994's *Out in L.A.*, it's given the full title of "You Always Sing the Same." To complicate things further, on two handwritten set lists, written three days apart in June 2002, Anthony picked both ways to name the track.

Chili Peppers were about getting in and getting out without boring their audience, and so they gladly gave up the extra time knowing they had captured something special. With the recordings finished, they finally had a version of themselves that was permanent, and not a wild affair that existed on a dimly lit stage for a moment only. This was their entire repertoire as it currently stood, and it's a perfect representation of the early Chili Peppers sound—jagged funk attack from Hillel, lead lines disguised as basslines from Flea, catchy rhyming from Anthony (with the odd, occasional genius turn of phrase), and steady yet interesting beats from Jack. All exciting, all unique. Each instrument is represented equally, and each member gets their own time in the spotlight. While there is little in the way of typical verse-chorus-verse structure, one can see where this band might head with a little refinement and a little focus. In essence, it was all raw talent.

This was, in a certain sense, the perfect *demonstration* recording, the real reason to record a demo in the first place. With a recording, they could hear themselves from the outside, and use that to see what worked and what didn't. On stage it was all adrenaline, but here was the chance to listen critically.

It's unclear if the sessions were mixed that day or at a later point: two different versions of the tracks exist—mixed, which have been released officially on 1994's *Out in L.A.* compilation and the 2003 reissues of *The Red Hot Chili Peppers* and *Freaky Styley*, and unmixed, which leaked to the internet in the mid-2000s from a cassette—so it's likely the versions the band took with them on the day were quick dubs, and the serious mixing work was performed on them in the days or weeks later.*

* Spit Stix recounts a story featuring Flea rubbing his naked body on the studio glass during a late-night mixing session in Jeff Apter's *Fornication* biography (68). But this may have also taken place during the recording of a different set of demos, early the following year, with a different version of the band.

Shortly after the recording session, Flea, Anthony, and Fabrice Drouet traveled to New York on a whim, helping their friend Pete Weiss move his employer—director and screenwriter Paul Schrader, who had just received torrents of critical acclaim with his scripts for *Taxi Driver* and *Raging Bull*—across the country.* Flea had met Weiss on the set of *Suburbia*, where he was a boom mic operator, and the two had quickly become ensconced in each other's worlds: Anthony also became a close friend over the next few months. Weiss would orbit the Chili Peppers circle for the next thirty years, drumming with Thelonious Monster, and even playing the jaw harp on "Give It Away" in 1991.

According to Weiss, the group picked up a copy of the demo tape on their way out of the city. If the bright yellow Ryder van had a tape deck, or perhaps if there was a boombox handy, the short recording surely would have sound-tracked their way east into the deserts. Aside from a "few run-ins with some crazy-assed truckers," Anthony's memories of the trip to New York don't amount to much, but that's perhaps because early on, Drouet took him aside and showed him the bundle of China White† he had taken along with him. Several of Drouet's photographs taken during the trip have surfaced; in one of them, Anthony is astride the thirty-foot-high statue of Marcus Aurelius outside Caesar's Palace casino in Las Vegas (he always did like climbing into high-up places, and being where he shouldn't be). Other photos show them mugging for the camera on the casino floor, but it's unlikely the motley crew of four were welcome guests or had much in the way of spare cash to throw around, unless it was a per diem from Paul Schrader.

---

* Flea mentions in *An Oral/Visual History of the Red Hot Chili Peppers* that Hillel also went on the trip, but Anthony doesn't mention him being there in his autobiography, and he doesn't appear in any pictures.

† Though now a term for a potent heroin-fentanyl mixture, in early 1980s L.A., China White referred to a form of unadulterated white powder heroin from Southeast Asia.

Anthony, always adventurous, astride a statue of Marcus Aurelius outside Ceaser's Palace in Las Vegas, shortly after his band recorded its blistering first demo. May 1983. *fabulosfab*

Once in New York, with Schrader's belongings safely delivered and Anthony, Fabrice Drouet, and Flea holed up in a friend's apartment on Broome Street, the idea was to use the new demo tape to book shows in New York City for some future tour. "We weren't quite clear on the workings of the music business," Anthony remembered. "We just thought we would go to clubs." Sadly, and perhaps understandably, the only positive reaction they got was from the owner of the Peppermint Lounge—then in its third iteration on Fifth Avenue—and, less expectedly, from children. Playing their demo tape in Central Park, the duo would get "scornful looks from people who thought we were obnoxious to play such loud music, but amazingly, every kid who came within earshot completely rocked out to it." This impression would stay in the forefront of their minds, and when they returned to Los Angeles about a week later,* they would build a song around it. But aside from a song idea and an eye-opening look into the inner workings of the live-music business, the trip to New York would be fruitless, and they wouldn't actually play in the city until August the next year.

Shortly after returning from the East Coast, Flea and Anthony found themselves homeless when Hillel moved in with his girlfriend, Georgia-born musician and actress Addie Brik, and the two remaining tenants let the rent at their Leland Way house fall into arrears (Flea had also managed to burn the kitchen down almost immediately after arriving, and a few of his kittens had "pooped all over the joint"). Out on Hollywood Boulevard on one of these midspring days with no real worldly possessions but the clothes on their back, they ran into Bob Forrest.† Flea had briefly met Forrest the year before when he had stormed the booth and flipped a Defunkt record over midsong while Forrest was DJ'ing at the Cathay de Grande, and Anthony and Forrest knew each other by sight after seeing one another at shows around Los Angeles. A recent Los Angeles City College dropout, Forrest had been given the gig by the Cathay's owner, Michael Brennan, earlier that year. For fifteen bucks a night he would spin records in between bands and keep the crowd occupied, or be the main attraction when no bands were playing at all; the free beer helped too.

* How they got back to Los Angeles is unknown. Perhaps they returned in the truck they drove east with.

† Flea's bass and amp were most likely being kept at FEAR's rehearsal space.

After a more substantial introduction took place, Forrest—newly divorced and in need of some company and rent assistance—invited Flea and Anthony to stay with him, and they quickly moved into apartment 307 at 1737 North Whitley Avenue. The building, just off Hollywood Boulevard, was a six-story architectural masterpiece built in 1927 known as the La Leyenda apartments, which according to Anthony had seen "better times." In 2005 it was dedicated a historical cultural monument by the city of Los Angeles, and is in much better shape today than it was in the spring of 1983.

Bob Forrest, Anthony, and Flea were all natural fits for one another, although as is the case in any triangle of dominant personalities, there were the inevitable spats and pairing-off of two of the trio for a quickly forgotten reason. In his autobiography, Forrest offers some insight into the interesting yin and yang aspect between Anthony and Flea that probably resulted in the two of them having such a lasting relationship, but which also created power dynamic problems down the line. After Forrest and Flea realized that they both revered bass virtuoso Jaco Pastorious, they spent a day poring over records that he appeared on, and discussing his work:

> It was then that I noticed Anthony had come into the room. He looked at us like we were idiots. His arms were folded and a smirk was on his face. Okay, this deserved an explanation.
>
> "What?" I asked as I threw up my hands.
>
> "Why do you guys do that?" he sneered.
>
> "Do what?" asked Flea.
>
> "This fucking idolatry, man. It's kind of sick, you know?"
>
> "Wait," I said. "You mean to tell me that you've never admired or idolized anyone in your entire life?"
>
> Anthony didn't even take the time to think about his answer. "No. Never." He gave a derisive snort and went out to buy cigarettes.

It may be a lightly fictionalized account of the interaction, but Anthony reaffirms this mentality in his foreword to the band's photobook *Fandemonium*. "Growing up, I was never really a 'fan' of anyone, as we normally think of being a fan," he wrote. "In some respects, to be a fan is to give up some of your own identity."

Where Anthony was distant and reserved, Flea and Bob Forrest (and Jack and Hillel) were more willing to devote their entire selves to their craft, even if it meant giving up a piece of that self. Anthony was always a little aloof, a little cooler, which some surely would have taken as arrogance. That Anthony still remains, more or less, to this day.

At the La Leyenda apartments, three musical tastes aligned, drugs flowed, and life was easy if not chaotic. Bob Forrest even introduced the duo to a number of artists that the Chili Peppers would wind up covering in the years to come, such as Hank Williams, and it would have been Forrest's close proximity with the Chili Peppers that inspired him to form Thelonious Monster with Pete Weiss, whom he had also met through the Chili Peppers, the following year. In a very loose sense, Forrest became their first manager, though perhaps booking agent was more appropriate. "For six months, he [Anthony] and I booked the band's gigs," he wrote in his autobiography. "I'd go to the shows, hang out backstage, and feel like I was part of something. I was connected to the music in a way that my DJ jobs didn't fulfil."

And with Anthony and Flea back in Los Angeles, their housing situation under relative control, and the demo tape burning a hole in their pocket, the Red Hot Chili Peppers were about to kick into a higher gear.

SHOW #10

MAY 20, 1983

Fiesta House, 2353 East Olympic Boulevard, Los Angeles, CA

IN MAY, What Is This played their first show at the Plant (the first in many instances in which the Chili Peppers, the younger of the two bands, would get somewhere first) and once more at the Club Lingerie. The next Chili Peppers show was organized by Jack Marquette, of the Anti Club, at his new project Fiesta House.

Marquette had a long history in the L.A. club scene. His former club, Brave Dog, had been shuttered unceremoniously in 1981, and in the aftermath, he was arrested for operating without permits. Working by the book this time, the Fiesta House was east of Hollywood, in an artsy warehouse district that was only a few blocks from the Los Angeles River. Here was another place that had a long history of being a restaurant during the week—Mexican, this time around (the haute cuisine Paul's Duck Press had occupied the space until the 1950s)—but a club for underground acts for a few hours at the end of it. And it was here, on a Friday night in mid-May, that the Chili Peppers returned to the stage after almost a month away.

Joining the band this time around were Outer Circle, an interesting act that were chaotic and abrasive in their own way, but quite a different act from the Red Hot Chili Peppers. Outer Circle fleshed out their sound with clarinets, lap steel guitar, and even synthesizer, which the Chili Peppers considered anathema to their worldview at the time.

Peter Bastone DJ'd the show, under the name Peter Wesley, his middle name. Born in Connecticut, he was the cousin of Anthony's former roommate Dondi Bastone and a friend of Jack Marquette's. Bastone had been spinning discs for about a year at various L.A. clubs, including the Anti Club, the Cathay de Grande, and Marquette's Brave Dog parties. Bastone also manned the sound for this show, roped in because the Fiesta Club's usual engineer was working that day at the US Festival, happening in San Bernardino.

The Chili Peppers apparently only played for fifteen minutes. "Two songs," Bastone remembers, "but the crowd dug them." This brevity is an important aspect when considering the band's early days; they were not a club act designed to entertain distracted or drunken guests for an entire night—this was no Hamburg Star-Club, and they were not the Beatles, doling out their endless repertoire of covers for hours on end. The Red Hot Chili Peppers were a spark that you would miss if you were only a few minutes late. Part of this is because they simply lacked the songs, but it was also part of the very nature of the band. They were loud, exciting, abrasive, and over before anyone could get bored and look at their watch.

Newspaper listings from the day suggest that What Is This played a show on this night as well, at the O.N. Klub on Sunset Boulevard, where they supported rockabilly dancehall favorites Los Lobos. Formed in 1973, Los Lobos were relative veterans and had just released an EP that would wind up winning them a Grammy; they had also played the Plant the day after the Chili Peppers did in April.

It's odd that the band members would spread themselves so thinly here, especially when What Is This would have normally taken immediate precedence as the senior band. But it wasn't impossible for the two acts to play on the same night; the venues were only fifteen minutes away from each other if traffic was good, and they could have played hours apart, with plenty of time in between to tear down and set up stages. If time *was* tight, one could imagine the first glimmers of frustration arriving from Alain Johannes; not only were his guitarist and drummer off playing shows and recording demos for this jokey new band, but also their more and more frequent shows were now starting to interfere with lucrative support slots for the act they were supposed to be focusing on. Years later, Jack Irons backed this up, recalling that at the time there were some surface-level tensions between the two acts, even if it hadn't yet become a real problem between the band members themselves: "There were definitely some bizarre feelings starting to grow between the two groups, because the Red Hot Chili Peppers were taking off a lot quicker. What Is This's appeal was a lot more of a struggle to get across, and that, in itself, became a little conflict." They weren't immune from interpersonal spats entirely, Hillel's refusal to speak to Flea after he left What Is This for FEAR being one example. But how much longer could this tug-of-war last before the situation became serious?

In late May, Anthony managed to make a nuisance of himself by getting caught having sex with a young woman named Germaine on the roof of the Zero One club, a spiritual successor to the Zero Zero, receiving a ban from the beloved venue in the process. Anthony himself said he was being treated unfairly by a vengeful and jealous bouncer who was after Germaine's attention himself, and that he was reinstated a short time later at the club owner's insistence.

Normally this event wouldn't be the kind of thing recounted in a story like this. But in a move that proved they were making waves thanks to their new band, this altercation and related fallout even made it into a L.A.-Dee-Da column a week later: "The most recent 86'd Zero patron is the lead screamer for the Red Hot Chili Peppers, who was caught choking the bird with a red hot chili-ette on the roof." This is the beginning of Anthony Kiedis as a public personality, who would go on to be the major outward face of the band. As a budding actor, in this period he was always the most comfortable with publicity, and in most cases was more than happy to jump onstage, in front of a camera, or—as the band grew in stature—in front of a reporter's microphone. Only six months after his first show as a musician, here was his personal life being published for all to see. Anthony's future—one filled with high-profile relationships with actresses, models, and other musicians, altercations with the paparazzi, entry after entry in gossip columns—can be seen in its infancy right here.

But it wasn't just the *LA Weekly* giving the band column inches, and it wasn't just Anthony getting noticed. At some point in late April or May, *NOMAG*, a punk street zine edited by Bruce Kalberg and put out on and off between 1978 and 1985, published what is most likely the first-ever interview by a member of the Red Hot Chili Peppers. Flea is given the honors, and technically it's his involvement with FEAR that gets him in the zine's pages, as part of a "Close-Ups '83" portraits special (Lee Ving and *Suburbia*'s Penelope Spheeris are also present and photographed). After being introduced as the punk act's new bass player and a forthcoming star of *Suburbia*, Kalberg asks Michael "Balcary" about his new band:

> The thing I like about the Chili Peppers is that we really don't take ourselves seriously at all. In most other bands that I've been in we've been like . . . Ohhh managers . . . what are we going to do . . . when's this going to happen . . . when's that going to happen. In the Chili Peppers we just sort of play for fun and we don't really rehearse or anything like that. We've only rehearsed about 6 or 7 times in our entire

> existence. We just get together and get as wild as possible. The main concept is just making people bounce off the walls. We lose our minds when we play pretty much. We do a lot of things that we don't really plan on. At every concert so far we've broken equipment and hurt ourselves and hurt other people, and things always go wrong and it's always great.

Flea's backhanded derision in these comments of an unnamed What Is This (and their struggle in getting the band more attention and stability) speaks volumes about his state of mind at this point in his career. First, to roll his eyes at Alain, Hillel, and Jack's understandable desire for their band to be bigger and better is ironic knowing what lay ahead for the Red Hot Chili Peppers. In fact, if they hadn't already recorded their demo—designed to get them more attention and more bookings—at the time the interview took place, they were just about to. Whether he realized it, they were more forward-thinking than he was letting on. But his comments also ignore the fact the band he left What Is This for already had a manager, a record deal, and substantial fame across the country. Easy to lament and disrespect the work when the work had already been done for you.

Second, it could just be simple braggadocio from a young man who knew his punk audience, or perhaps the reality was that the future of the Chili Peppers really wasn't given much thought in these early months. But this kind of thinking is in line with how Anthony later described it: "We saw playing our songs as a fun thing to do, not as a career move." In the interview, Flea makes it clear that FEAR is his predominant focus, not the Chili Peppers. "FEAR is the main thing that I'm doing right now. I'm the bass player for FEAR."

He also has a few concerns to get off his chest about live music and its ability to cut through cliques within the Los Angeles punk scene. "No matter where we play and no matter what we do it just seems that music takes a back seat to everything," he complains. "People aren't concerned with the music, they're concerned with the fucking scene and all that bullshit. . . . They don't really care about the music, they care about what's cool. And what's not."

Elsewhere, he makes some interesting comments representing a worldview that's a far cry from the open-minded musician he is today. He has harsh words for drum machines—"Most people don't understand the difference between someone who works hard to play and plays real good and is jamming, giving their performance, giving all they can, giving 100% into playing . . . and some stupid asshole jerk who programs a computer," which is a feeling reinforced by the band in their 1987 track "Organic Anti-Beat Box Band." He similarly disparages rap music—"I hate most of that shit . . . the disc-spinning scratch bullshit. Fuck that. It makes me sick. I haven't really seen a rap band I like. Grandmaster Flash is pretty cool." But he does compliment one local musician he had played with at Janet Cunningham's CASH club—"Cliff Martinez is a great drummer."

SHOW #11

MAY 30, 1983

China Club, 8338 West Third Street, Los Angeles, CA

THE CHINA CLUB was another Los Angeles restaurant that occasionally doubled as a concert venue and a gallery. Owned by Japanese mega-corporation Nisshin, it opened in late 1980 and achieved immediate success thanks to some high-profile visitors and artists on display; David Bowie was one of the very first to put on a show in the space. Queen even booked the club in the later months of 1983 to celebrate their new record deal, and star-struck Hillel Slovak attended the party.

But where the China Club was a swanky upmarket restaurant with "oriental influence" that was a great place to be seen by the staff of the *LA Weekly* and its columnists, starting late on Monday nights in May it undertook a transformation and became the Chain Club.

Inspired by Gaz Mayall's "Rockin' Blues" nights at the famous London club Gossip's, there was no real difference between this night and the next; it was just another in a long line of themed "clubs"—like the Rhythm Lounge—a compartmentalized little pocket of divergence that allowed a venue to put on a new face or play a specific type of music for a few hours at a time. In a way, concert venues became another type of gallery: a blank space for someone to transform into whatever they wished, for however long they were able to.

The Chain Club got its name not just from the easy anagram of China, but from the booker's band: Tupelo Chain Sex, a punk-rockabilly band fronted by the supposedly narcoleptic Dave "Limey Dave" Dahlson, who played just about every week around Los Angeles, in clubs that the Red Hot Chili Peppers (and What Is This, and everyone else) would also play. Tupelo Chain Sex played the first ever night at the Chain Club on May 23, and the Chili Peppers fronted the second entry a week later, for a $350 fee.* The show was announced in the *LA Weekly* with a two-page spread, featuring an appallingly dated and racist cartoon (a man of apparent Asian heritage biting into a chili pepper), and what is mostly likely the band's first photo session, probably taken for this very advertisement: all four are topless, horsing around outside on some sunny day, the joy evident on their faces. The unedited photo, seen later in the year, reveals them to be in a rundown, industrial area; graffiti adorns the alleyway walls, and the dilapidated wooden house they leap in front of is laced with piping and gauges.

On either side of the image are some choice words that promised to "bring red heat to your lead feet," informing readers that the band would be "doing the groove down to the ground, bone crunching mayhem funk!" That expression—"mayhem funk"—had appeared ahead of the show with the Minutemen in March, but here some damage to one's bones was added for good measure. This was a well-worn expression before long; Flea would describe the band's music

* Like many other clubs around L.A., this particular night would be shuttered before the year was out—this time only a month later—for not having correct permits. The China Club had to continue on without Limey Dave's weekly contributions.

as "bone-crunching mayhem funk" in an August 1984 interview with MTV, and Hillel used the expression "bone-crunching mayhem" as late as April 1988.

We can hear for ourselves if that promise of mayhem funk was delivered, as May ended with another recording. This time we're provided with our earliest chance to hear the band onstage, thanks to a tape that was made at the soundboard that night, most likely by a member of the band themselves, and inspired by how pleased they were with the in-studio demo recording. Fading in toward the end of Hillel's solo on "Out in L.A.," the recording picks up the odd cheer from the midsized crowd (probably made up of friends and girlfriends, being 10:30 PM on Monday night, after all). This recording highlights the band's stage presence as much as it does their music; they spend just as much time talking and yelping (and tuning up) in between songs as they do actually playing their songs, and one can imagine the band members' eyes scanning the crowd, each member with a microphone, picking on an audience member of their choice. If there weren't instruments nearby, one could imagine them as comedians in some New York City basement nightclub.

The Red Hot Chili Peppers' first promotional shoot, taken by an unknown photographer in an unknown location, seen here in the *LA Weekly* in July ahead of their show with Bad Brains. Circa April–May 1983.

"Sex Rap"—or "a sexist rap," as Anthony calls it—is up next, followed by "Police Helicopter," and then more tuning, and more stage banter: "We're gonna put some grins on your chins," Flea suggests. The lack of polished professionalism even extends to the silence in between songs; it's not clear if they actually have a set list, or if they're simply playing whatever comes to mind. That said, when "Stranded" pops up in between "Sex Rap" and "Police Helicopter," its timing is perfect, and they're all on the same page, which either speaks to a musical telepathy that many would kill for, or some sort of plan.

"Green Heaven" comes after, but there's a slight derailment when Flea stops the song halfway through the first verse because "we have to start over again, we're really out of tune, we don't wanna sound bad." After they tune up—again—they kick right back into the song with perfect, rehearsed timing. Of note is a lack of talk box from Hillel; further evidence that its appearance on the demo recording earlier in the month may have been a one-time thing.

"Get Up and Jump" follows, and it's a better performance than the stilted awkwardness of their demo take recorded earlier in the month. Flea even toys with his bassline in the second verse, taking a break from the knotty slap line to play something slower and groovier, a direction he evidently decided not to pursue.

After "Oom Chucka Willy," there's another chanted ditty, led mostly by Flea and Anthony: "2-4-6-8, who do we appreciate? China Club! China Club! Yay, China Club!" They certainly liked playing at the venue because they decided it was the right place to debut their first ever cover, the first of many that they would play in their career, across all their iterations.* Of course, it's a Jimi Hendrix song—he was the obvious choice, the childhood hero who never went away.

"Fire," recorded by the Jimi Hendrix Experience in the early months of 1967, was released on the band's debut album *Are You*

* If we don't count "Stranded" or "Oom Chucka Willy" as covers.

Experienced later that year. As far as Hendrix songs went, it was a deep cut of sorts; hidden on the second side of the album, it was never released as a single, and hadn't entered the public consciousness the way "Foxey Lady" or "Purple Haze" had by that point. This makes sense when considering that the cover was done at Hillel's request: he was the Hendrix obsessive, and Hendrix was his permanent lodestar, and he would be more likely to know and love the songs that others may not. This performance is an early look at the more polished, refined version the band would record in 1987. Interestingly, Hillel doesn't seem to know how to play the chorus, but he gets the solo note perfect.

This performance of "Fire" is an historic one considering what lay ahead for the band. On this night, it's the first in a long line of covers the band would perform and for which they'd be known for; their first five albums are laden with covers. Later, they would record it in the famous Capitol Studios during the sessions for their third album, play it live as the final song at Hillel's last ever show with the band in June 1988, then release the song on their fourth, breakthrough album as a tribute to him. In 2017 the band would bring Jack Irons—then on tour as an opening act—onstage at a number of shows, and play the track again, this time as a "classic" from the '80s. "Fire" followed the Red Hot Chili Peppers through everything: the highs and the lows, the clubs and the university ballrooms and the stadiums. This is most likely its first performance, the first of hundreds.

The cassette containing this recording, which surfaced online in 2006 thanks to James Slovak (brother of Hillel), is a raw, straight transfer of what was going through the desk.* But what it may lack in fidelity and dynamics it makes up for in its essence as a notable historical document. Here they are, wild things with no clue where

* On the other side of the tape was a copy of the band's demo session, recorded a few weeks earlier. They were probably considered companion pieces.

they were going, or what they were really doing beyond the chaotic twenty minutes they spent onstage. It's lucky that they decided to record the night; it's a miracle that the recording still exists.

Right after the show, a photo was snapped of Flea, Anthony (in what appears to be a swimming cap), and Hillel mugging for a *Scratch* magazine camera. "Quick," the caption says, "I need a glass of water. The Red Hot Chilli [*sic*] Peppers after eating too many of their own kind." Outside fliers, this is one of the first times the band's image was ever put into print, and it's no real shock that they were able to get there so soon. "Any time there was an opportunity to be in front of a camera I was right there and turning it on," Flea said, and here's another early surviving example.

"Appearing in print or in photo in *Scratch* is something of an honor," the *LA Weekly* would say later that year. "As the magazine has become this summer's trendiest reading material on the clubs, in part because it does give people a chance to be 'discovered.'" *Scratch* was a photocopied "zine" that had been started by Ruben Lee Lopez, who went by the name Ruben MacBlue. Hailing from Michigan, MacBlue had a bachelor's in behavioral psychology from Western Michigan University but moved to Los Angeles in 1976. In early 1983 he launched his zine, and it slotted nicely into the community; it had concerts, photos, gossip, interviews, and was a perfect representation of the L.A. scene at the time, even going a step further than the comparatively narrow L.A.-Dee-Da column in many respects. It started, MacBlue said, as "a reaction against in-crowd snobbishness at the *LA Weekly*. I thought there was a whole bunch of other interesting people and bands doing great things, but they were getting ignored by the *Weekly*'s L.A.-Dee-Da column because Craig Lee and his circle didn't consider them cool enough."

Luckily for the Chili Peppers, both MacBlue *and* the *LA Weekly* crowd thought they were cool enough, and their presence in both pages throughout the year allows for a clear look at their movements in and around the scene. It did have its downsides; this rivalry between the two publications might have explained the snide comments from the *LA Weekly* regarding Anthony's public sexual exploits at the Zero Club; his female companion, Germaine, was said to be a columnist for *Scratch* magazine, who had been denigrating the *Weekly* in her column.

SHOW #12

JUNE 4, 1983

Anti Club at Helen's Place,
4658 Melrose Avenue, Los Angeles, CA

THE BAND PLAYED another show at Jessum, Marquette, and Van Tyne's Anti Club as summer arrived in Los Angeles, alongside Tex and the Horseheads, the BEAT-EE-O's (another one of those acts who seem to have existed for this show only), and Carmaig de Forest.

Considered one of the foremost bands to play the unfortunately named "cowpunk," Tex and the Horseheads were fronted by Linda Yacoubian, better known as Texacala Jones. The band had formed in 1980 and played many of the same haunts that the Chili Peppers did in 1983; the following year they released their debut self-titled album on a local record label named Enigma. They were a rollicking act that combined the jangly, twangy rhythms of country and western with the intensity of punk, and would play with the Chili Peppers many times in the coming years.

An interesting flier was created for the night, which featured (once again) the Chili Peppers in pole position on top, headlining over the much more established Tex and the Horseheads. In each corner of the bright yellow piece is a glyph of sorts representing each band member: a swan for Anthony, a flea for (of course) Flea, a cowboy for Hillel (the Israeli cowboy), and Jughead from the *Archie* comics for Jack.*

One wonders if this is a calculated attempt to carve out marketable identities for each of the band members. Instead of becoming lost in the sea of musicians that played up and down Melrose Avenue each night, here were four different men, each with their own unique characters. They weren't quite a four-headed monster like the Beatles or some cookie-cutter rip-off with four distinct personalities—the cute one, the shy one, the sarcastic one, and the brooding one. But with Flea and Anthony immediately making a name for themselves—and their band—not just in the word-of-mouth scene on the street but in *Scratch*, *LA Weekly*, and even the *Los Angeles Reader*, too—there was the palpable sense early on that this venture was something unique that wouldn't soon be forgotten when other plans got in the way, and this establishing of personalities suggests some forward thinking.

Also playing that night was Carmaig de Forest. Worlds away from the Chili Peppers and the Horseheads, de Forest was a solo singer-songwriter who played the ukulele, with short, angry, folksy songs making up his repertoire. He had previously fronted garage bands but had struck out on his own a few years previous; his 1987 album *I Shall Be Released*, produced by Alex Chilton of Big Star, is a cult classic.

Based in San Francisco, de Forest had traveled down to Los Angeles a few months previously for a show with the Minutemen (another strange pairing) after being told to get in touch with Anti Club booker Russell Jessum. Jessum was a fan, and after the Minutemen show, he asked him to come back for another slot with the Chili Peppers a few weeks later.

* Jughead was the drummer in the Archies, after all.

But de Forest doesn't remember too much about this night. "I was just getting my feet wet," he says, and this one night has blurred into the rest of a full and varied career. "I was just getting a sense of what L.A. was." But the dominant memory was how full the club was during the show—"It was a crowded, sweaty room"—and that Flea pulled him aside during the night. "He dug what I did. . . . He gave me some props backstage. That always feels good when you're young and starting out."

The fact that a "cowpunk" band, a funk-thrash band, and a one-man ukulele act all played on the same bill didn't strike anyone as odd at the time. "That was the scene," de Forest remembers. "It wasn't cliquey in a genre way. You had serious composers, and fun-loving youngsters like the Chili Peppers, and a transvestite dance troupe all on the same bill." The one thing that every act had in common, de Forest says, "is that we were young and we didn't fit in the mainstream culture."

SHOW #13

JUNE 5, 1983

Sunday Club at Golden Village Supper Club, 6541 Hollywood Boulevard, Los Angeles, CA*

IN THE EARLY DAYS of the Red Hot Chili Peppers, before their recording and management contracts, booking shows around Los Angeles could manifest in two different ways. It could be a tricky, often-doomed affair that involved bended-knee pleading with an all-powerful club owner, or it could be a much easier process, in which the band members relied on the connections of friends and friends of friends who booked shows at nightclubs. This show is an example of the latter, for the man running this night at the Golden Village Supper Club was Anthony and Flea's roommate, Bob Forrest. Appearing with the band at this show was, once again, the Minutemen, who were beginning to become a recurring presence in the Chili Peppers' orbit.

In addition to his Wednesday night DJ gig at the Cathay de Grande, Bob Forrest had previously run After Everything Else, a

* Contemporary fliers also list the address as 6547 Hollywood Boulevard.

debauched after-hours show at a gallery called On the Fringe, at 4328 Melrose Avenue. When that ended, he tried something a little different. Starting its run in early May, the Sunday Club was meant to be a hangover cure for the Hollywood punk community, assisting anyone who was still a little wired from the night before with a beer-induced comedown—or inversely, helping anyone who needed a little pick-me-up to confront a difficult week ahead. Intended to be a low-key event that didn't draw much attention to itself, it only ran from 4:00 to 8:00 PM, with less risk of it turning into a night of debauchery. The first show featured both Black Flag and a fun, new, all-female band called the Bangles, who had just released their debut EP.

There were also softball games in the vacant lot across the street, which quite often became so involved that shows would start late if a band member got too invested. "Everyone came in their clothes from the night before," Pleasant Gehman, who occasionally helped run the afternoon, remembered. "Chicks slid into the flattened beer cartoon functioning as home plate in thigh-high spiked-heeled boots, fishnets, and miniskirts."

Perhaps unsurprisingly at this point, this show took place in another building with a long and storied history in Hollywood. The address 6541 Hollywood Boulevard was also known as Janes House, and by 1983 was the oldest Victorian-style home on the four-mile-long Hollywood Boulevard. Built in 1903 when "the boulevard was a gravel road and the Cahuenga Valley [a historical name encompassing modern-day Hollywood] was covered with orchards," it was home to the famous and family-run Misses Janes School of Hollywood, which counted (among others) the children of Charlie Chaplin and Cecil B. DeMille among its pupils. Having opened in 1911, the school shut in 1926, but the building remained in the Janes family, becoming at first a gas station and then a florist. Over the course of the next five decades, the plot of land passed into decrepitude, and when the last remaining Jane sister, Carrie, died in January 1983, the future of the house was up in the air. It would be sold to developers in 1984, but in that year or so that it remained empty, an industrious Armenian by the name of Marty moved the short-lived Golden Village Supper Club in and supplemented his income by holding the odd punk show.

While the "Sunday Club" was definitely held this weekend, there is also the chance that a show with this particular lineup never actually happened. A listing for a Red Hot Chili Peppers / Minutemen edition of the club appears in the June 9 edition of the *LA Weekly*, and the Minutemen, who performed at the Plant the night before, were definitely in the area at the time, willing and ready to play. However, there also exist fliers, listings, concert reviews, and even memories of a show by Tex and the Horseheads at the same venue on the same day, with support by the punk bands Redd Kross—an L.A.-based punk act started by brothers Steven and Jeff McDonald while they were both still in middle school, and whose affiliations include the Circle Jerks and Black Flag—and the Texas-based Big Boys.

According to Redd Kross bass player Steven McDonald, the Horseheads show definitely happened, and this is backed up by a review for the show that appeared in the *Los Angeles Times* shortly afterward. In this review, it's noted that the show was "last-minute," and so it's most likely that it was a replacement for the original show by the Minutemen and the Red Hot Chili Peppers that was canceled for whatever reason.*

If the Chili Peppers show *did* happen, one of the makeshift softball games would have just wrapped up (or perhaps it was running long) when the band made their way onstage. Perhaps the waning daylight and the Sunday evening gave the show a different quality, and things onstage were more subdued.

---

* A note accompanying most concert listings in *LA Weekly* throughout 1983 reads: "Due to the erratic lives of L.A. musicians and the capricious personalities of booking agents, all of the following bookings are subject to change for no apparent reason."

SHOW #14

JUNE 11, 1983

The Vex, 2580 North Soto Street, Los Angeles, CA

THE VEX WAS ANOTHER ONE of those Los Angeles clubs that had little luck finding a permanent venue during the early years of the decade. The proprietor, Joe Vex, was unluckier than most, with various attempts of his closed down due to punk violence, or disastrous, ill-attended attempts at fundraisers that wound up costing more money than they brought in.

Reopened in this latest iteration on April 2, 1983, this Vex was so far east of Los Angeles it was practically in the neighboring city of Alhambra, but the quieter locale ideally would have suited the after-hours atmosphere (the venue only opened at 11:00 PM) that the owners were attempting to cultivate. The seclusion did not always assure privacy, however, with one show by the Odd Squad and Blood on the Saddle being shut down by police in May before the bands could even reach the stage. But by the time the Chili Peppers played in June, the Vex management had ironed out the wrinkles, with themselves and with the local law enforcement, and Green on Red, the Meat Puppets, and the Damned all performed at the venue in the preceding weeks without any hiccups.

Playing this night alongside the Chili Peppers were San Francisco art-punk band the Mutants, who had formed in 1977 and by then released a multitude of singles and one LP, best known for their stage props and huge array of members (at one point, three singers in one lineup).

This show once again made the pages of L.A.-Dee-Da, with the roaming columnist gushing about the band's stage presence: "Good bands seen this week: Red Hot Chili Peppers burning up the stage at the Vex. Shirtless, funky, sexy and chaotic, these crazed hypo-teens slam their instruments into James Brown overdrive while throwing their bodies around like Mexican jumpin' beans. Color them intense!" At this stage, it seemed as if all they had to do was play live somewhere within the city limits to get into the column, and before long their reputation was preceding them.

They were an undeniable hit. But could it be sustained?

Where would they go from here?

SHOW #15

JUNE 17, 1983

Anti Club at Helen's Place, 4658 Melrose Avenue, Los Angeles, CA

THE CHILI PEPPERS rocked the Anti Club on Melrose again, opening this time for the Alley Cats, a punk trio that featured the husband-and-wife duo Randy Stodola and Dianne Chai on guitar and bass. The band had formed in 1977, had released two albums to date, and had even appeared in the British concert film *Urgh! A Music War* alongside more established acts like the Police and Echo & the Bunnymen.

Alley Cat Stodola only remembers asking the band to open for him, having found them interesting. But others remember the night a little more clearly, including Anthony's father. Coming onstage after the rest of the band and dressed in a tuxedo and a bowler hat, Anthony tripped on the "medusa" of cords and electrical wires, and in the course of doing so, managed to turn the gaffe into a flip. "His bowler cap flew high into the air, and, as he landed perfectly on his feet, the cap came down right on his head." It wasn't his first flip onstage, and it wouldn't be the last time a cord has upturned his performing world,* but it was a direct representation of the luck and flash-in-the-pan energy they were exuding. "The kid was ordained," as Blackie Dammett told it.

Another memory from the night, albeit a brief one, came from Anthony himself, in an interview that he and Flea gave to punk zine *Scratch* later in the month:

> Q: Anthony, how long has your band been playing around town?
> A: We've been playing around town about five months and it's absolutely amazing how much success we've had. We've got strong fundamental concepts. That's what it's all about.
> Q: Do you think your strong fundamental concepts will take you to New York and make you successful there?
> A: I think we can be successful all over the world.
> Q: Is this band priority or should I ask the others that question?
> A: Everybody will go with the flow.
> Q: So far, is this the only band flowing?
> A: It's got as much potential as any other band in the world, so yeah.
> Q: Who writes the lyrics to your songs?
> A: I write the lyrics and Michael and Hillel write the music.
> Q: Where was your favorite gig so far?
> A: At the Anticlub.

For a short interview that doesn't seem to give much away, this is still a revealing piece of documentation. For one, it's historical, in

* Sometimes with catastrophic results: at two different shows in 1996, Anthony tripped while on stage, tearing his calf on one occasion and dislocating his sacrum on the other.

that it may well be only the second interview Anthony Kiedis ever gave as a member of the Chili Peppers.* There's also the sly little hint to the Flow, the band's former name. Interesting, too, is the reference to Michael—Flea's nickname had not yet solidified, but it was getting close. And last, the assertion from Anthony that the Anti Club show had been their best show. He could be talking about the April 13 show, but given that this interview took place at the end of June, there's a good chance he was talking about the show that had *just* taken place, which would have been far fresher in his memory.

Flea was also interviewed alongside Anthony for *Scratch*, but his answers are (by design) far less illuminating:

> Q: Michael, your [*sic*] the bass player for The Red Hot Chili Peppers; is that true?
>
> A: No.
>
> Q: If you had been playing bass for the Red Hot Chili Peppers, which I know is preposterous, how long would you say you'd been playing with them?
>
> A: Oh, well, kind of a medium amount of time but somewhere in-between a really big amount of time and a small amount of time and not anything less than a large amount of time.
>
> Q: Before you played with the Chili Peppers, who would you say influenced you to play the bass like you do?

* What was probably the first interview the full band ever gave is actually referenced earlier on in the *Scratch* interview. On June 21, the band appeared on KXLU 88.9 FM's *Stray Pop*, which was broadcast out of Loyola Marymount University between 11:00 PM and 2:00 AM, and played just about everything, with local bands brought on for interviews as well. Anthony, typically, appeared to make a deviant nuisance of himself on the show: "Q: I talked to Stella from KXLU about your live interview and she said that Anthony was trying to unzip her dress with his teeth. Is that true?" Ruben MacBlue asked him. Sadly, no recording seems to have survived. This is especially vexing, as the band may have played live in-studio during the session.

A: Well, it was kind [of] the guys that I really like, then again, it was some of the guys that I really like a lot.

Q: Did you like them?

A: Well, I kinda liked them but I didn't like them as much as I liked them before I really started liking them.

The rest of the interview is more of the same; the joke runs cold quickly, and his disdain for the very exercise itself is evident.

A return to the Plant should have come the following night for the Chili Peppers, with another support slot opening for Tex and the Horseheads. They would also be sharing the stage with the Mentors, a band that featured on drums and vocals Eldon "El Duce" Hoke—who is perhaps best known now for his infamous interview, given just two days before his death, in which he claimed that Courtney Love had offered to pay him to kill Kurt Cobain. The Mentors were a shock-rock act that put FEAR's antics to shame, with band members with stage names like Sickie Wifebeater (Eric Carlson) performing in executioner hoods. But where FEAR seemed to have, at the very least, some sort of sardonic cultural criticism behind their actions, the Mentors were firmly in the shock-for-its-own-sake camp.

Nonetheless, in a sign that, while the Red Hot Chili Peppers might have been making inroads, it was still lower in the hierarchy of its members' commitments than FEAR and What Is This, this show was cancelled. Around the same time the June 18 show at the Plant was booked, FEAR also booked a show in San Francisco at On Broadway, the site of their April performance in the city. When one act needed to give way, it was FEAR that won out, and the Chili Peppers' slot at the Plant was jettisoned.

Joining FEAR in San Francisco were local act Pariah and Redd Kross. Flea made a great impression on Steven McDonald at this show, telling his fellow bassist that he thought he was a great player. Flea was never one to avoid praising the musicians he shared stages with.

Shortly afterward, What Is This played for the first time in a month, at a June 30 show at the Music Machine with bands Choir Invisible, Grand Manner, and Sound Delight. The next day, they had an engagement at the Plant with Outer Circle and Second Language. FEAR also played on July 1, their first show in over two months, at a seven-band show in Santa Fe that promised raucous chaos.

Two events occurred in late June and early July that signaled to the band that they were going places. The first took place on June 24, at the Los Angeles Memorial Sports Arena, when Grandmaster Flash and the Furious Five headlined the Master Slam Jam Dunk! with support from acts like the Chi-Lites and the Jonzun Crew. After the lengthy performance, the band somehow managed to go backstage and meet Grandmaster Flash himself, even performing some of their songs for him a cappella. For the band—especially Anthony, despite his adamant antifandom—to be this close to Flash, who had inspired Anthony to get onstage, must have been a thrill. And the Jonzun Crew, too: the soundtrack to their first show, and legends in a scene that they were now blossoming in parallel to. Adding to the thrills, Flash liked what he heard, and word on the street was that he would offer the band a support slot for a future tour. Alas, that was not to be, but by then the band may have been too busy to accept anyway. It's a shock that the band never mentioned this event in the future, but it's understandable that some memories would get lost in the busy whirlwind of years to come.

The second event took place in early July, when Flea and Anthony were doing the rounds of local clubs, playing their demo tape to owners and booking agents, or anyone who would listen, in an attempt to set up further engagements for their band. One of these people was Brendan Mullen, the booker for Club Lingerie.

Mullen, who would begin crafting the Chili Peppers' *Oral/Visual History* before his untimely death in 2010, looked back on this meeting with Anthony and Flea fondly in that tome's opening pages: "I first encountered Flea and Anthony one afternoon in early summer '83 when they whirled unannounced into my office at Club Lingerie in Hollywood, waving an audio cassette in my face and insisting I listen to it on the spot," he wrote. "What fool-ass club promoter listens to unsolicited tapes in front of some sorry band?"

Mullen demurred, but the "high-energy young pups who finished each other's sentences" weren't taking no for an answer and pleaded with him to listen to just two songs.* Capitalizing on his well-known love of FEAR and funk music, they tracked down a tape deck from the janitor downstairs, and hit play. The music, Mullen said, was "immediately captivating."

Reconsidering his earlier apprehension that the "skinny white rug rats playing funk" wouldn't be up to snuff, on the spot he offered them a support slot for an upcoming show at the Lingerie on July 18, headlined by punk legends Bad Brains. "They danced out of the club all the way up the street, as if I'd just told them they'd won the lottery," Mullen said. And in a sense, they had.

Originally a jazz fusion group called Mind Power that had discovered punk and renamed themselves after a Ramones song, Bad Brains had burst out of Washington, DC, in the late 1970s, touring extensively across the country and releasing their legendary debut single "Pay to Cum" in June 1980. The early part of the decade had been full of strife; having been banned from the majority of DC clubs, they were forced to move to New York City and recorded an entire album that would only see release in 1996. But by 1982 the band settled somewhat and had released their classic debut self-titled album. Issued on cassette only, it sounds like it was recorded with one microphone in an untuned room, and with the levels too hot.† In early 1983 they

* Probably "Out in L.A." and "Green Heaven," but the tape is so short they could easily have listened to the whole thing.

† This is not necessarily a bad thing.

recorded and released *Rock for Light*, a more polished album produced by Ric Ocasek of the pop-rock monsters the Cars, playing some of their first shows outside the United States, even opening for punk legends UK Subs at a number of shows only six months after FEAR had done so in San Francisco.

The Chili Peppers opening for Bad Brains was a little like winning the lottery. Bad Brains were legends on the scene already, a few years older and with two records under their belt, one of them produced by a bona fide rock legend in Ric Ocasek. They were bigger than the most established bands that the Chili Peppers had already opened for, bigger than FEAR in some respects, even if they hadn't been on *Saturday Night Live*. The band themselves were aware of the comparative enormity of this gig: "Damn, better really have our shit together for this one!" Anthony remembered. "Biggest stage, biggest P.A. system yet—a real club!"

Of course, the Chili Peppers had already *played* Club Lingerie, on March 31—only a few months previous. But if Mullen's earliest memory of Anthony and Flea is the duo waving their demo tape around in the early stages of summer, then the two possibilities are that either Mullen had forgotten that he had already met them, which is understandable if the March version of the band was a little more subdued, or perhaps that March show happened without Mullen's direct involvement.*

But before they could open for Bad Brains, there were a few more momentous happenings to take care of first, as summer continued to bloom, and a brand-new month unfurled across the avenues and boulevards of Los Angeles.

---

* Mullen sadly passed away in October 2010, inspiring the 2011 Red Hot Chili Peppers track "Brendan's Death Song," later a single.

SHOW #16

JULY 3, 1983

Kit Kat Club, 6550 Santa Monica Boulevard, Hollywood, CA

IF THE BAND had to pick one show that would sum up their inaugural year—one that made the biggest and most lasting impression, one that they kept coming back to in interviews and memories as the years tore on, one that solidified their ideals—it would probably be this show on the night of Sunday, July 3, at the Kit Kat Club, on Santa Monica Boulevard.

Starting as a supper club named Davy Jones, by the mid-1970s the usual Los Angeles seediness had set in, and waitresses applying for jobs at the newly christened Kit Kat Club were preferred if they could also dance on the side; by that time, it was a full-fledged strip joint that held Monday night nude dance contests, where hand-painted signs advised that "customers pick the winner!"

A strip club might have seemed like a strange place to hold a punk rock performance, but starting around May 1982, there had been regular new wave and punk nights held there, once every four weeks or so on Sunday nights, with burlesque and dance shows entertaining the crowd in between sets. "It wasn't like playing for sleazy old guys who'd come to see strippers," Flea remembered. "It was for people who wanted to hear good music. The people who booked it were really into the arty L.A. scene." In fact, by mid 1982 it had become a regular haunt with many people in the orbit of the Chili Peppers.

Two fliers were produced for this show, the first given an entire page in *Scratch* magazine.* Hand scrawled, again, this flier is adorned on each side by roadside photo-booth snapshots of Flea and Anthony with mohawk haircuts, taken on their 1982 trip to San Francisco. Was it just an interesting set of photographs to use, or was this a sign that Anthony and Flea were becoming recognizable enough that their very faces were enough to advertise the band? Up above, a cutout of the band's first ever photoshoot, taken in April or May. The foursome leap into the air in various stages of undress, some with inexplicable bowler hats, and some without; costumes and outfits were never far from their minds.

The second advertisement, placed in the *LA Weekly*, was a little different, featuring what appears to be the band again in various costumes (Jack has a blonde wig on) with four matching ladies, identities unknown, provocatively bent over in front of them. It's unclear what the source of the photograph is, or where it was taken; it may have been done specifically for the Kit Kat Club.

"Kit Kat Club is fast becoming one of the most popular places in town," the *LA Weekly* wrote in July 1982, just under a year before this show. "Far from being a 'seedy' strip joint, the staff and girls who work there are very nice, the place is clean (so clean in fact, that the waitresses walk around *handing* you ashtrays!)." The *Weekly* went on to report about a gig that weekend, featuring Wayzata de Camerone's Brainiacs, with occasional vocalist Tequila Mockingbird, soon

* Most likely the same issue from June, which featured the joint interviews with Anthony and Flea.

to provide backup vocals for Gary Allen at the first-ever Chili Peppers gig in December. Before long, the Kit Kat Club became a regular venue for local bands to play, and further performances by Top Jimmy & the Rhythm Pigs cemented its place in the scene. Soon a band with the provocative name Roid Rogers and the Whirling Butt Cherries would climb onstage amid the oil and glitter at one of the Kit Kat's "bands and bosoms" nights.

Aside from their friend's performances, this also wasn't the first time the Kit Kat Club and the paths of the Red Hot Chili Peppers crossed, Flea's in particular: the bar was the filming location for one of the final scenes of *Suburbia*'s denouement, in which Jim and Bob, the two "Citizens Against Crime" members—the major representative of The State in the film—meet to discuss their plan for revenge against the punk runaways. In the scene right beforehand, baby-faced Mike B. the Flea holds court in the kid's house, detailing his plan to siphon gas from a car and set the house on fire in a scorched earth attempt at fighting back against their oppressors. One can get a real sense of the venue through this scene, and it's not hard to imagine a rock band up on its stage in place of (or perhaps in addition to) a scantily clad young woman or two.

Joining the band for this performance were the aforementioned Roid Rogers and the Whirling Butt Cherries, who would be returning to Kit Kat's stage for the second time. An experimental act that was the product of "too much coffee," the Whirling Butt Cherries were a supergroup of sorts that included vocalist Marci Malibu; guitarist Bobby Mann; vocalist and *LA Weekly* columnist Shari Famous, whose name was on most of the L.A.-Dee-Da columns that had featured the band throughout the year; saxophonist Bruce "Spyder" Mittleman, best known from his role with punk act the Resistors; and synth player Cliff Martinez, a veteran drummer who had worked with artists as varied as Captain Beefheart, Lydia Lunch, and the Weirdos. Martinez had also been a part of a casual group called Two Balls and a Bat, which at various times had featured Joel Virgel-Vierset, Nickey Beat from the Weirdos, Bobby Mann from the Butt Cherries, and Richard Snyder, whom Martinez had met while they were both playing with Captain Beefheart.

Two Balls and a Bat were a drum- and synthesizer-based group that had played Chili Peppers haunts such as the Rhythm Lounge and had a revolving door of members. At one show in February 1983, they were accompanied by erotic beat poetry. It was pure performance art, or in some cases "underwear rock." Reflecting twenty-five years later, Martinez was quite sure he had played with Flea in the group at some point, most likely when they played at CASH, and the connections didn't stop there; the Whirling Butt Cherries had performed for the first time at CASH in June 1982 at the request of owner Janet Cunningham herself. The intertwined world of the L.A. punk community continued to thrive and piggyback off each other.

Much like the Chili Peppers, the Butt Cherries were the result of a group of friends living together and sharing interests, though the music was a little less conventional than the Chili Peppers' already-unconventional brand of punk funk. They were a zany crew, frequently in costumes concocted out of diapers and turbans, and had appeared on local arts show *New Wave Theater* only a few weeks after forming. They never actually released any of their recorded music but did film a fairly elaborate video for the track "Who Put Timmy in the Trash?" in early 1983 at Bronson Caves in Griffith Park. The video was directed by May Zone, an artist who had just worked on videos for Fleetwood Mac, Eric Clapton, and most notably Michael Jackson's "Billie Jean," one of the biggest songs of the year.

The clip, and the song itself, is representative of the type of humor the band was founded on and based around; inspired by a real-life case in which a father abandoned his child in a garbage can, it's sparse, electronic, repetitive, and very catchy. One is reminded of the dark comedic aspects in the works of David Lynch—a fitting comparison, as the band had been the opening act for weekly screenings of Lynch's film *Eraserhead* at the Nuart Theatre on Santa Monica Boulevard throughout that year. Later in 1983 the video was featured on MTV's *Basement Tapes*, which showcased unsigned and independent artists, and became a viewer favorite.

Upon arriving at the Kit Kat, the band were given a dressing room normally reserved for dancers, and somebody broke out a joint. Upon inhalation, paranoia broke out, and there was the concern that it would interfere with their performance. "I went for a run around the block to clear my head," Anthony remembered. Luckily for him, "it worked." The band weren't exactly known for turning down a mind-altering substance or two, but the clarity they required for this show implies they were taking this one a little more seriously than usual.

The Butt Cherries played first and were their usual fantastic selves. Cliff Martinez performed with a tampon sticking out of his rear end, and the rest of the band were clad in gorilla-hair loincloths and strap-on marital aids. Among the crowd, there was the feeling in the air instantly that this was a special gig, and the Chili Peppers weren't keen to be upstaged.

As the band came out for their encore, which most likely consisted singularly of "Fire," the crowd were stunned to see the band completely nude, with socks fitting snugly over their private parts.* Backstage, in the interval between the main set and the encore, the band were on edge, unsure that they should go through with the plan, and "levitating with nervous energy." But when they appeared, the crowd "audibly gasped. We weren't deterred for one moment by the collective state of shock that the audience was experiencing," Anthony remembered. The audience had seen a naked person before, obviously—they were

* In future years, when this stunt had become part of the band's regular routine, the socks were usually specially set-aside pairs of athletic tube socks. On this night, when it was more spur of the moment, there's no telling what they used. Perhaps the pairs off their own sweaty feet.

in a strip club after all—and the Chili Peppers had played in various states of undress in the months leading up to this performance, but this instantly became legend. It was a manic, over-the-top, and (most importantly) just plain funny stunt. The crowd even got involved, with one friend, in particular, trying to swipe Anthony's sock away from him as he did his best to focus on his vocals.

The band might have come to resent the image in the next few years and decades, but on this night, it was a genius move that shocked the audience, and it's most likely no one paid much attention to the dancers onstage either, let alone the music. "It felt great to be on stage naked," Anthony remembered in 1999. "With this exaggerated phallus dangling between our legs."

The iconic, arguably notorious "socks on cocks" routine was born, but exactly when the band decided to pull off the stunt is unclear. In an early 1988 interview Anthony implied it was a decision *made* on the night, as a way to win back the crowd's attention from the female dancers, whose presence the band weren't expecting. This theory was repeated in the 2004 biography *Fornication*, which quotes friend of the band and likely attendee Keith Barry, who said it was a "spontaneous thing to do." But in *Scar Tissue* Anthony claims that the idea to use the socks was already in motion in the lead-up to the gig: "Since we were playing at a strip club and the girls would be dancing onstage with us, we decided that the appropriate encore would be for us to come out naked." In fact, listings for shows throughout the year (including the week before this performance) even advertised the "Kit Kat Kittens," almost as if they were a supporting act to the main event.

In this case, the idea that the socks were a last-minute switcheroo is less compelling than the idea that it had been planned in advance as something to one-up not only the house dancers but Roid Rogers and the Whirling Butt Cherries, who were often scantily dressed themselves. Later, Flea couldn't even remember whose idea it was. "It might have been Hillel's," he wondered aloud, evidently bored with the hackneyed question after twenty-three years, and six whole years since they had done the routine last.

No matter when the plans were put in motion for this particular performance, the idea of putting a sock around one's genitalia for a laugh had been around for years. Anthony had come up with the idea in 1979 or 1980 while trying to rebuff the advances of a young female customer of his housemate Dondi Bastone, who was then dealing marijuana out of his house. Anthony already had a girlfriend and found that declining the girl's advances politely wasn't getting him anywhere. "So, as a razz, when she came over one day I went into my room and put a sock over my cock and nut sack and walked out to greet her as if nothing was different—casual, like a Monty Python episode. It was actually a great phallic look." How this overt display of sexuality was meant to push her away is not clear; in another telling of the story, in 2000 to *Juice* magazine, he admitted he was actually trying to impress her. Flea and Hillel frequently joined in during reenactments once they had all moved in together: "People would come over, and we'd hang out, drink beer, put socks on our dicks and run around." It was another instance of their friendship spilling out onto the stage. There's no written record of Jack Irons doing it before this July night, but he was excited about the idea, breaking out into nervous laughter just before taking the stage: "It was so funny I started to pee in my sock," he said. "We were laughing so hard!"

Tantalizingly, in the early 1990s, Anthony recalled that the show was recorded, and that he had even seen the footage. Being such a pivotal moment in the band's career and yet not having surfaced in a documentary or anywhere online, it's unlikely that the footage has survived. If it had, it would be the earliest of the band, predating the current holder of that record by a good eight months.

Representatives of the *LA Weekly* were there, of course, and in the following week's edition they recounted witnessing the band in full flight onstage, "giving the bare breasted dancers some competition by showing their young flesh au naturel. Well, actually they had socks over their private specimens, except for bassist Flea, who couldn't keep his on."

The stunt over, the attention of the crowd won, and a permanent element of their careers set down, the band then had to deal with an angry club manager. He ambushed them on the way back to their dressing room: "No pubes!" he screamed, terrified that he was about to be shut down by police. "I told you guys no pubes!" As the *LA Weekly* had already noted, Flea had trouble keeping his sock on,* and the public display of pubic hair was (and still is) illegal in licensed venues in California. The Kit Kat Club, which had been owned by infamous underworld figure Eddie Nash, had already received enough police attention for a lifetime, and the manager didn't need any more undue attention.† But after a dressing down, they were free to go.

This was not the first problem that had accompanied this show for the owner of the club; in fact, it almost didn't happen. Suzanne Schott, the Kit Kat booker/promoter and the woman responsible for these monthly music nights (who also appeared as a dancer in *Suburbia*'s strip scene, filmed at the Kit Kat Club), had recently left the venue after a dispute with the owner over her pay and the performing band's percentages, leaving the already booked engagements up in the air. Asked to stay for the July 3 performance, then fired once again, this particular show only happened in the end owing to the protests of the Chili Peppers and the Butt Cherries; Schott's involvement with the final performance is actually unclear, and the weekly shows were held under new management shortly afterward.

* Which must have been doubly embarrassing, as his mother was in the crowd.

† Nash, whose real name was Adel Nasrallah, had been the focus of police investigation for some time, most notably for the 1981 Wonderland murders, the subject of many true crime reports since. Nash also owned the Starwood along with several other clubs around Los Angeles, creating quite the live music empire.

After the show, the band went off into the night with pockets flush with cash and even more hype around the L.A. scene than before. But perhaps the biggest impression they made that night was on someone they weren't initially aware of.

In the audience was Lindy Goetz. Born in New York in December 1947, Goetz had been in the music business for decades in various forms. His first break was thanks to a childhood friendship that his stage actor brother Stuart had with Davy Jones (not yet of the Monkees). Stuart and Davy starred in *Oliver* on Broadway together, but Lindy and Davy became roommates. When Jones went west to Los Angeles, Lindy, a drummer, went with him.

An assortment of USO shows for the US Armed Forces in Japan and Europe followed, and some time in a group too: there were stints in Max Frost and the Troopers, a fictional band in the vein of the Monkees, created for the 1968 film *Wild in the Streets*. After the success of that film, versions of the "band" were sent out on tour, and Goetz played in at least one iteration with a number of other anonymous, roped-in session musicians.

There were even a few appearances behind the kit with the Monkees themselves, but toward the end of the 1960s, as the band petered out into an anticlimactic end. Never quite reaching success, and mostly playing other people's music, it's no real surprise that by the 1970s Goetz had relocated from behind the drums to behind the scenes, taking a promotional job in Los Angeles, where he worked closely with rockabilly and country-rock pioneer Rick Nelson, before joining Mercury Records in 1974.

Goetz quickly had a variety of upward moves; he was Los Angeles promotions manager for MCA Records and then its promotions executive. In July 1978 he joined EMI's Screen Gems and Colgems publishing divisions as director of national promotions. Aside from the work that his production company, Ziponki Enterprises, provided for him, in early 1980 Goetz was tapped to run START, an independent company designed to help get black artists on the airwaves. Throughout this time, he helped promote a litany of different acts, like Nicky Hopkins, the Bar-Kays, and Bachman-Turner Overdrive, on several labels. The Ohio Players, on Mercury, were one particular favorite, so much so that toward the end of the '70s, as their fame waned, Goetz tried to get them moved to a different, more appreciative label simply because he liked their music so much.

While the Chili Peppers formed and developed their repertoire in late 1982 and early 1983, for Goetz that period was dedicated to a pop-rock band called the Automatix out of Detroit, Michigan, that had formed in 1979 and were made up of Bruce Nazarian, a polymath musician, engineer, and software developer,* and session drummer Jerome Jones, along with a number of other players. The band had been signed first to Ziponki Enterprises and then to MCA Records under Goetz's management and guidance; the deal was made because Goetz was still friendly with the president of MCA Records. The Automatix recorded and released their debut album *Night Rider* in 1983 and were achieving the first glimmering hope of a following on album-oriented radio shortly thereafter. But upon a corporate restructuring halfway through the year, they were dropped from the label, just on the precipice of some real success. A crushing disappointment to band and manager alike.

This means that when Goetz witnessed the Chili Peppers on that July night, he had just had his hopes with the Automatix dashed and was looking for a new act to hitch his wagon to. He was thrilled by what he had just seen on that tiny strip club stage, recalling that they were "painted green" (a factoid that has never been mentioned elsewhere) and were "out of their fucking minds."

Goetz had been introduced to the band by Mark Richardson, who had previously tried to set up a meeting between himself, the Chili

* Nazarian, who died in 2015, was later brought into the Chili Peppers fold when he mixed "Yertle the Turtle" off their 1985 album *Freaky Styley*.

Peppers, Anthony's father, and their mutual friend Jay Brown back in April—a rendezvous the band had not shown up to. But in the months since, Richardson had kept at it, hounding the elder Kiedis for more opportunities, and even passing copies of their demo tape around town, one of which came Goetz's way: "I thought they were black," was his earliest impression. Perhaps Mark Richardson corrected him ahead of time, or perhaps he discovered the truth when he saw them in person, seeing their true colors—even if their skin was painted green. Regardless, the live show impressed Goetz at least as much as the demo tape had. Leaving that night, he quickly made plans to see the band again.

SHOW #17

JULY 4, 1983

Music Machine, 12220 West Pico Boulevard, Los Angeles, CA

PROBABLY NURSING HEAVY HANGOVERS, if not from drinks or drugs then from adrenaline, the band played again the very next night at the Music Machine, a club southwest of Hollywood where What Is This had already played a number of times. The venue was new to the scene, opening in 1981 as the Cowboy, a country-centric place that only lasted in that form for about a year before it was rebranded to better suit the exploding punk community. The newly minted Music Machine was ostensibly a punk club, with instantly recognizable silver streamers lining the walls behind the stage, but it kept its options open in a tough environment, still hosting the odd country show well into the decade.

This was a busy night, with many bands on the bill, and the Chili Peppers probably played first or second to a half-full club. Onstage before the Chili Peppers were Electric Peace (mistakenly named Electric Teeth on the flier), a Reseda-based psychedelic punk band led by singer Brian Kild, who only had disparaging thoughts about the band's name and Anthony's lyrics when asked for his memories of the night.

Also playing were Blood on the Saddle, one more genuinely unique band that was unfortunately branded under the all-encompassing cow-punk genre, and gothic, sludgy headliners the Flesh Eaters, who were touring their recent album *A Hard Road to Follow*.

Several photographs from this show have surfaced, in full-fidelity color from Fernando Mallory, who got so close to the action that Anthony's dilated pupils are visible, as is the evident joy on his face. It's hard to tell with any real certainty, but thanks to the previous nights' shenanigans the band seem to have shed their clothing at a faster rate than normal at this show; the entire band is shirtless, in almost-matching black jeans. Soon, they'd be getting onstage practically naked to begin with, but that level of freedom and comfort that the band become famous (or infamous) for seems to be emerging here, as the weather warmed up in the early summer of 1983, and they realized they could make as much of a scene dressing down as dressing up.

Scene photographer Lynda Burdick took a few more shots of the band most likely later this night, for the Nite Life section of gay men's magazine *In Touch*. The photos show the band on the street outside the Music Machine, a vertical liquor store sign glowing like a beacon behind them. Stripped to the waist, the four grin and grimace into the camera lens, still hopped up from another successful show. In one of the photos, Flea is holding a peace ornament up to the camera, and the rest of the band are flashing peace signs (or are they bunny ears?) behind him. In another, Hillel is whispering something, no doubt sarcastic, into Anthony's ear. When the photos appeared in the November issue of the magazine, it became apparent that "Southern California's badest [sic] bad-boy rock band" knew their target audience. "When our friend Lynda

A day after their "socks on cocks" stunt, the Red Hot Chili Peppers perform at the Music Machine on Pico Boulevard. July 4, 1983.
Fernando Mallory

Burdick told them that this show was for IN TOUCH, off came the shirts and belts," the caption read. "Thanks guys. You're the greatest."*

---

* Burdick may have taken another photo on this night of Flea and Anthony onstage, which has surfaced on the internet in low quality.

SHOW #18

JULY 18, 1983

Club Lingerie, 6507 Sunset Boulevard, Hollywood, CA

ON A WHIRLWIND TOUR across the United States in support of their new album, Bad Brains had played in Detroit, New Orleans, and Chicago in the lead-up to this show in Los Angeles on Monday, July 18. The DC band didn't take a support act with them the way most bands do when on tour, instead preferring to have a local act open for them at every stop along the way.* And it was in Los Angeles that the Chili Peppers got their chance, thanks to their demo tape, and thanks to Brendan Mullen.

Even within a close-knit music community, usually the first time a support act sees their main act, legend or not, would be at the show. Perhaps that first meeting would be for a moment or two only, in a backstage green room somewhere. Not so for Flea. On the morning of July 18, he later recalled, "I was psyched sitting there in my crib practicing bass, waiting, thinking over and over again like a little kid,

* Beastie Boys, still in their early punk phase, opened for them July 13 in New York.

oh my god, we're playing with Bad Brains tonight." But this crib was on Leland Way (or Pot Alley, as the locals called it), only around the corner from Club Lingerie, and outside his window he spies Bad Brains' lead singer H.R. "come rollin' down the street looking to buy herb. How the fuck did he divine so fast where the action was?" But rather than shy away from introducing himself, Flea offered him some of his own supply, and the two "got stoned out and then played that night, and it was a blast."

It was a blast, indeed, as the recording from the night shows. The second-earliest that exists of the band onstage, it was recorded by an unknown audience member and unleashed online at some point in the mid-2000s. The recording picks up just after "Green Heaven," probably the third song of the night, has begun.* While the late start means that Hillel's talk box, if it was present, isn't recorded, his regular (fantastic) guitar solo at the end seems to imply that he wasn't using the device here.

After an ad-lib by Anthony that implements a couple of lines of his "Nevermind" intro (a few songs early), "Baby Appeal" is next, the earliest appearance of this song, and its possible live debut. Structurally, it's much the same as the version that would appear on *The Red Hot Chili Peppers* the following year, though the instrumental portions last a few measures longer.

After a charming pun from Flea ("This song is very dedicated!"), all eleven seconds of "You Always Sing the Same" follow. Afterward, while the band tune up, the crowd make their own fun, calling for "Fire." Perhaps not the wisest thing to call out in a crowded room (even a half-crowded one, as this night seemed to be).

Up next is "Get Up and Jump," and once again Anthony seems to lose himself in the cacophony halfway through, but otherwise the

* "Out in L.A." and "Sex Rap," most likely the first and second songs, are missing from the recording. But there is the slim chance that the band played a shorter set without them.

song sounds much the same as the demo recording from two months earlier. For whatever reason, a beatbox-backed rendition of the theme for the CBS show *The Beverly Hillbillies* arrives next. Having been off the air for twelve years by the time the band played this night, it's not entirely clear why they performed the song; if they had a reason, it isn't obvious from listening to the recording. But it wouldn't be the only time they pulled something like this out of thin air; throughout 1986, the band would frequently open shows with the theme song to "Rocky." Like most in-jokes, to an outsider it isn't as funny, but that's the whole point.

After the TV theme cover comes "Nevermind," and as they finish, the band step offstage, then on again, for their encore of "Fire"; understandably, being in a support position, no socks routine accompanies it.

This was the end of the Chili Peppers show, but it wasn't the end of their time onstage. In a show of goodwill that might have been borne out of Flea's sharing of his weed stash earlier in the day, or just a representation of the easygoing natures of the headlining act, the "Red Chili Peppers" were invited back onstage to jam at the end of the Bad Brains set.*

What follows are a few loose jams—reggae guitars, the odd lick, and a steady beat over slap bass beds from Flea—that don't impress all that much, or inspire the listener as much as they could, or should, considering the caliber of musicians onstage. The crowd seem politely attentive: but at one point, an audience member that the recording captures is heard turning to a friend, murmuring "you wanna hang around much longer?"

But onstage there are some moments of interest. As Anthony raps and scats, searching for something to ad-lib, he evidently falls back on

* There's also the possibility that after two short sets, they needed to fill a bit more time onstage to give the crowd their money's worth.

a few pieces of writing that were at the forefront of this mind. One of these pieces is the "dolphins" verse from "Green Heaven," probably familiar to the audience—or at least those that were listening—as the band had performed the song only an hour beforehand. Another is a few lines from a song that Anthony and Flea had recently written for Nina Hagen.

After meeting in March after one of the early Chili Peppers shows at the Cathay de Grande, Hagen and Anthony had a physical relationship for about a month, cooling off once Hagen's more-serious boyfriend returned from out of town. But a more platonic relationship continued, and at one point in midspring, Hagen had asked Anthony to write her a song to include on her next album, set to be recorded that autumn.

Seven years his senior, Hagen was an experienced "wise soul" and a worldly mentor of sorts to Anthony; his exposure to her way of life and her vastly different worldview led to many changes in his lifestyle. One mantra of giving away valuable, expensive, or even cherished items in order to make the world a better place would later resurface as the genesis for the 1991 *Blood Sugar Sex Magik* track "Give it Away."*

Hagen's song, written by Flea and Anthony early in the summer, was entitled "What It Is."† Some of the themes present in Anthony's lyrics for "Green Heaven" resurface here, refined somewhat by Hagen's influence: "People have to know that it's not about money, cash is not the way to make your life sunny."‡

A demo, recorded on the night it was written on a boom box with just Flea's slap bass as a backing, was released on the *Out in L.A.*

---

* Hagen was probably on Anthony's mind that year because of a song from her 1991 album *Street*, "Nina 4 President," which incorporated lyrics from "What It Is," handing him a writing credit.

† Though judging from its appearance on the 2003 reissue of the band's debut album, it was also given the placeholder title "Nina's Song."

‡ The themes to "Green Heaven" don't just resurface; some of the lyrics do too. What Anthony planned to do about that if both songs became Chili Peppers staples isn't clear. It seems he wasn't thinking that far ahead.

compilation in 1994. "Anthony and I stayed up all night, wrote it, and recorded it in the wee hours of the morning on our blaster to show to Jackie and Hillel that day," Flea recalled in its liner notes. They probably recorded many demos just like it that are, sadly, yet to see the light of day, if they have even survived.

It's unclear what the immediate plan for the song was. It isn't known if the rest of the band ever worked on it as a full-fledged Red Hot Chili Peppers song, or if it was given straight to Hagen and only intended for her—but the latter is more likely. The band actually recorded a version of the song with Hagen on vocals in midsummer, right around the time of this show. Unfortunately, the band's instrumentation was taken off at the last minute by producer Keith Forsey, who "wanted it nice and clean." Karl Rucker replaced Flea on bass, Steve Schiff redid Hillel's guitar, and Jack's drums were taken over—to their horror—by a drum machine. While the band's demo predates this recording, and Anthony wouldn't have appeared, this is still an early recording of the original lineup of the Red Hot Chili Peppers, and to this day remains an unreleased and sought after recording.* The song, obviously still fresh in Anthony's mind, made an appearance here onstage on this night. It would resurface at least twice more in the coming months.

The night's entertainment was reviewed by Richard Cromelin in the *Los Angeles Times,* and within is the Chili Peppers' first mention outside concert listings in their hometown newspaper. The band, Cromelin said, "were great when they were playing their hot, taut, James Brown-derived riffs, not so great when they were playing around. The adolescent horseplay between songs seemed to amuse them and a few onlookers, but they'd better shape up if they expect to impress unconverted audiences." To the band's

* Hagen's album, *Fearless*, was released in November 1983, and made it to no. 151 on the Billboard 200. The Chili Peppers are thanked several times in the album's liner notes.

credit, the recording shows the horseplay was fairly restrained, *Beverly Hillbillies* theme song aside, and it seems as if Cromelin might have simply been filling space by repeating the work of others; the reference to James Brown is lifted straight from a previous concert listing advertising the band.

Elsewhere in the review, Cromelin notices the relative timidity of the crowd (a detail evident in the recording), wondering if it was a result of the Bad Brains' shift to more outright reggae stylings, or the fact that Club Lingerie's twenty-one age limit reduced the punks in the audience.* This would have been a problem for half the band; Jack Irons celebrated his twenty-first birthday on this very day, leaving just Anthony and Flea as the only underage members of the band. This age restriction didn't seem to negatively affect them; they had been playing clubs for many years now, and in the worst-case scenario, club owners would simply make the offending members wait outside until it was their time to go onstage.

After the two bands finished and had packed away their instruments, and as the DJ, Japanese musician Hisao Shinagawa, returned to play reggae tunes to lead out, the band grabbed a drink in the large, brick-lined room that doubled as the dance floor. Mark Richardson, friend of Blackie Dammett, approached Anthony, seeing his opportunity at last. "I met a guy at the Lingerie from Atlanta. This tall rocker-looking bass player dude came up asking who manages me," Anthony remembered. "I said, 'You are looking at him.'" Having evidently given up on trying to manage the band himself, Richardson was there to introduce them to Lindy Goetz, who had been waiting to see the band again since that night at the Kit Kat Club. Accounts differ: either Goetz was there himself, and suggested that the band visit him at his offices on Ventura Boulevard the next day, or Richardson

* The show being on a Monday night may have also had something to do with it, but this wasn't exactly a crowd of people with day jobs.

suggested it in Goetz's absence. Whatever the case, Anthony, delighted to have this opportunity fall into his lap, agreed to take a meeting, and headed off into the night.

The next day or shortly thereafter, Flea and Anthony headed fifteen miles north into the Valley, where the offices for Goetz's Ziponki Enterprises were located. The two men may have been surprised (or considered it fortuitous) to discover that Goetz's offices were only a few doors down from the Plant, at 12400 Ventura Boulevard; by that point, their August 4 show at the venue may have already been booked. Curiously, neither Hillel nor Jack apparently attended this informal meeting. That said, of the four members of the band, the bass player and lead singer were the two that, at least looking back, seemed to be the ones leading the way; Hillel (who, as Anthony noted, disappeared whenever he had a girlfriend) and Jack already had their other band—due to perform at the Music Machine for the first time on July 21, alongside "avant-ska" band Skanksters*—and while Flea was in FEAR, who were themselves set to play again in early August, it was hardly *his* band; he was simply the bassist, playing someone else's parts. Add that to the fact Flea and Anthony lived together, and it's understandable that it was them, and just them, whom Goetz greeted on this warm summer's day.

"That afternoon we smoked some pot and did a line or two of coke and swapped stories," Anthony remembered. Already, the artists and their prospective manager were on the same level. While Goetz was fifteen years older than the rest of the group, there was no overtly paternal relationship here, despite the father-figure role Goetz would eventually play in their lives—especially in Anthony's, when his drug use spiraled out of control. Here it was simply three men shooting the shit and sharing a love for the Ohio Players, whose records lined

* This show was filmed by TV station Channel 7, and the following week broadcast on *Goodnight L.A.*, a program dedicated to local acts. Unfortunately, a recording does not seem to have survived.

Goetz's office wall. (This was a connection dear to the band's heart; after all, they quoted the Ohio Players in every performance of "Out in L.A.")

Looking back, Flea and Anthony didn't seem to realize at the time that the wheels had come off Goetz's plans, that perhaps he might have needed the band more than the band needed him. But despite his "pretty lame one-liners," he was friendly and looked like someone they could work happily with. If Goetz was straighter—if the cocaine hadn't come out of the top desk drawer—things might have gone very differently. If they hadn't "actually really liked Lindy," they might have passed on his eventual offer. As it happened, they saw in each other potential and opportunity, and perhaps most important, the possibility of a real friendship.

Goetz asked them if they were willing to come to a management agreement, promising that he would get them a record deal within six months. Flea and Anthony asked for a moment alone. This would be the first time that a decision they made, with respect to the band, would have any real, lasting effect. A low-key show here and there, booked with a handshake, was easy; so was a demo session to which they owned all the rights. Now Goetz was suggesting they ink and notarize a binding contract.

Flea offered a litmus test of sorts. If Goetz agreed to take the two of them to lunch, they would let him manage their band.

"We got moo shu pork and a new manager."

SHOW #19

JULY 25, 1983

Music Machine, 12220
West Pico Boulevard, Los Angeles, CA

THE RED HOT CHILI PEPPERS returned to the Music Machine on West Pico only a few days after What Is This had graced its stage, playing with Psychobud, an Orange County new wave and synth-pop band led by Joseph Marx that would release their self-titled debut EP the following year, and Citizen Smith, another band that seem to have existed for this show only; no record of them exists elsewhere.

The Chili Peppers (and Blood on the Saddle, who were playing with the band for the second time that month) were possibly a last-minute replacement for an act with a similar name, but not a similar sound: postpunk act Chill Factor. Along with surf band Ten Foot Faces, they don't appear on the flier but appeared in newspaper ads in the lead-up to the show.* An example of the casual nature of the

* This could have been the other way around, with Chill Factor and Ten Foot Faces replacing the Red Hot Chili Peppers and Blood on the Saddle. Of course, there's also the chance

scene, these last-minute switches were not uncommon, but luckily a rarity throughout the year. Unfortunately, no other memories from the show have surfaced. However, there is the slight chance that the photos taken by Fernando Mallory and Lynda Burdick at the July 5 performance at the Music Machine were actually taken on this night, only being a few weeks apart.

that there were no replacements, and all five bands played on the night. Quite often bands would be left out of advertisements either for a lack of space or lack of name recognition.

SHOW #20

JULY 31, 1983

Al's Bar, 712 Traction Street, Los Angeles, CA

IF THERE WERE a list of Los Angeles venues that an up-and-coming rock band needed to play to obtain their bona fides, the Chili Peppers were, over the course of a few months, managing to play the majority of them with considerable ease. It probably wasn't intentional; there was no real plan here, and it's more likely that the band were exciting, cheap, and well connected, and these factors became evident when the band spread across various Los Angeles venues without really having to try. At this show they played, for the first and only time, Al's Bar.

Already legendary by 1983,* Al's Bar was situated on the ground floor of the American Hotel, in downtown Los Angeles. Originally called the Canadian when it was constructed in 1905, this was the first hotel in Los Angeles that catered to African Americans. A year

* In his memoir, Anthony admitted to being exposed to what real heroin use looked like at Al's Bar in 1981.

later, one of L.A.'s only Black police officers at the time, Berry Randolph, retired from the force in order to manage it. But despite Randolph's best attempts, over the next decade the hotel and its ground-floor café, the Golden West, was dragged into infamy and closed after a series of salacious (and fabricated) articles in the *Los Angeles Record* were published that claimed "Fast and Furious" orgies were "Pulled Off at the Negroes' Rendezvous." The unfortunate relationship with institutionalized racism didn't end there; into the next decade, after knee-jerk responses to immigration culminated in the Asian Exclusion Act of 1924, an enterprising Japanese man named Kintaro Asano took over the hotel—right in the middle of what is now known as Little Tokyo—and provided lodgings for other Japanese immigrants.*

The building—its uses and its occupants—shifted regularly over the years, remaining closely entwined with the Japanese population of Los Angeles and the Black residents; after the 1941 attack on Pearl Harbor, the mostly Japanese population of the city wound up in internment camps, but Black families replaced them. A variety of restaurants took up residence in that ground-floor space, but in 1973, Alfonso Vasquez took over and opened Al's Bar, staying in business until the end of the decade. In 1979 multitalented artist Marc Kreisel took over the hotel *and* the bar on the ground floor, keeping the name Al's Bar, until its closure in 2001.

The new phase of the building was designed as a source of income not just for Kreisel, but for the arts community as a whole; it was designed specifically to funnel money back into the community, a place "created by artists for artists to hang out in," as Jack Marquette said, and this artistic community spirit was mirrored in the party known as Theoretical.

---

* Not all the history of the building is unfortunate; in the early 1910s the Golden West was the site of some of the first jazz gigs in Los Angeles.

Theoretical grew out of the ashes of Brave Dog, which had been shut down for good in 1982, and had been the site of several Anthym shows, before the name change to What Is This. It was also where the members of the Chili Peppers had first met Gary Allen and Joel Virgel-Vierset, among many other new friends. After its closure, hoping that a similar event could spring up, Jack Marquette had given *Brave Dog*'s members-only contact list to Jim Van Tyne so he could start another party; the two would also collaborate on the Anti Club together. Brave Dog was, in theory, a private party, and the only way to gain access to the party was to have an invitation, mailed out on a postcard shortly beforehand. This didn't always work to keep things private; that they advertised shows in the newspaper ahead of time probably didn't help.

Working with art director John Barry, the three lifted the name from the San Francisco drag act Theoretical Girls and held the first event on July 25, 1982, at a leather bar in Silverlake called One Way. The first show featured Age of Consent, whose members David Hughes and John Callahan had DJ'd the first show the band played under the name the Red Hot Chili Peppers back in March. These continued on throughout the next year, until Theoretical's first birthday celebration, which was held at Al's Bar on July 31. It had been held at Al's at least once before, shocking the management, who had thought that a "gay guy" party would be "nice and sedate"—but this was evidently not the case.

Also on the bill were Necropolis of Love, a synth-pop band formed in 1981 from Berkeley that described themselves as "hostile disco." They had been invited down from San Francisco specifically for the Theoretical party. After playing a show at the Lhasa Club the night before, they drove to the venue the afternoon of the show and promptly got lost on the way. The band found themselves endlessly crossing the Los Angeles River, whose famous viaducts they knew from countless Hollywood TV shows and movies. "We kept going over it trying to find where we had to go," David Velasquez, keyboardist and vocalist remembers. "And staring at this clump of buildings . . . suddenly looking up to see one of those small Cessna planes, looking like it had been nailed to the side of the building. We quickly guessed that was where we had to go."

They were right; attached to the side of the American Hotel was a fully painted Cessna 150, put there by sculptor/artist Dustin Shuler, who called the piece *Pinned Butterfly*.* Meeting the Chili Peppers inside, each band did their sound checks, rudimentary in a club with only the simplest of sound systems and a tiny stage. Velasquez remembered the Chili Peppers as "very friendly guys," and that one of them, maybe Jack, was wearing a "goofy blonde wig" when they showed up.

The other act playing that night were Jes Grew, a duo consisting of William "Skip" King and his boyfriend, Jet Compton; they were to debut at this performance after a dare from Jim Van Tyne. King and Compton had attended several Theoretical nights, and Van Tyne had asked them to form a band for the party each time. "We kept putting it off until one day he said, 'What would your band name be?'" After giving it some thought, Compton replied off the top of his head with "Jes Grew," a term first used in *Mumbo Jumbo*, a 1972 novel by Ishmael Reed to give a solidifying name to the Black influence on American culture from the 1920s.

Completely nonmusical, King and Compton were unable to avoid the offer for much longer, and "suddenly a week or so later there's us opening that show." They weren't entirely well received—"We cleared the room with the exception of two people"†—but the performance was enough fun that first time that the duo gave it six more shots before finally giving it up in 1985.

---

* Having been attached in 1982, the plane remained in place until 1986.

† One of those remaining people was Alex Gibson, who performed the soundtrack for *Suburbia* and would later receive great acclaim in Hollywood, winning an Academy Award for his sound design work for 2017's *Dunkirk*.

After Jes Grew and Necropolis of Love performed, the Chili Peppers jumped onstage and did their thing. From all accounts it was a great show, and spirits were high. They had a number of props onstage: Skip King recalls Anthony taking out a pack of playing cards adorned (knowing his audience) with naked men, and flinging them into the audience, who went wild for it. The other prop was Rod Serling's face.

Serling, the host and writer of *The Twilight Zone*, was the visual theme for this iteration of Theoretical. Why that was so, if there *was* a reason, is now unknown, but his face was also featured on one side of the invite to the show, and larger-than-life-size cutouts of his top half were everywhere inside Al's Bar that night. At one point, Flea and Anthony fashioned a creepy mask out of one and wore it while they played.

Flea, Anthony, and Jack midflight at Al's Bar, on Traction Street, for a Theoretical party. July 31, 1983. *Rob Allen*

We know this thanks to Rob Allen, a scene regular who had been to most of the Theoretical events and captured in high fidelity several photographs of the band. Evident in Allen's photos were their interesting sartorial choices for the night: Anthony's hat with one word blazoned across it, somehow related to his father—DAMMETT—and his sleeveless shirt, an old piece of Steely Dan merchandise from their *Aja* days. But that doesn't last long—Flea is topless from note one, and Anthony, the muscular Adonis, works his eager crowd even further by taking his shirt off shortly into the set.

Visible on Flea's bare left shoulder is his fresh tattoo, the first of many that the members of this band would get and earn—fairly or not—them notoriety. His very first tattoo was a small grin on his right shoulder resembling his gap-toothed grin. It's unclear when that piece was done, but it's visible in photos taken at the Anti Club in April and was probably done in late 1982 or early 1983, maybe around the time he joined FEAR.

This newer piece of art is a portrait of Jimi Hendrix, done by Bob Roberts, who ran the renowned Spotlight Tattoo on Melrose Avenue. Roberts, who tattooed many in the scene over a period of many years, later give Anthony his famous tattoo of the band's asterisk logo on his wrist. When exactly Flea got Jimi's face inked can't be definitively stated, but he isn't sporting it in a photo taken on July 4, so it must have been done at some point this month.* Rick Cox, who was living in the American Hotel above Al's Bar at the time and witnessed the performance, remembers Flea sitting outside beforehand showing his fresh ink off, and so it was probably very freshly done.

While Rob Allen's wonderful photos have survived, sadly no audio recording or clues about a potential set list has, and we can only guess as to what the band played that night. All signs point to it being identical, albeit perhaps reshuffled, to the set on July 18.

* Is there perhaps a connection between the year Flea got this tattoo and the Jimi Hendrix Experience song set in the same year, "1983 . . . (A Merman I Should Turn to Be)"?

SHOW #21

AUGUST 4, 1983

The Plant, 12446 Ventura Boulevard, Studio City, CA

AUGUST GAVE THE BAND another show at The Plant, their second of three for the year, this time headlining over Tex and the Horseheads and Tupelo Chain Sex. Craig Lee, who was an *LA Weekly* mainstay and music reviewer for the *Los Angeles Times*, DJ'd between the bands on this night.

A day later, Hillel and Jack suffered a bout of déjà vu as What Is This played the same venue, supporting short-lived rock band Choir Invisible, who would fizzle out of the scene before the end of 1984. FEAR were busy as well, playing twice in San Francisco on August 5 and 6 with Circle Jerks, and once more back in Los Angeles a day later for another one of Bob Forrest's Sunday Clubs at its new location of the Cathay de Grande. This FEAR performance was a not-so-secret secret show—secret in the sense that the band played under the name the Fighting Cocks, and not so secret in that their faces were plastered all over the fliers, and hints as subtle as Lee Ving's lyrics were placed in local newspapers in the week leading up to the show. This run of performances was perhaps the busiest that the four members of the Chili Peppers had all year: six shows in seven days, across three bands, in two different cities. While it was unlikely that they had to do so, if there was any need to prove to the world that these four were serious about a career in music, the events of this week might have been it.

But that wasn't all. On Friday, August 12, Anthony and Flea accompanied Nina Hagen to the FM Station nightclub in North Hollywood, where she was the main attraction for a night of break dancing and rapping put on by *Funk* magazine. According to a report from the night by *LA Weekly*, Hagen lip-synched to a couple of songs before leaving the stage in retreat after a drink was thrown on the turntable. Whether the duo accompanied her onstage is unclear, but reference is made in the report to "What It Is," which Hagen had recently recorded. "What It Is" was to shortly make another appearance onstage, so there's a chance the trio performed it for the crowd on this night, given the opportunity to rehearse it.

If their current schedules weren't busy enough, *LA Weekly* also broke the news that Flea was planning on teaming up with brothers John and Dix Denney, of the seminal punk act the Weirdos. This group (who would have drummed can only be guessed) never manifested anywhere other than this small mention, but a connection to the Weirdos, specifically Dix, would prove useful in a few short months.

The Red Hot Chili Peppers may have played another show within this period, but its existence is not confirmed. In his memoir, Blackie Dammett writes that in July or August he "went north with the band to open for Bad Brains at the Warwick Theater in San Francisco." Bad Brains did, in fact, play in San Francisco on July 21—three days after the Club Lingerie show in Los Angeles with the Chili Peppers—with three cheery-sounding local bands: Personality

Crisis, Executioners, and Firing Squad. But this was held at a classic punk club called On Broadway, not the Warwick Theatre. The Warwick Theatre doesn't exist; Dammett was most likely referring to the *Warfield* Theatre, a rock club about a mile and a half away from On Broadway.

No other evidence has surfaced to confirm that the Chili Peppers played a show in San Francisco at this time; if they did, they were asked to at the last minute, and their names didn't make it onto fliers or newspaper ads. Flea may have referenced it in a 2019 Instagram post: "I remember the first time the red hots played outside of la in 1983, I was beyond thrilled. We drove up to San Francisco and performed at I-Beam club." I-Beam was yet another club frequented by punk acts; the mistake is understandable, akin to confusing a show played at the Cathay de Grande for one at the Club Lingerie from a distance of decades, and with thousands of other shows clouding your memory.

However, there's no mention anywhere else about the show Flea may be referring to—such as in Anthony's autobiography, or any other biography of the band—nor are there any surviving clippings or fliers that confirm it took place. And as it would have been the first show the band played outside Los Angeles, one can imagine that it would have been worth writing about, or at least remembered specifically in the years since. The first recorded show that the band played in San Francisco was in October *1984*—at the I-Beam, which may be the show Flea is referring to, just a year later than remembered. Likewise, the band *did* go on to play several shows at the Warfield Theatre in the years to come—opening for Run DMC in 1985—which may be the source of Dammett's mention.

If the Chili Peppers *did* open for Bad Brains in San Francisco during their 1983 tour, there is no surviving confirmation that the show happened. Dammett may be remembering incorrectly, or is perhaps getting the location or timing incorrect for a show that did actually happen. Likewise, Flea may be misremembering the October 1984 show as happening a year earlier.

Also possible is that the show did happen, and all trace of it was missed by contemporary sources; for now, it is a yet to be confirmed performance.

SHOW #22

AUGUST 13, 1983

Pomona Valley Auditorium, 235 West Third Street, Pomona, CA

FROM GARY ALLEN to the Minutemen to Bad Brains to Oingo Boingo, the early Chili Peppers managed to put themselves in front of an impressive variety of acts, and these two shows for Oingo Boingo—one at the Pomona Valley Auditorium and another four days later at the Universal Amphitheater—were perhaps their most impressive yet, and certainly to their biggest audiences yet.

One might assume that these slots were a result of the band's newly minted management agreement with Lindy Goetz. After all, Oingo Boingo were an established, famous act, even if they were on an independent label, and this was a prestigious gig that few would turn down. Why else would they take a chance on a wild pack of nobodies if not for the intervention of a seasoned professional like Lindy Goetz? But indeed, they were actually the result of Flea's relationship with Oingo Boingo's trumpet player, Dale Turner, and their keyboardist, Richard Gibbs, who offered them the slot. Flea would often attend

Oingo Boingo rehearsals, and Turner and Gibbs were impressed by his energy and talent. The Chili Peppers were given the support slots only a few weeks before the show, and only for these two out of four that the band played in town that week; the Bangles opened for them on August 18, and X on August 20, at the Pacific Amphitheater in Costa Mesa.

By August 1983 the Chili Peppers had already crossed paths with the band a number of times. Anthym had played ahead of them at the Orange County Fair in 1980, and a year later the newly minted What Is This opened for Oingo Boingo at the Reseda Country Club, as they toured their debut album. FEAR had also supported the band in December 1982, a week before the first Red Hot Chili Peppers show, at that chaotic night under the Big Top in Long Beach. Neighbor's Voices, friends of the Chili Peppers, had also opened for them at least once in 1981, and the list goes on.

The history of Oingo Boingo is long and complicated and befits their unique sound. Originally a street theater troupe called the Mystic Knights of the Oingo Boingo, musician Danny Elfman joined the existing act in 1974 and quickly made it his own. After a number of lineup and stylistic changes the band was reformed as Oingo Boingo in 1979, releasing a number of well-received EPs and their debut, *Only a Lad*, in 1982. A mix of ska, punk, and comedy, Oingo Boingo were an eight-piece act that didn't exactly seem like the kind of band that would set the Los Angeles scene on fire. But that they did, even if they didn't make many commercial waves.

Sadly, while opening for Oingo Boingo might have seemed like a boon, the reality was much different, and Flea knew this from experience. Having opened for them three times already in consecutive years (with two different bands), each time the band he played with was treated with disdain and, at times, outright abuse from the crowd, who seemed to have no interest in anything other than the band they were really there to see. Though Oingo Boingo can in no way be considered a White supremacist act and had nothing to do with that scene, Anthym were pelted with beer bottles by a crowd of neo-Nazis at the Orange County fair in 1980, and FEAR caused a riot of sorts when they played before another restless crowd two years later. And while FEAR may have relished the chaos, the less-intense What Is This probably didn't, especially after Alain Johannes was hit in the face with a beer bottle.

Would it be fourth time's the charm? ("That ought to be a Chili Pepper trial by fire," the *LA Weekly* forecasted, perhaps keenly anticipating where this was going.)

But any lingering idea in Flea's mind that Oingo Boingo fans had changed in the nine months since he had played before them was quickly removed. They were, he remembered several months later, "a cruel new wave audience." Oingo Boingo rarely had an opening act, and so in the times when one *was* brought out, the expectant audience didn't take too kindly to their favorite band being delayed by some scrappy punk act they'd never heard of. And the Chili Peppers, pulling their usual over-the-top routine, may have caused some further friction. As "boos and objects thrown by the audience rained on the musicians throughout the set," the band played the best they could. But Flea, evidently having enough of this kind of treatment after what was now three hopeless shows supporting Oingo Boingo, gave the crowd a parting shot by dropping his pants.

How that stunt went down, one can only guess.

This show was the first held at the newly christened Pomona Valley Auditorium, which had been a cinema when it was first built in 1923; in this case, the Chili Peppers had the honor of being the very first act to play the new venue, being the opening act. Sadly, as is the case with the majority of these later-year performances, no photos or recordings have surfaced.

SHOW #23

AUGUST 17, 1983

Universal Amphitheater, 100 Universal City Plaza, Los Angeles, CA

ORIGINALLY BUILT SO tour groups could watch a Western shootout during the Universal Studio Tour, the Universal Amphitheater was quickly repurposed to hold rock concerts after dark, when the stage was free of score settlin' cowboys. The venue, just north of Hollywood, proved a successful moneymaker for Universal Studios, but the lack of a proper roof caused problems whenever inclement weather was involved. An extensive renovation that began in 1980 and finished two years later followed, upping the seating capacity and keeping the rain out.*

While in his memoir Anthony either forgot about or neglected to mention the Pomona Valley show a few days previous, he still seemed to understand the severity of this second night, and appreciate the

* The Universal Amphitheater is a venue closely linked with Oingo Boingo; they would play the venue dozens of times throughout their career, and in fact would play their final show at the venue over two nights during 1995.

bizarre gift that had been handed to the band: "Here we were with no record deal, a ten-song repertoire, and we were going from playing in a club before two hundred people to playing to an audience of four thousand." But that didn't stop him from almost ruining the show before it even happened.

As Blackie Dammett tells it in his memoir, his son had climbed onto the Amphitheater's roof and was "running amok" before the show. Apprehended and maybe even detained when he finally returned to the ground, security and venue staff canceled the Chili Peppers slot. Oingo Boingo lead singer Danny Elfman and the show's promoter, Larry Vallon, had to step in for it to go ahead, under the proviso that Anthony behaved himself and stayed away from the backstage bar.

This last-minute rescue did not improve the reception the band received once they made it onstage, dressed in rainbow wigs and their "weirdest clothes," and the same torrent of boos was rained down upon them as at the Pomona show. There were added stresses; Flea broke a bass string early on, and in the ensuing interruption that changing it required, Anthony and the rest of the band had to vamp the best they could. But either out of nerves, or just because he was wound up too tight, Flea broke another string shortly afterward, and the crowd laid into them while the proverbial crickets filled the spaces in between the abuse. It wasn't all bad. Blackie Dammett said the "lobby concessions applauded RHCP for driving people out of the auditorium and into their eateries."

But even if the crowd wasn't happy, the band had at least one fan in the building—and an important one, at that—Danny Elfman. He had already come to their rescue once and was willing to do it again, even if it meant scolding his own adoring fans. As the punks wailed and hissed, he strode onstage in "a bathrobe and with a face full of shaving cream" and excoriated the crowd for being so disrespectful. Anthony believed Elfman's attempt was helpful, if only moderately, but "by the time we finished, I think we let them know we were for real and that they had just been hit with something they wouldn't soon forget."

He was correct. The Chili Peppers *did* make an impression on a number of Oingo Boingo fans in the crowd that night. One of them, Emilio Loza, remembers that the band "exploded on to the stage jumping around shirtless like prizefighters. I didn't know what to think like most of the crowd and I started booing them along with everyone else. . . . They powered through their set and from what I could tell eventually they won over most of the crowd. I was certainly impressed by the end of it." With some amusement, Loza also recalled that portions of the crowd were shouting "go back to New York" out of some mistaken belief that, because Anthony was rapping, the band must have hailed from the East Coast.

The set featured a special guest in Nina Hagen, who joined the band to perform "What It Is," which she had just recorded for her own album. As a recording of this performance hasn't surfaced, we sadly can't hear what a full-band version of this song might sound like. If it was a full-band performance, and Hillel and Jack did add their own pieces to Flea's bassline, this can be considered a lost early-era Chili Peppers song. However, if it was merely a trio performance, with Flea on bass and Hagen and Anthony on alternating vocals, then it's no wonder it didn't receive a rapturous reception from the already-on-edge crowd.

A point worth some consideration is *why* Hagen joined them onstage. Anthony writing a song for the musician he was casually seeing is one thing, and it's no surprise that he and Flea found themselves accompanying her on various nights out; they wouldn't miss an opportunity to be seen somewhere and get their names in the mouths and minds of others.* But to have her join them onstage is a curious move.

* Their physical relationship was most likely over by this point; by August, Anthony had met fashion designer Jennifer Bruce, whom he would start officially dating by October or November. Anthony and Jennifer dated on and off until 1987.

On one hand, she added star power and punk authenticity to their relatively lowly presence: Hagen was a *bona fide*, a genuine star who had escaped from the intimidating and strictly ruled West Germany to flourish artistically in the United States like it was no big deal. Though 1983 may have felt like the future in many ways to those in the scene, here was a woman ahead of her time, someone truly alien to the kids of Hollywood, as forward thinking as they may have been. The Chili Peppers hitched a ride with many acts during the year: Gary Allen, Minutemen, Bad Brains—even FEAR, in some respects—but Hagen was perhaps the act they associated with the most. A lot of this was Anthony by himself, "acting all big-time and shit," but the band definitely benefited from her being around, if only briefly.

This association could have gone *too* far, for Hagen also had the ability to overshadow the rest of the band. She was a well-known musician—not quite a celebrity, but not exactly a D-lister, and "What It Is" would have been the centerpiece of the show no matter where in the set it appeared. Many audience members going home that night may have simply remembered the band as a strange, chaotic blur that featured, of all people, Nina Hagen. Good performance or not, it's most likely that the only reason their set is remembered at all is because they went on to become a cultural phenomenon ten times the size of Oingo Boingo.

And to complicate matters, the song was one that would have sounded familiar if they had already played "Green Heaven," which was highly likely, seeing as they considered it the best of their early pieces. And on the off chance an Oingo Boingo fan had gone home humming "What It Is," hoping to hear it again, they'd be out of luck. Hagen's album, which featured a fairly different version of the song, wouldn't be out for another three months, and the band (most likely) wouldn't play the song live ever again.

Though the *LA Weekly* would say afterward that Hagen's appearance onstage would lead to a delighted audience, how the surprise guest really went down is unknown. Why she was there *at all* is also unknown: Were they filling out a sparse set, still only about ten songs and twenty minutes long? Were they trying to flex their punk muscles by showing off their connection to a scene legend? Were they simply playing a song they enjoyed with a person they all liked? All are possibilities.

Backstage after the show, Blackie Dammett presented his son with two round-trip tickets to London as a "gift for all he had accomplished in just six amazing months." After a series of strains arose that had resulted in Anthony leaving his father's home for the streets at a young age, over late 1982 and early 1983 the relationship had recovered enough that his father was at many early Chili Peppers shows, cheering his son on and ensuring that he too was seen somewhere in vogue after dark. "After all the negative commotion about my fathering," Dammett wrote, "I was finally vindicated."

Dammett told his son to take his best friend, Flea, with him overseas, and Flea ecstatically accepted a ticket of his own. The two wouldn't be departing for some time—most likely, late September or early October—and much would occur before they left that would send their world spinning, starting the next chapter of their story. But for now, they had that excitement to look forward to.

Almost ten years to the day after this show, Flea and Anthony—by then Grammy-winning, world-famous rock stars and the twin front men for the Red Hot Chili Peppers—presented Video of the Year at the MTV Video Music Awards at this very venue. As they stood onstage that night presenting an award with, of all people, Tony Bennett, one has to wonder if they realized how much had changed in the meantime, and what hadn't.

SHOW #24

SEPTEMBER 9, 1983

Radio City,
945 South Knott Avenue, Anaheim, CA

AFTER A THREE-WEEK STRETCH OF relative quiet that only saw a single performance by What Is This (on September 6th, with another engagement at the Club Lingerie), the band headed southeast to Anaheim for this show at Radio City on September 9th. Contained within a strip mall that held a variety of nightclubs, including the more mainstream Woodstock, Radio City was the heavy metal venue. In March the previous year Metallica played their first-ever show at this location. This would be the first and only time that the band played this club, which closed in 1986.

Supporting the band on this night was the gothic electropop act Cathedral of Tears, showing once again their uncanny talent for managing to play with bands that might not seem like a perfect fit on the surface. Cathedral of Tears were the brainchild of Jack Grisham, who had recently departed the Long Beach-based T.S.O.L. (True Sounds of Liberty) along with several of his bandmates. The reshuffled T.S.O.L would remain close to the Chili Peppers in the years ahead, playing shows with them as late as 1988.

Also listed as playing tonight are the little-known Cause for Concern, who would go through various lineup changes in the ensuing years, including an all-girl reboot under the same name later in the 1980s.

SHOW #25

SEPTEMBER 10, 1983

Kit Kat Club, 6550 Santa Monica Boulevard, Hollywood, CA

DESCRIBED AS A "TRIUMPHANT RETURN" to the Kit Kat, this show was a direct repeat of the July 3 performance, down to the returning support act of Roid Rogers and the Whirling Butt Cherries. Besides its happening, no other memories from the night have surfaced—such as whether the band performed their socks routine once again, this time to an expectant crowd. They most likely did, judging from the "by popular demand" notice gracing the advertisements; word had gotten around quickly about the first show, and its promoters would be keen to replicate its success.

More action was happening away from the stage. *LA Weekly* reported that present at the September Kit Kat Club show were executives from record labels Chrysalis and EMI/Enigma. Goetz had told Flea and Anthony that his primary goal as their manager was to get the band a record deal. In typical fashion, for Anthony, this was something he wasn't too concerned with; a deal was only a "cool and exciting thing," but to the bands around Los Angeles, a record deal was a status symbol, a money maker, a sign that they were a step above every other unsigned act playing mostly empty rooms. Goetz had come from deep within the industry and knew that there was only so far that an act could go without one. Hillel and Jack, in particular, would have been keenly aware that What Is This was toiling in obscurity without a deal of their own, forever unable to take the next step of their career—that is, until they were courted by MCA in the autumn of 1983.

The Chili Peppers may have been the joke party band with only a few pieces that could be considered legitimate "songs," but they were gaining attention, and they were already one step ahead of their peers in one important way: they had a demo tape. Their blistering, short, and sweet May recording was the perfect demonstration of the kind of act they were, and with that already out of the way, Goetz could focus on the next steps. Throughout August and September he worked tirelessly to get the band into the sights of record label A&R men, shipping the tape around and cycling through the contacts in his stuffed Rolodex. Anthony wrote of the meetings that he and Flea would have with their manager and his wife, Paulette "Patty" Durham Goetz, at their West Hollywood apartment; fried chicken, the odd line, and big plans for the future.

EMI/Enigma was a newly created partnership that was the result of two companies with long and convoluted histories. Enigma was formed originally as a distribution company called Greenworld in Torrance, California, in 1978. The owners—brothers William and Wesley Hein, and Steve Boudreau—had formed the spin-off Leathür Records in 1981 after they were approached by the then-unknown Mötley Crüe, who were after a distribution company for their self-produced debut album. Within a few months, that album, and Leathür's distribution work, had gotten the band signed to the much bigger Elektra Records, and worldwide fame followed soon after.

Realizing that there was more fun and more success to be had in a full-service record label than ordinary distribution, the Hein brothers and Boudreau changed their name from Leathür to Enigma, and started looking for more acts to work with. Their third-ever release, Berlin's *Pleasure Victim*, also saw that act reach greater success once they had jumped ship and signed with another label, Geffen.

Enigma grew exponentially throughout 1982 and early 1983, hiring additional staff and expanding their output, often utilizing one-off deals with other independent labels (including repackaging some existing albums from overseas) to release records in a partnership. In 1983, with and without the help of outside labels, they released albums by Green on Red, who had played with the Chili Peppers in April, a solo release from former Stooges front man Iggy Pop, and Slayer's *Show No Mercy*.

This growth was further boosted in July 1983 when Enigma signed an agreement with EMI Records. Similar to but more permanent than their traditional one-off deals, this gave the two labels an almost equal footing with each other. Speaking about it a few years later, it was referred to as an agreement "whereby the two labels mutually select acts they feel could use alternative marketing." In essence, both labels were given the opportunity to try something new; EMI could tap into a feverish underground scene, knowing there was good money to be made there, and Enigma could utilize EMI's massive corporate reach to boost artists that they liked but didn't have the desired funding for. Enigma/EMI was born, and their first release was *Playback* by the synth-pop act SSQ.

By the time this deal had been worked out in Los Angeles boardrooms, EMI had been through their own extensive maneuverings over a fifty-year history. One of the main tentpoles of the recording industry, EMI (Electric and Musical Industries) had formed in England in 1931, when two similar-sounding phonograph makers—Columbia Gramophone Company and The Gramophone Company—merged to develop a more closely knit hold on the market. Not content with just producing the playback equipment, they wanted to make the music, too, and furthered the success that The Gramophone Company had previously had with their occasional His Master's Voice releases.

These early deals among the first titans of the new industry caused confusing ripples down the line; early on, Radio Corporation of America (RCA) holding shares in the Victor Talking Machine Company—another gramophone producer—meant that RCA now automatically owned shares in the newly created EMI, all because Victor had *previously* owned half the now-obsolete Columbia Gramophone Company. When an antitrust lawsuit caused EMI to sell off its share of Columbia, it lost its presence in the United States all thanks to this complicated history. This issue was dealt with once flour magnate Sir Joseph Lockwood took over the company in the mid-1950s: EMI purchased 96 percent of Capitol Records, home to Frank Sinatra, Judy Garland, and countless other American stars, and oversaw the American market from across the pond.* In 1978 it started a second presence in the states with EMI America, which ran, confusingly, as a subsidiary of both Capitol *and* EMI.†

By 1983 the recording industry was one of mergers, acquisitions, rebrandings, and corporate shake-ups that weren't always obvious. To the average fan on the street, these connections meant nothing; many wouldn't think to look past the album cover to the ever-changing logos on the disc label and the copyright information contained in the tiny print on the back. But these connections and agreements—some of them made fifty years previously—created the exact circumstances that put EMI/Enigma in the room that night.

---

* Shortly afterward, they built the world-famous Capitol Records building, whose basement studio would be the site of the *Uplift Mofo Party Plan* recording sessions in 1987.

† The relative fortunes of each company would reverse in the coming years. By the time the Red Hot Chili Peppers' EMI catalog was reissued in 2003, the four albums bore the Capitol label most predominately, and EMI was barely mentioned.

That EMI were one of the final contenders made sense, given Goetz's previous relationship working for the label, and he was most likely responsible for Jamie Cohen being at the Kit Kat Club that night.* But this may not have been the first time a label rep had seen the band or openly expressed interest; the previous month *LA Weekly* reported that the group was "recording demos for an interested label"—most likely mistakenly referring to the already-complete May recordings. But, as the *Weekly* said, "The Flea, for once, is keeping his yap shut," and so that information might have been based purely on speculation, and not entirely accurate.

Born June 1, 1953, Jamie Cohen was originally from Chagrin Falls, Ohio, the son of a music industry entrepreneur and record store owner and was an avid music fan from his childhood. He joined A&M Records in the late '70s, then Slash Records (home to FEAR) as an A&R rep in 1981, before being poached by EMI America in mid-1983 as their West Coast representative. Being new to the company and eager to impress, he would have been on the prowl for new talent. Whatever he saw that night, he liked. As Anthony remembered it, Cohen was "particularly aggressive in going after" the band, and it was most likely in the weeks after this show that EMI/Enigma started the negotiation process that preceded them signing the Chili Peppers to this new venture.

Assisting the Chili Peppers on their end was their new lawyer, whom they joined forces with shortly after meeting Lindy Goetz. Anthony modestly describes the process in his autobiography: "If we were going to try and get a record deal, we'd need a lawyer. Someone gave us a recommendation for a guy named Eric Greenspan." Here was another partnership that got off on the right foot purely because of shared interests; Greenspan had artwork on his wall by his client

* It can't be confirmed that Cohen was actually in the crowd that night, but all signs point to his attendance. Sadly, Cohen died too young in 2008, at the age of fifty-five.

Gary Panter, an artist and cartoonist who had close ties with the punk community, and who would go on to create the covers for the Red Hot Chili Peppers debut in 1984 and 1987's *The Uplift Mofo Party Plan*. Evidently, this was all the duo needed. Much like Lindy Goetz's display of Ohio Players records on his wall, to Anthony and Flea this was a sign that Greenspan was on their level, that he wasn't just some corporate *other*, or a stooge. He was cool; he had even booked a Grateful Dead show as a college student.

Greenspan seemed to like the duo just fine himself. In his office at the firm of Shagin & Myman on Wiltshire Boulevard, the three worked out a deal: Greenspan would be the band's attorney, but he wouldn't take a cut until the band made some real money. Then, he would take a typical 5 percent fee.* Maybe he saw something in them, or maybe he just took a risk, thinking that if they imploded it wouldn't waste too much of his time. Greenspan, now the head of the music department at his firm, Myman Greenspan Fineman Fox Rosenberg & Light, remains the band's lawyer to this very day. In 1997 he was briefly their manager.

* In his retelling, Anthony only ever implies that it was he and Flea who attended these meetings—likewise with the initial get-together with Lindy Goetz. Hillel and Jack never appear to be involved; or if they were, Anthony has erased them from his perspective of the events. Narrative technique, or a sign of things to come?

SHOW #26

SEPTEMBER 18, 1983

Sunday Club at the Cathay de Grande, 1600 Argyle Avenue, Los Angeles, CA

ON SEPTEMBER 11 What Is This played their own show at FM Station after Flea, Anthony, and Nina Hagen's appearance, and a week later the Chili Peppers performed at another of Bob Forrest's Sunday Club shows. These weekly sessions had moved from the Golden Village Supper Club on Hollywood Boulevard to the Cathay de Grande, only about a mile away on Sunset Boulevard, and the site of the first performance the band played under the name Red Hot Chili Peppers.

This afternoon's frivolities were the twenty-eighth birthday party for Circle Jerks lead singer Keith Morris, who had recently returned from a country-wide tour for his band's third album, *Golden Shower of Hits*. Morris had previously been in the original lineup of Black Flag for the three years leading up to 1979 but had split out on his own once creative differences and drug problems got too out of hand. He formed the Circle Jerks shortly thereafter;

their first album, *Group Sex*, is arguably the classic Los Angeles punk record—fourteen irreverent songs in fifteen wild minutes. The Chili Peppers would have close ties with the band in the years and decades to come.

Also present was Flea's FEAR-mate Derf Scratch, who emceed the night, and a "special guest," whose identity was spoiled in the accompanying newspaper listing: the Stains, another local punk band.

Once again, Fabrice Drouet brought his camera along, documenting the band close-up and in stunning fidelity. Notable is Anthony's outfit: a tartan shirt and matching pants ensemble—though, of course, everyone's clothes are quickly dispensed with—and Flea's clean-shaven head. To each side of the band sit the crowd, arms folded, listening with cool detachment. One wouldn't know it to look at them, but the band is on the edge of a major transformation. It was certainly lucky that Drouet was present to take these photos because they may well have been the last of the original Chili

The Red Hot Chili Peppers perform at the Cathay de Grande on Argyle Avenue. September 18, 1983. *fabulosfab*

Peppers lineup until September 1986; no photos circulate of the band for the rest of the year.*

This performance would have also been a sending-off party for Anthony and Flea, who most likely left for their Europe trip, paid for by Anthony's father, in the days shortly after this show.† In their immediate futures were exotic locales, strange new sights, and interesting people, and their excitement would be palpable. But one more life-changing event had to happen first.

The exact date that the Red Hot Chili Peppers were signed can't be identified, and the process—the offer from EMI/Enigma, the contract negotiations, and all the internal machinations involved—would have taken several months to iron out before it was finalized by both parties and their legal teams. The earliest glimmers of deal-related news circulated in the Los Angeles press in August and seemed to kick into a higher gear in September.

As Anthony relates it in his memoir, the offer, which would wind up being an eight-album deal, was filtered down to him from the boardrooms of EMI and through new lawyer Eric Greenspan and new manager Lindy Goetz just before the two left for Europe. "One night Flea and I were hanging out at La Leyenda when we got a call from Lindy," he wrote. "He told us that we had a record deal with EMI/Enigma."

While this was an incredible, unlikely achievement for such a young act, there was one problem. What Is This had also finally

---

* Flea published a photo from this set in his 2019 autobiography, incorrectly stating that it was from the May 1983 demo sessions at Studio 9 Sound Labs. But the Cathay de Grande's decrepit tiled roof is unmistakable, and the rest of the photos in the set, not published in the book, are obviously from a live show at the Cathay de Grande.

† They may have left for the trip in late August, directly after being given tickets by Anthony's father backstage at the Oingo Boingo show on August 17. The band did have a quiet period in the later weeks of that month, which might have been explained by the pair being overseas. But this doesn't fit with how Anthony later described their year going, and would entail the pair immediately leaving with virtually no preparation.

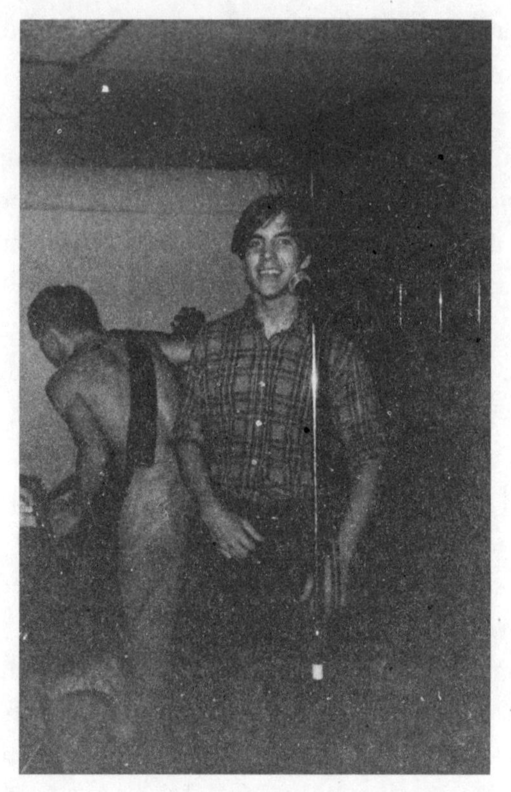

All smiles from Anthony, finally in his element. Cathay de Grande on Argyle Avenue. September 18, 1983. *fabulosfab*

attracted record company attention of their own throughout that same summer and early autumn period, and it was, incredibly, this very day that they too received some good news of their own. Anthony, writing about the same day that he and Flea found out the Chili Peppers were signed, recalled that "I was still excited about our deal when the phone rang again. Flea answered it. I heard him say, 'Are you sure? Wow, wow, that's really bad news.'"

When the call was over, Flea then turned to his bandmate, suddenly the only bandmate he had left, and told him that Jack Irons and Hillel Slovak had just quit the band. They were siding with What Is This, who had just obtained their own offer from record label MCA. Crestfallen, finally finding themselves where they wanted to be, they were suddenly without half of their crew. Anthony and Flea were a two-headed monster, that much is undeniable, but how could they go forward without Hillel's blistering guitar work and Jack's propulsive percussion? Even from the perspective of decades later, knowing where this band would eventually head, Hillel and Jack's performances throughout 1983 are undeniably magical. The band was built around Anthony's rapping and Flea's bass work, but they were far less effective in these early days without Hillel and Jack behind them.

"It wasn't like these were incidental guys," Anthony graciously observed. "They made up our vibe. We were kids from high school, we were a team, you can't go shopping for a new mom and dad, it doesn't happen."

The Chili Peppers would lose members in the future, of course. In fact, they would lose these two exact members again almost five years later, in much more tragic circumstances. But those losses happened to a more established act, with ongoing contracts to fulfill, a nearly worldwide fan base, and three major-label records already out. Here they were fragile and new, not even a year old, and this schism could have broken them prematurely. Stunned by this parabolic journey that their fortunes had taken over the course of two phone calls, Anthony, "emotionally devastated," broke down on the couch crying, while Flea mumbled over and over in disbelief to himself.

Was it over? Of course it wasn't, but it certainly must have felt like it at the time.

Repeated above is how Anthony remembers the moment happening, and that's how it's been retold in band biographies and interviews over the years—that, unbelievably, the two acts got their deal at the exact same time, and the drummer and guitarist that the two acts shared had to make a quick, on-the-spot choice, which was a shock to all parties.

However, the most probable scenario is that What Is This got their recording contract offer weeks, if not a whole month, before the Red Hot Chili Peppers did, and it's hard to imagine that Anthony and Flea didn't know about it. According to the *LA Weekly,* Jack and Hillel's band were being considered by MCA in early September, either before or around the same time that EMI/Enigma representatives attended the Chili Peppers' September 10 show at the Kit Kat Club, and certainly before EMI/Enigma made their own offer. The newspaper had been inaccurate in the past, of course, but MCA signing What Is This is exactly what ended up happening, and so this report had some basis in reality. This all meant, in essence, that Hillel and Jack had been walking around knowing about their impending deal with MCA, playing shows with the Chili Peppers and most likely telling their friends (telling enough people, in fact, that it showed up in a gossip column) about this exciting new chapter about to unfurl in their lives. But it was only when their bluff was called, and the Red Hot Chili Peppers had an offer of their own, that Hillel and Jack had to seriously consider which direction their future would take. The Chili Peppers could well have stayed at their current level, playing a club show every few weeks and never progressing further. But that wasn't what was happening. They had a manager; they had a demo; they had plans. Did Hillel and Jack really think it wouldn't become an issue?

If Anthony and Flea were shocked about the decision their drummer and guitarist had made, Lindy Goetz was doubly so. According to him, he wasn't even aware that Hillel and Jack played in another *band,* let alone one with an impending record deal. When he told them the news of EMI/Enigma's offer, "Hillel and Jack told me they couldn't do it, because they were already in another band. . . . 'What are you talking about? What other fucking band? Whoa. . . . Now you're telling me this?'" This has to be a mistake in his recollection. It's highly unlikely he really had no idea that the two were in another

Hillel and Jack, the soon to be departing members, at the Cathay de Grande on Argyle Avenue. These are the last-known images of the original lineup until their reformation in 1986. September 18, 1983. *fabulosfab*

band; they were actively playing in the same scene, possible scheduling conflicts had to be mutually agreed upon, and he had even previously worked for the record company that was involved in signing What Is This: MCA. If Hillel and Jack had really kept their involvement with What Is This from him, they had to have done so for a reason, or were being plain negligent. Furthermore, it was clear that being in another act wasn't an issue; Flea was playing with FEAR with no evident concerns from all parties (for the time being).

While it might have been a difficult decision for Hillel and Jack to leave the band, it's not a strain to see why they might have chosen to do so. The Chili Peppers had surpassed What Is This in many ways—the amount of attention they were getting, their fan base, even the number of shows played throughout the year—but the elder band never stopped being the main focus of their attention. The

Chili Peppers were fun; What Is This was *work*, the thing that was going to fulfill them for years to come, the vessel for their rock star dreams that had been percolating since their early teens, when they first graduated from miming KISS, to playing covers, and to playing music of their own.

One couldn't possibly know where this strange new funk-punk joke band was heading, with its ninety-second songs and lewd stage gimmicks. Would they get bored with it? Would the shows dry up? Would it flame out in a month with a needle in its arm? Nobody could have imagined the insane heights they would eventually reach about a decade later.

At first, there was the thought that the two could remain in both bands, but Alain Johannes nixed that idea with the wise reality check that it "would never have worked out." As Jack Irons put it, staying with What Is This was partly a practical decision, but it was also sentimental: "We'd been with this group, as Anthym and What Is This, ever since Junior High," he recalled. "So we figured that when we had the chance to actually make a record, after all these years together, that was who we should do it with."

Making a record was key, and at first it might not have mattered which band they made a record with. Touring the United States, the rest of the world, building up a fan base, and all the other glory that came with a record deal would come afterward. But what record did they want to make—one with the act that they had dedicated six part-time months of their lives to, or six mostly full-time years? One who had a handful of actual songs, and who relied mostly on jokes and skits to pad out their repertoire, or the cultivated, refined band that had continually grown over the years, throwing away old songs that they considered weren't good enough, even changing the name they had outgrown.

It was a no-brainer. And while Anthony and Flea were disappointed, they both seemed to understand why it was happening, and forgave them quickly—if forgiveness was even needed. Flea, having already quit What Is This for FEAR, hardly had a leg to stand on. He immediately suggested that they hire new musicians to replace their departing friends.

Anthony's mood quickly turned around as he realized that losing their guitarist and drummer didn't mean that the band had to end. "Once I started thinking about it, I realized that we had the songs, we had a record contract, we had Flea, we had me, we still loved what we did," he wrote. "We just hadn't done it yet, so we needed to find a way to make it happen." This was the first time—the first of many—that the band had been saved from breaking up, and it was thanks to both their passion for playing together and their capable practicality. Flea was the more experienced of the two and had keen experience in recent years of what the realities of band life were like; sometimes members left, but that wasn't always a negative. The record deal certainly helped. If they didn't have it looming over them as a responsibility, they might have found it easier to give up and put an end to this fun new endeavor. But the thing that truly kept them together was the fun they had onstage, and this musical connection they shared. A great deal of the fun they'd had throughout the year, and the closer connection they had forged, had been something the band provided them. There was no way they could stop now.

What should have been a tormenting experience finding two new band members at such short notice was made easy by the tight-knit Los Angeles punk community. Flea "immediately suggested" Cliff Martinez, whom he had grown close to over the previous year. Flea and Martinez had already played together several times in Two Balls and a Bat, had recorded together in one instance, and they had all seen him up close at both Kit Kat Club gigs that year, when Martinez manned the skins for Roid Rogers and the Whirling Butt Cherries. Never mind that they shared a rehearsal space, and his already incredible CV: Captain Beefheart, Lydia Lunch, and the Weirdos. He was the perfect candidate.*

Cliff Martinez was born in New York on February 5, 1954—eight years older than the other band members, virtually ancient†—and moved to Ohio with his family shortly afterward, developing an interest in drumming while playing the snare in his grade school orchestra. His career in music followed a familiar pattern. The Beatles on *Ed Sullivan* sparked a passion for rock, and a Museum of Modern Art exhibit featuring sound sculptures by the Baschet Brothers confirmed his destiny: "I not only wanted to be a musician, but a weird musician." Within a few years he had his own rock band, playing top-forty covers to whoever he could. In 1976 he moved to Los Angeles and enrolled at the Dick Grove School of Music in the San Fernando Valley to hone his skills and join a proper band. That was a seminal year for punk, but it took until 1980, four years later, for Cliff to be exposed to it.

While rehearsing with a now-forgotten band one day, Cliff heard another extraordinarily loud act playing in an adjoining room. It was the aptly named Screamers, whose vocalist David "Tomata du Plenty" Harrigan would eventually become close friends with the Chili Peppers.‡ At first, Cliff was disgusted by the "ungodly racket," but experiencing this strange band's intensity, he changed his mind. "I just turned on a dime," he later remembered. "I went from hating it to loving it. And that's when I started checking out punk rock."

---

* At some point during the latter half of 1982, Flea and Cliff played together on a demo recording by Ivy Ney, a musician who was also an incredibly talented fashion and portrait photographer. The track, "Kill You Tonight," also featured folk guitarist Randy Burns and Top Jimmy & the Rhythm Pigs saxophonist Steve Berlin. A sparse, moody video was filmed for it a few months later (though neither Flea or Cliff appear), and aired on NBC's *Friday Night Videos*.

† Cliff humorously recalls being treated like an old man by a twenty-year-old Anthony in the *Oral/Visual History* book (29).

‡ "Grand Pappy du Plenty," the final track on the band's debut album, was named in honor of the man, who was also an accomplished painter.

Within a year, Cliff was in the Weirdos with brothers Dix and John Denney, and left the cover bands behind him forever.* In 1982 he played in Lydia Lunch's *13.13* project, and with Captain Beefheart on his album *Ice Cream for Crow*; he got the Beefheart job because after seventy-two straight hours of practice he could play every rhythm track on Beefheart's polarizing, influential, and damn-difficult *Trout Mask Replica*, a trick he showed off during auditions. But while the Beefheart gig was high profile and had street cred, it was a rough ride with an unforgiving boss, and no live dates followed the recording of the album. This left him free to pursue other musical interests, such as Two Balls and a Bat, who only played occasionally, and Roid Rogers and the Whirling Butt Cherries, who had a slightly more solid grounding, playing more often and even recording the occasional song and accompanying video, but were hardly a full-time gig. (If nothing else, he attracted bands with unusual names.)

Flea and Anthony approached Cliff with the offer to join the Chili Peppers at his home, a "wacky one-room apartment that you accessed through an underground parking garage on Harper," and, as Anthony put it, he was "goofy with joy" with the news. And despite his busy schedule, he didn't need to consider any other acts first. He took the job on the spot, without an audition. "I'd seen the Chili Peppers several times and knew what was expected," he remembered. Early rehearsals proved him to be more than capable, and the two were delighted with their new band member.†

Cliff had other reasons for wanting to join. For one, he was thrilled that the band had a record deal, but he was also interested in improving his funk chops. "It was a style that I wanted to be good at, but I didn't think it was my strong suit at the time." He had even dabbled with funk earlier in the year, playing with Flea's FEAR bandmate Derf

* Unfortunately, Cliff's recorded contributions with the Weirdos wouldn't be released until almost a decade later.

† It seems as if several three-man jam sessions took place before a guitarist was settled on.

Scratch and Wayzata de Camerone, booker of several early Chili Peppers' shows, in a short-lived project called Funk-A-Holics that played live at the Cathay de Grande. But with his joining the band, he would soon have his opportunity to really woodshed.

Finding a new drummer proved easy; if Flea and Anthony auditioned (or even considered) anyone else, they have never mentioned it. And as far as finding new members went, they were currently holding a 100 percent success rate. At first glance, finding a new guitarist seemed to be just as easy, and again they looked close to home. Shortly after joining the Chili Peppers, Cliff suggested Dix Denney, his former bandmate in the Weirdos and Lydia Lunch's *13.13* project, as a possible replacement for the recently departed Hillel Slovak.

Dix Newell Denney* was born in Kansas City, Missouri, in 1957, the younger brother of John. The family moved first to New York and then Los Angeles so that Nora Denney—born Dolores Teachenor—could follow her acting dreams. The move paid off; after a number of roles in prominent TV shows like *Get Smart* and *Bewitched*, in 1971 "Dodo" Denney starred as the television-obsessed Mike TeeVee's mother in the cult film adaptation of *Willy Wonka & the Chocolate Factory*.

Both Denney brothers took to music—the Stooges' *Raw Power* being a key inspiration—and in February 1977 they formed a band together. This was a low-key affair, for their amusement only. Just before their first show, opening for the Nerves, which some have considered the first punk show ever in Los Angeles, they lost their drummer. In a very punk move, they decided to play anyway.

As this was in the very early days of this newfangled thing called punk, they weren't actually inspired by the movement itself—they were out ahead of it. In the beginning the Weirdos (early names included the Barbies and the Luxurious Adults) resembled something

* Dix is his actual first name.

closer to a hard rock or rockabilly act with the amps overdriven and the speed turned way up. But the band quickly became entangled in the early days of the punk movement, becoming one of the first acts associated with Brendan Mullen's Masque club, and from the vantage of decades later, are usually considered one of the first real punk bands to come out of Los Angeles in the late 1970s. By the time the Chili Peppers became active in the early 1980s, the Weirdos were elder statesmen, and Denney, being five years older than Flea or Anthony, had the similar kind of age difference that Cliff Martinez had with these original members of the band. Somehow, these two young kids—neither of them twenty-one yet, with comparatively little experience onstage—had roped in actual *adults*, who had made real names for themselves, and who had played with actual *legends*.

But for all the long-lasting cred from the Weirdos' live shows and recordings (their early singles "Destroy All Music!" and "We Got the Neutron Bomb" are some of a handful of seminal early punk recordings), the band never quite took off, and they somehow managed to blow every chance they had to record a debut album, though many demo recordings were made, some with their short-lived drummer Cliff Martinez. Instead, fans had to subsist on a variety of sporadic singles and a few EPs, and in 1981 they broke up without ever touring or signing a record deal. But the Denney brothers remained active, forming the group If-Then-Else, which released an album late in the year.*

Aside from the Martinez connection, Flea had played with Dix at various points throughout the year, including once with Keith Barry at the CASH club, and had even toyed with forming a band with him and his brother back in August, which never materialized. Anthony hadn't quite played with him yet but found him to be a "loveable

* The Weirdos would eventually reform in 1986 and have remained reasonably active ever since. It would take until 1990 for them to record a debut album.

fellow," and everyone—at least on first appearances—appeared to be on the same page when it came to the spirit of the band, and what the future would hold going forward.

And that was ostensibly that. With the new members roped in, Anthony and Flea could leave for Europe, safe with the knowledge that they once they were back, they could continue on with this new version of the band. They might have had two limbs torn from them at short notice, but they'd replaced them with two more-than-serviceable substitutes, and maybe with a little luck, and a few shows under their belt, everything would be OK. Who knew—perhaps these two would feel more like Chili Peppers than Hillel or Jack ever did.

Anthony and Flea had other reasons to consider themselves lucky that they had replaced the departing members of the band so painlessly. According to Lindy Goetz, the plan was for the switch to happen without EMI or Enigma catching wind of any lineup change at all: "Things were shaky enough as it was getting the deal we got, so I told the guys not to say anything to anybody," he remembered. Of course, that didn't prevent the spies at the *LA Weekly* from finding out, reporting in their October 13 issue that Cliff and Dix would be the "new Chili Peppers," and would debut after "Flea and Anthony return from England."

Either it wasn't really a problem for this brand-new band to quietly swap out a few members, or the executives at EMI/Enigma weren't keeping a close eye on the local punk scene's gossip pages. Previously, the *LA Weekly* had also reported in the lead-up to the trip that the whole band would be traveling, not just Anthony and Flea, and playing shows while they were there. In fact, the plan seemed to be for Anthony and Flea, alone together again, to simply hang out and experience faraway and exotic Europe—a holiday from the band and their lives at home (not that they really needed it)—and a sort of coming-of-age trip, for they would both be turning twenty-one in the very near future (Flea on October 16, Anthony on November

1). This would be their first trip to Europe—Anthony's first outside the United States.* England, in particular, was the source of much of the music and culture they had ingested and regurgitated over the previous half-decade; from the punk and new wave acts that had made such an impact on them over the previous few years, to the records that the Jimi Hendrix Experience had made in the late 1960s, England was a key location in everything that the Chili Peppers were now doing in 1983.

Memories of this trip have been scant in the years since; the duo visited London, Paris, and Amsterdam, but they may have stopped elsewhere during the trip. While in London, the two seemed to have spent the majority of their trip in the southeastern district of Catford, at one point managing to score some acid, and imbibing it in the cemetery. They also climbed out "hostel windows" at one point, as the lyrics to "Deep Kick," written a decade later, imply.

While (presumably) in London, the duo also met Gavin Bowden, a twenty-year-old British chap who was studying film production at the London International Film School. The three became close enough during the time they spent together that when Bowden later emigrated to the United States, he got back in touch with the band, and would wind up marrying Flea's older sister Karyn.†

As they wound their way east and landed in Paris, Anthony and Flea were separated; the reason has been chalked up either to a fight or because Anthony had "ditched" Flea for a Danish girl he met in the City of Love.

The short love affair over, Anthony, in an effort to put an end to the silent treatment Flea was giving him, purchased with some pocket

* Flea was born in Australia, of course, and returned to his home country a number of times in his youth. If Anthony ever traveled overseas before this trip, he has never mentioned it.

† In 1991 Bowden directed *Funky Monks*, a documentary detailing the recording of *Blood Sugar Sex Magik*. He also directed several music videos for the band in the 1990s. He and Karyn Balzary are still married.

change two sets of tin cups from a man on the street; perhaps one of the many *les bouquinistes* vendors that line the Seine selling their wares at riverside stalls. In a stroke of sartorial genius, he then attached them to the shoulder straps of their matching leather jackets, purchased in late May back in Los Angeles, and probably worn throughout their entire trip across Europe, then shrouded in the chill of autumn. The cups had a likeness to military epaulets, as if the two had been in battle together in a strange land and were awarded these odd medals for their efforts. Better yet, when they ran and banged them together, "it made a gonglike noise," something that would provide them with hours of fun in the years to come.

Flea's sour mood was broken, and the "Brothers Cup" was born.* This small moment of brotherly humor was indicative of the bond that Anthony and Flea were furthering, and perhaps helped cement a lot of what the next years of their lives would entail. The two were already close; they were bandmates, housemates, and were traveling across Europe together. But here was something new that they and they alone shared. Hillel and Jack didn't have the cups, or the jackets, or the yin and yang relationship. Nor (as the rest of the year will show) did they have the shared bed, or the journeys together in the dark of Los Angeles. Flea and Anthony—and Flea and Anthony *alone*—did. There was a series of circles growing ever smaller; the four (now six) band members, and then Los Faces, and then, with the Brothers Cup, just these two friends left.

Anthony and Flea would shortly be the only original members of the Chili Peppers left in the band—titles they still hold to this day—and their relationship defined and continues to define the way the

---

* The accessories were immortalized forever in a track on 1985's *Freaky Styley*, which incorporated some of Anthony's leftover lyrics from "What It Is (Nina's Song)." While in Amsterdam, Flea also bought Anthony a shirt, adorned with Soviet designs, that would go on to inspire lyrics in the band's song "Buckle Down" and would later be seen (worn by Flea) on *The Uplift Mofo Party Plan*'s cover.

band operates. That they would take a short trip out of the country and return with this new in-joke might not have seemed like a big deal at the time, but without this cementing of their relationship near the end of the band's first year, which compounded the trips and schemes and adventures they had already taken, the next thirty-five plus might not have happened at all.

The current whereabouts of the cups isn't known, and it's unlikely they're still with their owners. Anthony erroneously states in the opening pages of his autobiography that he lost the jacket and the cups in early 1985, but they can both be seen wearing them (cups attached) in the 1987 video for "Fight Like a Brave." The cups themselves changed over the years (if, by the end, they were indeed the same set originally purchased in Paris); initially, they were all one color—a pale blue or white—but in the next few years, Anthony had painted a variety of designs on his, and by their 1987 appearance—perhaps the latest available—his were black, and Flea's were red.

The exact date of the Europe trip is also unknown, though some clues narrow it down. There's no evidence of any Red Hot Chili Peppers shows between September 18 and the second week of October, as speculated below, so it most likely fell between those two dates; the L.A.-Dee-Da mention of the trip, which at that point was still forthcoming, is from late September. The next mention of it, implying that Flea and Anthony were still overseas at the time, is from mid-October.

While Flea and Anthony were away, What Is This kept busy and played at least two shows, one at the Plant on September 30 and another at the Club Lingerie, their fifth that year, the next day.* This Club Lingerie show would most likely be the last show they would play for two whole months, as the band—in another parallel with their brothers in the Red Hot Chili Peppers—parted ways with a member

* Jimi Hendrix Experience drummer Mitch Mitchell made an appearance at this show, which must have been a thrill for the Hendrix-obsessed in the band.

on the eve of them signing a record deal. In this case, it was with their bass player, Hans Reumschüssel. Within a week of the Club Lingerie show, Hillel was placing ads in the *LA Weekly*'s classifieds section looking for a "funky bass player with diverse musical interests who rocks out." Finding this new member would take some time, and they wouldn't play live again until December.

This complicated the situation considerably. Hillel and Jack had just left (or had announced their intentions to leave) the Chili Peppers in order to focus on their other band, but this other band had immediately been hamstrung by a member departure of its own. It kept them in a limbo, but it also delayed their departure from the Red Hot Chili Peppers. In the end, this may have been a net positive. Because What Is This were put on hold, Hillel and Jack were free to play the remaining shows the Chili Peppers booked for 1983, and it also gave Flea and Anthony more time to rehearse and prepare with their incoming replacements. They may have preferred a cleaner transition, but not much about this band was ever clean.*

The Chili Peppers themselves weren't forgotten while Flea and Anthony were away, with Lynda Burdick's July photo of the band—shirtless and in each other's arms outside the Music Machine—featured in a message from the Club Lingerie management that took up a whole page of the *LA Weekly*. "Thank you Los Angeles for another year of support," the ad read in a handwritten scrawl, "in particular thanks to all the artists who created fascinating diversity and who once again set the precedents and the style for the other clubs to follow and copy."

The Chili Peppers had only played the club twice that year, without headlining; they wouldn't *headline* the Club Lingerie until early

* It seems as if during the latter part of 1983, as Lindy Goetz negotiated the band's deal with EMI/Enigma, Flea and Anthony became the only "official" members of the band, and Hillel and Jack became temporary employees, in a sense. A necessary move perhaps, but one that inadvertently made it easier to swap out members down the line.

November, and yet there was the already-famous band (in a scene-wide sense) given ample room alongside many other acts. A sign of things to come?

As Flea and Anthony returned from their European jaunt, there were a few important tasks to attend to. The first was that within a week or two of their arrival back in the States they once again had no place to live. Paying rent was low on the list of priorities at the La Leyenda; since they had moved in a few months previously, the trio in apartment 307 had battled continuously with their landlord over the rent. This was mostly the fault of Bob Forrest, who had absconded with the rent money Flea and Anthony had given him. After the desperate landlord had removed the door, thinking that this drastic effort would surely drive them out, they simply tacked a bedsheet up to replace it. When the water was shut off, they washed elsewhere. But returning from Europe, "they posted notices that we were going straight to jail if we occupied the premises again," as Anthony recalled. Sufficiently spooked, Flea decamped with his sister Karyn, and Anthony followed for a spell before being asked to leave for—once again—being caught having sexual relations in a place he shouldn't have.

The second task to attend to was the band. Cliff Martinez and Dix Denney might have been roped in tentatively, but they wouldn't have been properly integrated and rehearsed yet. There were a number of shows booked before Flea and Anthony had gone to Europe; a number of shows, possibly, that had been booked even before the record deal with Enigma/EMI came about. Luckily, Hillel and Jack were still available while What Is This sought out their new bass player, and this strange limbo-stricken version of the band could play.

The first of these shows was a first in itself: the inaugural performance for the band outside the state of California.

SHOW #27

CIRCA OCTOBER 10–13, 1983

E'wu's Paradise,
450 South Galena Street, Aspen, CO

NESTLED in the *LA Weekly*'s report of the historic July 3 show at the Kit Kat Club was a notice that the Chili Peppers were "on their way to Aspen," followed with the dry quip that there were no arrangements for the band to "collaborate with Claudine Longet—but it's a long shot. Ow!" Claudine Longet was a French American actress who was convicted of negligent homicide after shooting her husband, Olympic skier Vladimir Sabich, in Aspen in 1976. Longet claimed Sabich was showing her how a gun worked when it accidentally went off. This was a claim that many found unbelievable, hence the *Weekly*'s pithy jab.

Some crossed wires must have made the authors of the *LA Weekly* report think that the trip out east was scheduled for July; it may have been booked in June, but it actually took place in early to mid-October.

Why had the band made the curious decision to up and leave Los Angeles just as they were really making waves in their hometown? And why Aspen? It was a bizarre choice; the Colorado resort town known for its abundant skiing trails and the music of John Denver is nine hundred miles east of Los Angeles and was hardly the kind of scene one associated with punk music, let alone punk infused with funk. But it goes to show how much can change in a short amount of time; when the trip was booked, there was no record deal, no sign of any membership change. Aspen, with its slopes and ritz and glamour, might have seemed to be enormously different to the streets of Los Angeles, but perhaps that was the point. Why not take the chance and head somewhere different? Here was the chance for a trip away together, and L.A. would always be there when they got back. And head there they did, breaking the bonds of California for the first time as a band in a rented van in early October, with their old friend Gary Allen going along for the ride.

The booking was the result of sisters Sherri and Deanne Franklin. Deanne lived in Los Angeles and was a fan of the punk scene, having witnessed the Chili Peppers at several of their first handful of shows earlier in the year. She was such a fan she had actually passed their demo tape along to her friend Ron Fair, who was an A&R executive at Chrysalis Records. The band, Deanne felt, were "truly going to be the next big thing," but it was sadly not to be. "He turned me down flat."

Still determined to help the band out, Deanne was reminded of something her sister Sherri, living in Aspen and running a hair salon, had told her a few months previously. David Moss, an Aspen native and a friend of Sherri's, ran a club-bar-restaurant called E'wu's Paradise, and wanted to "shake up" the mountain town with some punk music from out west. At Sherri's suggestion and through Deanne's connections, Moss visited Los Angeles and met the band in June, offering them a residency of two shows a night for three nights at his club later in the year—for $270 a night, it was a great deal for the unknown act, then without a deal or a manager. There was also a closer personal connection between David Moss and Anthony Kiedis. Moss was friends with Anthony's "godfather"* and one-time babysitter, Sonny Bono, who spent a great deal of time holidaying in Aspen. Bono, in the end, would wind up thanking Moss for giving his godson the opportunity to "make it big."

E'wu's Paradise opened in 1978 and was the project of David Moss and his wife, Nikki (born Nae Kyung Kim), who was said to be the first businesswoman of Asian descent in Aspen. After some experience running a Chinese restaurant called Arthur's in town, the pair converted the bankrupt Rick's American Cafe—infamous for its wet T-shirt concerts—and opened the Paradise Theater. That became E'wu's Paradise in early 1983, named for one of the restaurant's cooks, and was quickly one of the main attractions in the city; a bar, a restaurant, and a concert venue in one, much like the Grandia Room or the China Club back in Los Angeles.

For all Sherri, Deanne's, and David's good intentions, and despite how well the band was received back in Los Angeles, in rural, conservative Aspen, things didn't go particularly as planned. In retellings, Flea said that they managed to play an entire set, but Sherri Franklin remembers the band being asked to leave by Moss after only two songs, one of which, according to Gary Allen, was another rendition of the *Beverly Hillbillies* theme song.

"Asked to leave" may be putting it politely. They were, essentially, chased off the stage by an unruly crowd: "They told us to take our '[*n*-word] music' back to Hollywood."

There are a number of reasons why they got this kind of reception, but the simplest explanation is that it was still the off-season,

* Sonny Bono is frequently referred to as Anthony's official godfather, but this is not the case.

and the type of crowd there that night at E'wu's Paradise wasn't a fit for these rowdy punks from the far-out, progressive city back west. The locals already resented rich, Hollywood-based tourists filling the town every ski season, and this may have been another sign of that—and in the off-season, no less, when they *definitely* weren't welcome. It was not the first time that a band like the Chili Peppers would be met with derision, scorn, or even the threat of violence by a crowd not yet ready for them.

The band weren't happy with the violent reception, and were driven to anger; they were "so pissed," Sherri Franklin recalls. They might have been able to handle to outright hostility—they had been bottled before, abused by crowds, and told to go back to a town they weren't even from by Oingo Boingo fans—but this outright racism (after all, Gary Allen, who is Black, was with the band) and close-mindedness struck a nerve. And so they left the stage.

After the short show, they decamped to spend the night at a friend of Allen's, who, he remembers, "prepared a beautiful organic dinner [of] which very little was actually eaten, because we had [ecstasy] and went swimming in the heated pool in the rain."

Sherri Franklin joined them, and then it was time to head back to Los Angeles, early, underpaid, and with an all-round negative experience behind them. "We all got high and then they left in the middle of a snowstorm."

But while they might have had *some* fun after their residency came to a premature end, the way they had been treated left a bad taste in their mouths. "We left and will never play there again," Flea stated a few years later, the anger still evident. They've been true to their word; in the years since, the Red Hot Chili Peppers have played Colorado many times, but never Aspen, despite several opportunities, especially as they themselves eventually began to mingle with the glitterati that the town usually attracts.

It might have been strange that the band went out to Aspen in the first place—with the record deal looming, the incoming membership swap, and all the cataclysmic changes about to take place—but it's probably for those exact reasons that they found it so easy to return once they realized things weren't going to plan. They had a home base that was waiting for them, an in-built crowd that enjoyed, even egged on their antics, for the time being, and important work to do. Why waste their time in snowy Colorado playing to a bunch of hicks who didn't want to hear it?

The Red Hot Chili Peppers wouldn't play another show outside Los Angeles until April, and wouldn't leave California until August 1984—but here was a first taste of what the next year, and the next decade, would bring: the leaving of the bubble; the possibility of hostility; the long trips in rented vans through the snow to strange new worlds. It wasn't the first out-of-town show for some of them (and there *was* that mystery show in San Francisco in July), but it was the first show in an outwardly hostile territory, away from their home state and deep into something unknown.

The exact date of this show, and the intended residency, is unknown. No advertisements seem to have been placed in any of the Aspen daily or weekly newspapers in the lead-up, and none of the parties involved remember exactly when it took place—only that it was in autumn, as the town was gearing back up out of hibernation for the snowy season. The only identifying feature is that snowstorm that arrived as the band left. According to a Colorado Climate Center survey of the period, the year's first heavy snow fell over the state in between October 10 and October 13.

There is no evidence of any shows booked for the Red Hot Chili Peppers, What Is This, or FEAR between October 1 and October 26; this leaves that period in the middle of that month as the most probable for this ill-fated trek to Aspen. They would have already had the calendar cleared, having booked the shows back in June, and this also takes into account the Europe trip that Flea and Anthony took. Of course, a primary source would confirm the date of this shambolic, short-lived, and yet in some ways historical performance; the suggestion above may be incorrect.

Back home, Flea was put back at work in FEAR, playing a show in El Monte, northeast of Los Angeles, on October 26, the first for the band in several months and the beginning of a slightly more productive time for the act.

A recording of this El Monte show circulates in fairly decent quality. Performing twenty-one songs (most of them yet to be recorded or released) in just over an hour, it's a frantic document of this era of the band, full of sarcastic jibes—homophobic, racist, xenophobic—that might warrant an eye-roll in the third decade of the twenty-first century, but still would have retained at least some of its sting late in the twentieth. Anthony put it well when, years later, he recalled that "their onstage patter wasn't very PC for most people, but we just didn't take any of their crowd-baiting shit so seriously. It was fun. They tried to upset everyone in the room."

This is also one of the rare recordings of the lineup featuring Flea. Here we can catch a glimpse of his attempt at playing the tough-guy punk, and despite what he might later say ("I learned how to talk confidently into the microphone, that I could say anything, anything at all that would stir the pot"), it's not always convincing. Aside from his lazy homophobia (which, to his credit, he would later lament), during one early break caused by technical difficulties, he winds up merely making noises into the microphone, lost onstage in front of a crowd that is quickly growing disinterested. Lee Ving, who has the most experience onstage out of any of them, is occasionally wryly charming, but most of what the band say onstage has not aged well, and it's hard to imagine it was ever very compelling.

But when FEAR actually play, they don't sound half bad, even if the slide into the more metal-oriented territory—what Flea would later say was also one catalyst for him leaving—is already evident. Also of note is Flea's trumpet playing (including a solo) on the band's "New York's Alright If You Like Saxophones"—evidently a saxophone was unavailable, and the instrument swap was treated with good natured jibes at Flea's expense.*

* This is also the earliest available recording of Flea playing the trumpet, an instrument he would return to many times in the future, often with the Red Hot Chili Peppers.

SHOW #28

OCTOBER 29, 1983

The Plant, 12446 Ventura Boulevard, Studio City, CA

ONCE MORE, the band decamped to the Plant; this time the Chili Peppers headlined a show that featured a very familiar lineup of Minutemen, Blood on the Saddle, and the Mentors.

This night and the two performances that follow must have been strange, somewhat melancholy, and slightly frozen in time. Record deals for both the Red Hot Chili Peppers and What Is This were imminent. Hillel and Jack knew that they were leaving. And yet the act continued to perform. Staying with the Red Hot Chili Peppers for the time being was made possible because What Is This was without a bass player; that band wouldn't play again until December. So while Hillel and Jack had the freedom to stick with the Chili Peppers, all parties knew it wouldn't last.

What was going through their minds? That this was one of the last few blasts of fun before it all had to end? Or was it now a distraction before they could get to the band that they had decided to dedicate their time and energy to?

No photos seem to have survived from this show, except for one possibly taken the night of by Jennifer Finch, later the bass player for prominent punk act L7, of Flea (who looks particularly enrapt), Jack, and half of Anthony's shoulder, watching Minutemen in action.

Sadly, this would be the last show the band would ever play at this unique industrial venue with its garage-door stage. While it was beloved by fans and fair to the bands—not always the case around the clubs in Los Angeles—its location in the San Fernando Valley left a lot to be desired. "There is a deep-rooted provincial attitude amongst Hollyweird folk that one does not trek out into the terrible Valley under penalty of becoming some kind of socially-diseased nonentity," the *LA Weekly* wrote, and sadly the Plant was one more casualty of this mentality. With its shuttering, one more venue that the early Red Hot Chili Peppers performed at was closed forever.*

On Halloween night FEAR played a show at the Starlite Roller Rink in North Hollywood. A strange place for this type of show, maybe, but a frequent site of punk chaos—the Dead Kennedys, T.S.O.L., and Circle Jerks would play the same venue before the end of the year. An audience recording from this show also circulates, and it differs from the show from a week previous in that it shows a much tighter, much more professional-sounding band. The technical difficulties are gone, the time wasting is minimal, and the four men chug through a workmanlike set with minimal distraction. Strangely, because of all that, it inevitably sounds like a lot less fun to be there.

---

* On December 10 while the Chili Peppers were on a forced hiatus, Flea and Anthony joined a variety of other bands on stage for a boozy farewell party, ensuring, at least, that if the venue had to go out it would do so on a high note.

SHOW #29

NOVEMBER 7, 1983

Club Lingerie, 6507 Sunset Boulevard, Hollywood, CA

THIS EARLY NOVEMBER SHOW was a benefit for the Zero One club, then in urgent need of funding. A hand-drawn flier was circulated featuring four chili peppers, asking loyal club members to "protect the place you stand every Friday and Saturday night." Also playing, once again, were Tex and the Horseheads, and joining them the Screamin' Sirens, an all-girl band formed in early 1983 and in the middle of a flurry of club shows. Their members included the multi-talented Pleasant Gehman, Cathay de Grande booker and one of the revolving writers of the *LA Weekly*'s L.A.-Dee-Da column.

L.A.-Dee-Da had been the site of so much free publicity for the band that year, but after this show it became the site of one of their first real negative reviews, with the column stating that "some incrowders were claiming the group had already played out its novelty appeal." This anonymous response, while not unduly hostile, could perhaps suggest that the band, their music, and their antics had begun to wear thin on the audience that had seen so much of it throughout 1983. With a set list that had remained virtually identical since May and a forced holding pattern that had been over them since September, this is understandable; they were on a precipice, but the major changes hadn't been enacted yet. They were a band stuck in amber, with an aging routine. Something had to change.

But others in the room enjoyed the show, with Screamin' Sirens vocalist Rosie Flores remembering Flea's head-banging antics and worrying that he was going to hurt his neck.

While to the crowd it may have looked like the band was in a holding pattern, behind the scenes they were working hard, meeting up from time to time with their two new members, Dix Denney and Cliff Martinez, to go over their old material and begin writing new songs.

Unfortunately, when independent creative minds get together, issues can arise, even with the best of intentions. Cliff fit in immediately and learned his parts with the same kind of studiousness that he had shown during his time with Captain Beefheart. But while Dix was a great guitarist whom the band got along with easily in a social setting, it became evident that when it came to the band, he "wasn't cutting it," and that despite his chops, he "couldn't apply himself to other people's parts."

There may have been other reasons for Dix not connecting. His playing, far more suitable for the kind of role he would wind up playing in Thelonious Monster, which he would form with Bob Forrest and Pete Weiss the next year, never quite lent itself to the sparser, more jagged-edge funk of the Red Hot Chili Peppers. While Hillel's early parts weren't overcomplex, they had a spirit and feel in their economy that wasn't easily to replicate. Denney was also substantially older than Flea and Anthony; the age gap didn't seem to cause a problem when it came to Cliff Martinez, but perhaps it did in Denney's case.

But these are theories, and Anthony's recounting of the events in his autobiography are the only time any member of the band has spoken of his stint in the years since. In a nutshell, he just wasn't right for the band. That fact was evident almost immediately, and the sooner they all moved on, the better.

And so, Flea and Anthony came up with a farcical plan to fire him during the middle of a croquet game in a local park. This didn't go as planned. Denney misunderstood them, as neither Flea or Anthony could bring themselves to take the lead and say what needed to be said. The gentle firing turned into a blunt statement, leaving the singer and bassist heartbroken, and Dix forlorn. "We thought we would always be four knuckleheads from Hollywood," Anthony remembered. "But now we were learning that we would have to deal with the realities of life." This would be the first time the duo would have to fire a band member, quite a different experience than Hillel quitting out of a happy necessity. They would soon get used to it, but here was another first in a year full of new experiences.*

And just like that, there were now two ex-guitarists for the Red Hot Chili Peppers.† Flea, Anthony, and Martinez now needed to find another replacement for Hillel's vacant position, and the precious time they had spent with Dix had all been wasted, valuable lesson aside. But feelers were quickly put out; in the November 17 edition of *LA Weekly*'s classifieds, among the ads for phone sex operators and photocopier salespeople, was this tiny notice: "RED HOT CHILI

* There were no hard feelings, and this would not be the last time that Flea or Anthony played with Dix Denney. In early 1984 they formed the one-off band the Anarchy 4—backed by "the Mysterious Drummer," who is perhaps Cliff—for a show at Club Lingerie, supporting metal-spoofers Megadeath.

† In a 2019 interview with Nate Pottker for the Thelonious Monster website, Dix mentioned that he only *auditioned* for the band and never actually joined. However, contemporaneous mentions in *LA Weekly* specifically refer to him joining before the Europe trip, and Anthony states in *Scar Tissue* that Denney was present at several rehearsal sessions after agreeing to join. While he didn't play any shows, he can still be considered a legitimate member, much in the sense that Jesse Tobias was, with his short stint ten years later.

PEPPERS Need the wildest, funkiest, most intense guitar player to ever strut the face of this earth." Three spaces above the ad was a similar one for What Is This, who sought a "bassist for the ultimate groove down infl. Hendrix, early Gang of Four and Ohio Players. Image important." This ad was the band still seeking a replacement for Hans Reumschüssel, more than a month after his firing.

Flea, meanwhile, was busy elsewhere with FEAR—the busiest he had been with that band in some time—heading northeast to the city of Azusa to play another weekend show at the Timbers, with support from punk acts Mad Parade and Modern Industry.

Anthony was busy too, albeit in a more social sense. At one point in mid-November, he managed to meet Hugh Hefner, the editor in chief of *Playboy*, presumably at a party in Hollywood. A photo of the two taken by Gary Leonard was, naturally, put in a late November edition of L.A.-Dee-Da.

SHOW #30

NOVEMBER 23, 1983

Reseda Country Club, 18415 Sherman Way, Reseda, CA

THE GROUP'S FINAL PERFORMANCE of that groundbreaking year of 1983—and the last show that Hillel Slovak and Jack Irons would play with the band for fourteen and thirty-one months, respectively—was, anticlimactically, a support slot for the Plimsouls. They were a rock act founded in 1978 by Peter Case, who had released their major label debut *Everywhere at Once* earlier in the year. Also playing were the Plugz, a Latino punk act also formed in the mid-1970s that had played all around Los Angeles in the previous months and who were featured in *The Decline of Western Civilization* documentary directed by Penelope Spheeris.

The Reseda Country Club opened March 1980 under the helm of Chuck Landis, a veteran promoter well known around Los Angeles for being a partner in the world-famous Roxy, among a multitude of other Sunset Strip clubs. As the name might suggest, this new building was opened specifically to cater to country music, with Landis seeking "the cream of country music talent like Willie Nelson, Kenny

Rogers, Anne Murray and others of that stature" to play. And while outlaw country singer and fiddler Merle Haggard had opened the first night's festivities, it became evident fairly quickly to the management—another local legend, Jim Rissmiller, soon took over—that country alone wasn't going to keep the place afloat. By the end of the year, all types of music were being played in the thousand-seat room, and within a few years they were even hosting rap and hip-hop acts.

And so, it was fitting that this last show of the year took place at the Reseda Country Club, for this was the site of Anthony's awakening with rap and hip-hop the previous October, at the life-changing Grandmaster Flash concert. And thirteen short months later, look where it had taken him. The joy of that one-off performance had fanned a spark into the flames of a full-time commitment: a band with a repertoire, a record deal, and a bright future ahead, playing the very same stage that had led him there. What better place to put a bow on the year, to come full circle?

Sadly, there are no recordings or photographs from the show. But as Hillel and Jack made their way offstage—perhaps after playing "Fire," which seemed to close most of the band's shows since it had found its way into the set in May—did they realize that this would be their last-ever outing with the Chili Peppers? After eleven fun months, was this the end?

The Red Hot Chili Peppers had no more shows booked for the year,* and What is This had finally settled on a new bass player in late November or early December, drafting in Chris Hutchinson. This may have happened by the time of the Reseda Country Club show, which would have finally put an end to the prolonged denouement of Hillel and Jack's time in the band. In that sense, it was a shame they weren't able to go out as headliners, to have all their friends in the crowd, and to say goodbye to the band in a better way than via a support slot, in

* If any were booked, no fliers have survived, or they were canceled beforehand.

front of a group of patient people waiting to see another band. But that was not meant to be. Both the Plimsouls and the Plugz eclipsed the Red Hot Chili Peppers in terms of name recognition and success at that point, and third place on the bill was only fair.

Hillel and Jack may well have also felt a great deal of relief; after all, as they would later say, the "Chili Peppers was something that started to take off and was always a lot of fun, but What Is This was always the main group for us." Now, with Hutchinson drafted in and the band's bottom end intact again, they had the chance to focus on that "main group."

Unfortunately, Peter Case of the Plimsouls has no memories of the Chili Peppers at this show. And while Tony Marsico, bassist for the Plugz, also did not recall anything from this particular night, he had many fond memories of Flea, writing in his 2008 autobiography that "he was a great kid who he [sic] had a lot of guts and would do anything on a dare. I regret laughing at him one night at a party when he suggested that he and I start a band with two bass players!" Marsico had come to recognize Flea as someone who would "fight the crowds to get front and center at all the Plugz shows," which might explain why his band might have been given the lucrative slot in the first place; once again, loyalty and an open mind had paid off.

As the year wound down, Flea traveled north to Sacramento and San Francisco to play two shows with FEAR, at Club Minimal and On Broadway, respectively, and on November 29 played what was probably his final performance with the band as they supported the Circle Jerks at the Starlite Roller Rink in North Hollywood.

Flea had found himself becoming discouraged with FEAR throughout the year, culminating in a split early in 1984. What at first was an exciting and sometimes-overwhelming experience soon soured; FEAR were fun, but the Chili Peppers were unexpectedly more fun, and more important, they were fun to be had with his direct peers. Flea's FEAR bandmates were friends, but they weren't his *closest* friend, like

Anthony. And so in a peculiar turn of events, just over a year after leaving his friends in What Is This for FEAR, and having to contend with the hurt he would cause his friends in doing so, he would wind up leaving FEAR . . . in order to play with his friends.

Flea had also begun to find that FEAR's "vibe" of antagonism and tongue-in-cheek racism, sexism, and general xenophobia "was growing stale." While he could appreciate the humor, and admittedly didn't consider anything off-limits, he began to grow more and more uncomfortable with what was being said onstage night after night, to a crowd of fans that would either lap up the abuse or abuse the band right back. After one particular moment of inspiration involving Eldridge Cleaver's seminal yet controversial collection of essays on race, *Soul on Ice*, written while Cleaver was in a California prison on rape charges, a nervous Flea phoned Lee Ving to tell him he had to leave, only to be fired at that same moment. Ving had started to feel that Flea was stretching himself too thin between FEAR and the Red Hot Chili Peppers. Clearly, Flea wasn't the only one feeling disillusioned with his place in the band, but with this awkward conversation dealt with, now he was free. The experiment with his punk idols was over, and by February 1984 FEAR's new bass player was former Dickies member Lorenzo Buhne.*

As far as Flea's actual involvement in the band went, he wasn't a particularly impactful member, playing live with them under twenty times and only recording with the band in the studio once, and on an unreleased session at that. It wasn't for lack of trying. Flea was a full-time member of the band and wasn't intended as a stopgap or temporary member. According to drummer Spit Stix, the band

* FEAR released their second album, *More Beer*, in 1985. But the rest of the decade was quiet for the band, and they split up in 1993. In the meantime, Lee Ving continued to act; his most notable role was in the big-screen board game adaptation *Clue*. FEAR have reunited several times, with ringleader Ving being the only constant member. The classic lineup, featuring Tim "Spit Stix" Leitch and Philo Cramer, have played together again on a number of occasions since 2018. Fred "Derf Scratch" Milner passed away in 2010.

rehearsed Flea's original material extensively—material that, enticingly, apparently contained ideas that instead became Chili Peppers songs. But in the end, none of this made its way to the stage or the studio, and as Flea's time in FEAR drew to a close, he wound up making very little mark on the band; merely filling in between two bassists who would contribute more, and for longer periods.

Elsewhere, the new What Is This reemerged on the Los Angeles scene two days before Christmas for a show at the Music Machine, supporting Megadeath, a jokey spoof of hair metal featuring members of the Circle Jerks and the Plimsouls. Preparations were quickly underway for the band, finally back on their feet, to begin recording their debut EP for MCA Records.

As far as presences onstage went, that show wrapped up 1983; three different bands playing approximately seventy times across Los Angeles, with the occasional forays into cities further north and east, and for one of them, a chaotic journey to Aspen in October. For FEAR, it had been a quiet year, an off year especially after the tumult of 1982, with the members' side projects dominating proceedings to the point where some in the scene had wondered if they had broken up. What Is This had simmered for most of the year, with the departure of two different bass players, but they had finally broken through in autumn, obtaining the record deal they had been after for so many years, with the chance to move up finally upon them.

As for the Red Hot Chili Peppers, they had arrived fully formed and burst through almost immediately. Theirs was the flame that burned brightest and fastest. After those first performances the previous December, they had been on a continually upward trajectory; gaining attention, building their repertoire, and solidifying their base, and only recently had suffered their first bout of stillness and misfortune.

Three different bands, three different paths, three different years. And looking at them in the winter of 1983, as 1984 dawned and the next chapters of their careers were underway, one could never predict where each of these bands would end up; thrust into stardom, or stuck in stagnation?

Of all three bands, it was the Chili Peppers in the most precarious of positions. They were the youngest, and the most untested, especially away from their home base. It was they who had not only lost their drummer and guitarist at the end of the year, but had then lost a replacement member, thereby undoing all the precious breathing room that they had bought themselves in the meantime. But during November and December, Anthony, Flea, and Cliff had been putting in the work, for perhaps the first time actually treating the band with the seriousness it deserved. They were actively auditioning new guitarists, one with whom they would feel comfortable not just playing their existing repertoire but writing. Where before they had relied on friendships, immediate relationships, and contacts within the scene to find a new player, even settling on people that they had played with before, here they relied on wider sources, with newspaper ads taken out and friends further afield consulted. Rick Cox, a multi-instrumentalist whom Flea had played with throughout 1982, was approached but declined: "I just said straight up, I am not your guy."

After a grueling few weeks in which the band considered "a lot of people," they had at last settled on two final candidates: Jack Sherman and Mark Metcalf, who went by the stage name of Mark 9. Two guitarists who occupied very different worlds within the music industry but who would be, with any luck, perfect fits for the Chili Peppers. It is a credit to the uniqueness of the Chili Peppers' early sound that their guitarist didn't need to be a particular style of player. They could be a jagged and clean, chicken-scratch chuck funk player like Nile Rodgers or an acidic, wailing Eddie Hazel–like virtuoso. It is a testament to Hillel Slovak's playing that he so easily managed to be both. But Hillel Slovak had left the band.

Jack Morris Sherman was born January 18, 1956, in Miami, the son of an electrical engineer. Much like Flea and Anthony, Sherman's family moved around frequently in his early years—from stints in Lake Hiawatha, New Jersey, to Allentown, Pennsylvania, and to Rochester, New York, they finally settled on the West Coast, in San Diego, in Jack's early teens. His musical development comes from the usual sources; he had an interest as a child in the viola that ended in tears, but seeing the Beatles on the *Ed Sullivan Show* in February 1964 sparked a desire for guitar-based rock music, and a musical education from his older sister Gail soon followed. "Satisfaction" by the Rolling Stones was, in particular, an "air raid siren" for the young man when he heard it on the radio.

As far as deep influences also shared with the Red Hot Chili Peppers, an eleven-year-old Jack Sherman even had the supreme honor of seeing Jimi Hendrix perform live in the flesh, who (in a move immediately regretted by all parties) opened for the Monkees during a short-lived tour of the States during the summer of 1967.

When he was fourteen, Jack's parents bought him his first guitar and paid for his first lessons, and a natural talent for the instrument started to flourish. After high school (doubling up of credits and summer classes, he graduated a year early), he played in a variety of middling bands, like Funky Demon, who were a Grand Funk Railroad cover band, and Pagan Tumor, the types of bands someone just out of high school plays in while still trying to find themselves as a musician.

Seeking more fertile pastures, Sherman made it to Los Angeles in the fall of 1977 and was confronted straightaway with a bad omen when his car was stolen. But, set up in Santa Monica, moderate success as a guitarist followed. Thanks to a tip from his sister, who sung in a band called Little Itch, the most promising of his early work was as a lead in Toni & the Movers, which also featured future Bangles bassist Micki Steele. This gave Sherman his first proper recording in

1981 and a TV appearance shortly afterward.* Though his time as one of the Movers eventually stagnated and culminated in his abrupt resignation—"We were starting to spin our wheels playing the same songs over and over again . . . gig after gig"—the connections he made during his time in the band wound up paying off.

The most prominent of these was with singer John Hiatt, whom Sherman joined in 1982 as he toured his recently released record *All of a Sudden*. But that was a temporary position, and he departed the band late the next year, as the Chili Peppers found themselves needing a guitar player. Once again, he was looking for work, and once again his sister Gail—based in Hollywood while her younger brother toiled away in Santa Monica—offered him a lifeline. "She said a couple of guys she knew in Hollywood needed a guitar player," Sherman recalled. "And, I believe, gave me Flea's number and suggested I call him. I did." Sherman's life had changed in the months leading up to this moment; he was single, without a regular gig, and had recently changed his life to implement some Taoism-aligned principles, including a macrobiotic diet. In other words, the circle that the Red Hot Chili Peppers ran in was very far from his own. He had never heard of the band or caught wind of their performances throughout the year and had never heard of Anthony or Flea before his phone call. But the conversation with Flea went well: "It was a pleasant conversation and we arranged a time for me to come by and audition."

In a fact that showcases the still-close bond that Hillel Slovak had with his soon-to-be ex-bandmates, this audition—like the others undertaken that autumn—took place in a back room of the house and rehearsal studio belonging to Addie Brik, Hillel's girlfriend. The space was a converted pool hall on North Heliotrope named the Crooked Cue that Brik had taken over. What Is This had started to rehearse

* The single "Africa" backed with "Bitches and Bastards," issued under the name Nadia Kapiche, was tracked at Eldorado Studios and engineered by Dave Jerden—just as the Red Hot Chili Peppers' debut album would be a few years later.

there in the early 1980s, and the Chili Peppers most likely set up shop there once they started to become a serious endeavor in mid-1983.*

After arriving ("I remember seeing this guy [Flea] pull up in a large, old car, and thought that his head looked small inside the vehicle"), one of the first things Sherman noticed was that the band's lead singer was absent. This was a period of heavy drug use for Anthony, who seemed to ramp his self-destructive behavior in the latter months of 1983, while the band was in stasis. With Flea moving back in with his mother and easing off the drugs thanks to a newfound (but short-lived) appreciation for the straight-edge scene, Anthony's new girlfriend, Jennifer Bruce, and housemate, Bob Forrest, became his main partners in crime. It would take a few months before Sherman appreciated that Anthony's absence was a sign of troubling things to come. Before that, he was just happy to play with a promising and exciting new group of musicians.

Sherman's introduction with Flea and Cliff was a standard funk jam in the key of E, a way for each player to get a feel for each other and to find out what talents the other might hold. But in a repeat of *his* audition with FEAR a year earlier, Flea, either organically or in an attempt at self-conscious showmanship, spent the whole time acting out, "Shaking his head from side to side violently . . . pounding the bass," as Sherman recalled. "I didn't know whether to stare with my mouth hanging open or keep playing my guitar. It was so intense. I thought, 'This is somewhat appealing,' even though it wasn't anything new. It was pretty minimalistic." The type of music they were playing definitely appealed to him. Sherman, like Cliff Martinez, was interested in joining the band because it gave him a chance to work on his funk chops. "I always liked to play funk music, and I heard they weren't the typical horrible white funk band that this town is so proud of

* That said, aside from a few acoustic rehearsals in various living rooms around Hollywood, the band have never revealed where, if ever, they rehearsed during their first year together.

producing." In addition to the frenetic jam, Sherman remembered that the band may have played an early, rudimentary version of a track that would later come to be known as "True Men Don't Kill Coyotes," the opening track on their debut album.*

While this jam and audition was fun for all involved, it would be a few weeks before the two parties crossed paths again. While the Chili Peppers needed to be expeditious in finding this new guitarist, with a record deal and the eventual recording sessions for their debut album waiting, they seemed to have learned from the too-quick hiring and regrettable firing of Dix Denney a few months previous. Sure, someone might have been able to play the guitar incredibly well, and they weren't an immediately repulsive presence to the existing members of the band. But would they fit in with the other personalities beyond that first meeting? Could they write a song? Would their hiring simply lead to more regret and more instability, further down the line? This newfound carefulness may have stemmed from the influence of manager Lindy Goetz, who would have tempered Flea and Anthony's potential for rash decisions.

Sherman himself was unsure if he would join the band if they had asked; he had recently begun playing with a keyboard virtuoso named Barry Goldberg, who had played with Bob Dylan in the 1970s. Goldberg was putting a band together and had a record deal; this was the exact kind of situation Sherman was looking for. But Goldberg (and the rest of his band) was substantially older, and Sherman found the Chili Peppers more intriguing, even if their music wasn't as song oriented or structurally interesting as he might have liked. To him, the Chili Peppers' music was fairly "old-hat," and rap didn't interest him.

Musical differences aside, Jack Sherman was interested in playing with the Red Hot Chili Peppers for three main reasons. The first was that he relished the opportunity to play a starring role with the guitar,

* Though this may have taken place at the next audition, a few weeks later.

after so many years spent on the sidelines, playing other people's songs. He would be a main player in this band, taking solos and leads, and while they had an existing repertoire, he would be tasked with writing original music with them. A vastly different situation than what he had been in previously.

The second was that they had a record deal; after years of frustrating toiling in the Los Angeles scene, it was a "huge incentive." A deal meant (relative) financial stability, the chance to record in a proper studio with company backing, and the chance to further his career as a musician. No serious musician would admit it (or at least the ones that did would be laughed at), but the glory of rock stardom was never far from anyone's mind. Sherman also had a personal edict he was attempting to live by, even if he might not have been aware that he was living it at the time; if he was going to move from quiet San Diego to the hustle and bustle and drama of Los Angeles, he was going "to make it, and to do original music of some kind." The Red Hot Chili Peppers gave him that chance, however slight that chance might have been. "I wasn't just going to play in cover bands, I was going to go for it."

The third reason the band interested him was that he was already aware of Cliff Martinez as a player and was deeply interested in playing with the drummer. He might have never heard of the Chili Peppers, but Cliff, with his varied career, had made an impact on Jack Sherman. The two had already met on a few occasions, once at Amigo Studios in North Hollywood while Cliff was rehearsing with Captain Beefheart, whom Sherman adored, and again at a party for Beefheart a short while later. During the audition, Sherman was thrilled by Cliff's playing, finally getting the chance to see it in person: "He's drumming away, and striking me as very unique, making up these very tom-tom, almost Beefheart inspired [parts]."

But as fun as the initial experience was, the Chili Peppers didn't immediately offer Sherman the job, and Sherman didn't press the band for an immediate answer. Instead, they thanked each other and kept their respective searches open, holding their cards close to their chest and staying quiet for the next few weeks as they considered other directions.

One other player caught the Chili Peppers' eye. Mark 9 had a closer initial connection with the Chili Peppers than Sherman; a "hip avant-garde art school refugee," he previously played with postpunk poet Randall Kennedy, and in a short-lived lineup of Nina Hagen's band alongside a local hero, former Germs (and future Nirvana and Foo Fighters) member Pat Smear.* Mark 9 also had another connection to the Red Hot Chili Peppers, though it would take a few years before that connection became apparent. A highly skilled guitarist, he supplemented his income by giving lessons to other budding players, and throughout 1983 one of those students was John Frusciante, a thirteen-year-old prodigy from the Valley who lived for music, especially punk and new wave. Mark 9 had even given the young Frusciante his first ever taste of live performance earlier that year, bringing him up onstage with his psychedelic-inspired band Underworld, at a show at the Lhasa Club, on either April 1 or June 24 of 1983.

Mark 9 has never publicly mentioned auditioning for the Red Hot Chili Peppers, though Frusciante did recall being told about it during guitar lessons in those weeks in November and December: "I heard about them from him. He said there was this band he was waiting to find out if he was in." So while they may never have been mentioned in the years since, one can imagine that the auditions took a similar shape to Sherman's—an initial play together, and then radio silence. But while Mark 9 waited to hear back, and the band kept looking, another guitarist made his own move.

---

* This connection through Nina Hagen may be how Mark 9 and the Chili Peppers met in the first place. In *Scar Tissue* Anthony Kiedis refers to Mark 9 playing in Two Balls and a Bat with Cliff Martinez, but this may be a mistake, as that band, whenever advertised, did not feature a guitar player.

Curious about how the band were faring in the weeks since his audition, Sherman called Flea and was invited to come back and jam with the band again, this time with Lindy Goetz in attendance. The trio played another "roof-raising" jam in E, with Goetz marveling at Sherman's abilities. "How in the world do you play like that?" he recalled being asked by the band's stunned manager.

More familiar with the environment now, Sherman was starting to pick up on some red flags in the room that day. The first was the absence of Anthony Kiedis—the band's lead singer is missing in all of Sherman's recollections of these early days; though he was sure Anthony had to be there during the second audition, he didn't interact with him or the rest of the band. While Anthony might not have been able to involve himself in the jam as it happened—ad-libbing was never his strong suit—the fact he seemed to be leaving the hiring of a guitarist up to Flea and Cliff struck him as worrying. The bassist and drummer would have needed to ensure that their musical chemistries aligned, but shouldn't he have had more to say, or did he just see Sherman as filler that didn't require his complete attention?

The second red flag involved Flea. During another break in proceedings, the bassist approached Sherman in awe and disbelief, shaking his head in the still-charged atmosphere. "It's going to be really hard keeping up with you, man," he said. While Flea most likely intended the comment to be a compliment, Sherman found it "odd. . . . Almost like this resentful acceptance that I was going to have to be the guitar player." In Sherman's mind, it was a competitive outburst that had no place in a band that was supposed to be based around mutual appreciation, and it tied into what he felt that Anthony might have been thinking—that Sherman was only there because Hillel Slovak couldn't be. "Maybe there's already resentment from the get-go. . . . It was very weird, and it left me kind of scratching my head."

Years later, the resentment was there plain as day when Anthony recalled Jack's playing at the audition in his autobiography: "We played some of our songs, and though he didn't have a down-and-dirty nasty-dog element to his sound, he was technically efficient, hitting all the notes in the right places. His playing didn't have the same spirit as Hillel's, but at least he was playing the parts."

But red flag or not, after Sherman had left on this December day close to Christmas, the band put their heads together and decided to hire him. "He wasn't the raw, explosive hellcat of funk that we were looking for," Anthony admitted years later. "But he'd definitely be capable of going into the studio and putting down these parts." There was a respect there for his musicianship—Flea and Lindy Goetz would go on to call him a "really good player" and "an amazing guitar player" in later years—but there was also a seemingly immediate acknowledgment that he was a very different person to the rest of them, and especially to Hillel. For all they knew, that would wind up being a positive thing. A band is the sum of its human beings—not just their talents and their style of playing, but their personalities, their qualms, and their world views. And Sherman was an enormously different person to Anthony, Flea, and (to a lesser extent) Cliff. This needn't be a negative thing, and the band, as Anthony said, was "embracing" of Sherman's "nerd energy" and were cautiously willing to welcome him into the fold. At the end of the day, they needed a guitar player, and there was a guitar player available.

When Sherman got home that day, there was a message waiting for him on his answering machine. Three of the Chili Peppers welcomed their newest member into the fold with a tune in "cascading harmony," as Sherman put it, with the band sounding like they were covering the Beatles' take on "Twist and Shout": *You got the gig, you got the gig, you got the gig!*

This touched him. "Something in me wanted the acceptance," he remembered. "I remember me being in my little apartment hearing that, feeling very emotional that I was being accepted into something. And that's how I got in the Red Hot Chili Peppers."

That good feeling lasted a few weeks, and then a stretch of unease set in, which would not lift until the early months of 1985. After a number of quick and diligent rehearsals, the reconstituted Red Hot Chili Peppers lineup debuted on January 19, 1984, at the Music Machine, as they opened for Tex and the Horseheads alongside the dance-pop act Cambridge Apostles. Tex and the Horseheads would put out three albums on Enigma before disbanding in 1986, and Cambridge Apostles were associated with the label as well, having contributed to its *Hell Comes to Your House Part II* compilation the previous year.* With the Chili Peppers as their most recent signings as part of the new EMI partnership, this was an Enigma showcase of sorts; the beginning of an exciting year for the label.

As the new guy playing his first show, Jack Sherman was in for some roughhousing, but as he looked back with maturity and clarity years later, he could only see the red flags he had missed, more red flags after the many that had been present at those initial auditions: "I had my new girlfriend, Anne, who I would later marry, with me, and my friend Micki [Steele] was there from the Bangles. Lots of people." Jack was still deep into his macrobiotic diet and was avoiding dairy, and this seemed to give his bandmates an idea. "We were on stage, and all of a sudden, Flea and Anthony threw a bunch of stuff like cottage cheese or yogurt all over me and my guitar. . . . I was extremely humiliated." It was probably Anthony and Flea's idea of hazing, their version of a welcome, or perhaps a sort of celebration for Jack's birthday, which was the previous day. To Jack, however, it was "a horribly cruel thing to do to a new band member." It was Cliff's first show as well, but he seems to have already been integrated into the band

* In July 1983 the Red Hot Chili Peppers were announced as one of the many bands taking part in this compilation, but for whatever reason (perhaps their new deal with Lindy Goetz, or typical punk lack of organization) they never wound up doing so. If they had, it would have been their earliest appearance on record, though it's unclear what recording would have been used.

fully, and if any pranks—cruel or not—were directed his way, they've not been mentioned since, and perhaps they were interpreted by the more easygoing drummer differently.

As is typical for a small club show from the band's early years, no set list survives from this performance, but it most likely featured early versions of the new songs the band had been working on in rehearsal sessions with Jack and Cliff; "True Men Don't Kill Coyotes," an ode to California's roaming wild fauna that doubles as a tribute to X, one of the Chili Peppers' favorite L.A. bands;* "Buckle Down," a chugging, heavier song about pulling oneself up by the bootstraps that breaks into a jazzy prechorus; "Mommy, Where's Daddy?," a slow and funky groove based around a repeated D minor chord from Jack that was complemented by a ridiculous, even creepy, vocal duet between Anthony and Flea; and finally updated versions of "Get Up and Jump," "Baby Appeal," "Police Helicopter," "Green Heaven," and "Out in L.A.," with moved around sections, new riffs, refined parts, and added lyrics. The band had a busy few months ahead of them; having at last signed their record deal and solidified their lineup, they had to make up for the time they had lost late in 1983.

Preparations for the Red Hot Chili Peppers' debut album were also underway, with Jack and Cliff drawn into the band's contract with EMI/Enigma and the management agreement with Lindy Goetz. With the help of Eric Greenspan, whose initial gamble on the band was certainly starting to pay off, two partnership agreements were drawn up. One involved a new publishing company, Moebetoblame Music, named for a lyric in "Green Heaven," which the band used as a publishing arm until 2016.† Jack and Cliff were to be fully credited with all the work they had done since joining the band, though the credits seen on the debut album are obviously the result of some behind-the-scenes

* The band would open for X two days later, January 21, at the Palace.

† In 2021, the Red Hot Chili Peppers sold the Moebetoblame catalog to UK investment company Hipgnosis Songs Group for a rumored $140 million.

negotiations between current and former band members.* The other agreement was a four-part split on record sales and merchandise profits. In this aspect, the band agreed to divide everything equally, regardless of seniority in the band. According to Jack Sherman, this was his idea, but one that Flea was more than happy to sign off on.

Preliminary discussions were also being made with a series of potential record producers. The two final candidates were Gang of Four guitarist Andy Gill, and Doors keyboardist Ray Manzarek—two genuine legends, either would be a major boon for the band. In January or early February, they entered Bijou Studios on North Cahuenga Boulevard and cut a series of demos, with Flea's now-former bandmate Spit Stix involved again in a mixing (but not producing) capacity, which to this day have yet to surface. It's not known what exactly the band recorded, but Jack Sherman remembered a version of "Mommy, Where's Daddy?" being done, and elsewhere Andy Gill has referred to a demo version of "True Men Don't Kill Coyotes."†

Aside from the busy writing sessions, the first photoshoot with the new lineup, taken by local photography legend Ivy Ney, and a stack of performances to test out new songs and iron out the kinks with Jack and Cliff—two more shows at the Music Machine and a daytime show at UCLA in February, among other bookings—the band also had their most high-profile date to prepare for: their debut television appearance.

---

* New members Jack Sherman and Cliff Martinez would be credited on "True Men Don't Kill Coyotes," "Buckle Down," "Mommy, Where's Daddy?," and (along with Andy Gill) "Grand Pappy Du Plenty," all songs they had an equal part in writing. For the songs that existed before they joined, such as "Out in L.A.," only Anthony and Flea are credited, perhaps to avoid any clashes with Hillel Slovak and Jack Irons. But oddly enough, Hillel *and* Jack Sherman are credited on "Baby Appeal," even though the song existed long before Jack joined the band. Why Hillel was included on this single song and not any of the others can only be guessed at. The odd song out was "You Always Sing the Same," which was credited to Flea alone, even though Joel Virgel-Vierset wrote it.

† The band most likely recorded a demo version of their entire forthcoming album during this session, which only adds to the frustration over it never surfacing.

EPILOGUE

MARCH 9, 10, OR 11, 1984

KTTV Studios, Metromedia Square, 5746 Sunset Boulevard, Los Angeles, CA

FOR THE FIRST TWELVE MONTHS of their existence, the Red Hot Chili Peppers had inhabited a small bubble—the Hollywood areas of Los Angeles, mostly, with disastrous and short-lived forays into the rest of the United States. But their early-March appearance on *Thicke of the Night* was their first chance to spread the word of their band across the country, on a nationally syndicated talk show. This was another major score for the young band, and along with their preliminary talks with potential producers, a sign of what kind of connections they could leverage now that they were aligned with a major label, or even a smaller label, like Enigma, which was itself benefiting from its partnership with the much larger EMI-America.

The Red Hot Chili Peppers tended to make fans immediately. After all, everyone involved with the band seemed to realize they had something special after a single two-minute show. What kind of impact could they make on a national audience? This performance, taped on March 9, 10, or 11, 1984, could have been their moment—the moment they lit a real fire under their bourgeoning career, and take that momentum with them up to the release of their debut album.

There was just one problem with that dream. Nobody was watching.

Alan Thicke was a Canadian TV presenter, producer, and composer who was relatively unknown in the United States but had hosted a popular daytime talk show in his homeland in the early 1980s. Drafted by former NBC executive Fred Silverman to host a nighttime program devised to directly compete with Johnny Carson's ailing behemoth *The Tonight Show*, Thicke was referred to as the "second coming of comedy" during the initial coming-out press conference, and the hype ballooned dangerously from there. The expectation proved to be too much, and along with distribution problems and poor reviews, the new show was doomed from the beginning. The general public tired of the overexposed Thicke before the show even aired for the first time in September 1983, with some in the press pithily coining it *Sick of the Hype*. Worse yet, the second filmed episode was deemed so bad that it never aired, instead being chopped up, its pieces salvaged across several different future episodes. At one point during its short run, it was seen by so few people in one Nielsen ratings catchment in Philadelphia that it didn't even register a rating. *The Tonight Show* may have been ailing, but it still held its own against rivals.

Viewership wasn't the only issue that *Thicke of the Night* faced. Because *The Tonight Show* was so popular and had such a hold over talent agencies (and wasn't afraid to show it), the producers of *Thicke of the Night* had trouble booking more established acts for their rival show; one visit to *Thicke*, and they might not be invited back to see Johnny and Ed across town. This might well be why the Red Hot Chili Peppers, a relatively unknown act that didn't even have an album or single out—indeed, that hadn't even started *recording* their debut album—were given the chance to play on the show. Fred Wiseman, a former dentist, booked talent on the show. Wiseman was a fan of the Chili Peppers and had eclectic taste; he also pitched Midnight Oil, Cyndi Lauper, and Bon Jovi, but had *Thicke of the Night* been more successful, these smaller acts might never have been given the chance.

Two songs were played by the band during the recording. Up first, "True Men Don't Kill Coyotes," soon to be the opening track on their debut, self-titled album.* The band are immediately notable in their actions and their clothing choices; Anthony and Flea are wearing their Brothers Cup jackets (though Flea loses his immediately, revealing lines of fluorescent electrical tape wound up and down his torso), and the newly redheaded Anthony has on an unexplained foot-high headdress and patchwork-design pajama pants designed by girlfriend Jennifer Bruce. Jack Sherman is wearing his recently custom-made "gorilla-suit": a nicely tailored jacket and pants combination with carefully placed furry patches sewn into it. It's a hectic performance, so hectic that the chaos precedes the actual song; as Thicke tries to introduce the band, they interrupt him while plugging in their instruments, smothering the host with feedback as he laughs along.

One fact that is immediately clear is that Anthony and Flea are running the show, and the producers and camera crew seem to acknowledge that. During the song, Cliff Martinez is anonymous and basically unseen in a grey jumpsuit behind his kit, while Jack sticks to the side, playing his parts and occasionally glancing over at Anthony and Flea with a smirk and an eye-roll, as if he himself is a spectator. All focus is on the singer and the bassist; to look elsewhere is to miss the action.

The energy ramps up even further when "True Men Don't Kill Coyotes" finishes. Thicke joins them and asks the audience a few

* Curiously, while a video would be filmed and released for the song later in 1984, it was never released as a stand-alone single nor were promos sent to radio stations.

rhetorical questions: "What does it mean? What did they say? Where are they from?" and the band, seemingly with no other ideas, take this opportunity to tackle the straight man host. In this instance, they are a collective unit—even Cliff joins in—and it ensures that, while they might seem immature and bratty, they're certainly more interesting than the too-cool-for-this, immaculately presented pop acts that were in vogue and on top of the charts at the time. Conservative attitudes had reemerged throughout the United States, and while punk acts had been shocking audiences for years, it was still a rarity on late-night TV.

They are a spectacle, and the crowd loves them. For they are, after all, among their own: many of the Chili Peppers' friends and family were in the crowd for filming, including Blackie Dammett, and Jack's sister Gail, who was responsible for connecting him with the band in the first place.*

After a short, erratic interview (again, just Flea and Anthony) in which Thicke runs laps around the two amateurs, they launch into "Get Up and Jump." A rather different song from "True Men Don't Kill Coyotes," but it follows a similar trajectory; the band fling themselves around and the cameras do their best to follow, and while their playing is sloppy and cacophonous, they manage to stay in time with one another, and the song doesn't fall apart like it could. When the hurricane of the verse slides smoothly into the outro, it's impossible not to bob one's head along with it. Overall, "Get Up and Jump" sounds similar to the three versions of it available from the previous year, though Jack has fleshed out the guitar part, and the band sound, understandably, more rehearsed. When they finish, the crowd cheers again, the show fades to commercial, and their time in the spotlight is over, for now.

---

* Backstage, Gary Leonard took a photo of the Chili Peppers posing with Thicke that appeared in a L.A.-Dee-Da column the next week.

It may not have been to an audience of millions, but it was a slot any new band trying to make their name would kill for, and the Chili Peppers certainly made an impact on whoever might have been watching when the episode was broadcast on Friday March 16, 1984, with comedian Richard Belzer as the show's main guest. Thankfully, one of the few people watching thought to tape it, and decades later, the first television appearance of the Red Hot Chili Peppers is there for curious fans to watch—the ultimate curio, an ancient relic of an era forgotten almost entirely.*

This appearance on *Thicke of the Night* is, in a historical sense, only the beginning of the Red Hot Chili Peppers story. They are barely a year old, with a handful of demo recordings to their name, and only about fifty shows under their belt. Some of which, of course, are already legendary, but many of which have been lost to time, unrecorded and forgotten in a blurry sea of foggy memories. The Red Hot Chili Peppers onstage during Alan Thicke's short-lived show are yet to record their debut album, which in any case will not be the stunning, career-making piece of art made with their hero Andy Gill that they had hoped. Instead, *The Red Hot Chili Peppers*, released in August of 1984, will be an instantly dated disappointment that the band will always look back on with regret. Their first tour to accompany the album with Jack Sherman and Cliff Martinez is yet to take place. When it does, it will be a mostly unhappy experience, with too many shows played to too few people, packed into too little time.

There is much misery in this band's future, but there is also much hard-earned, joyous success. The lineup changes and the instability forced upon the band in their first year together will remain a frequent issue. Jack Sherman, who will never really fit in, will be fired in early 1985 to make way for Hillel Slovak, returning from a moribund What

* One recording even made it into a young John Frusciante's hands a few months later. It was instrumental in kick-starting his interest in the band.

Is This.* Cliff Martinez will leave on far more amicable terms a year later for Jack Irons, unexpectedly reuniting the original lineup. But the core group, the original Chili Peppers, the Fax City Four, Tony Flow and His Miraculously Majestic Masters of Mayhem, will be torn apart yet again after Hillel succumbs to a heroin overdose on June 25, 1988. Drugs were present in their lives recreationally throughout all of 1983, but they were not yet a problem. They quickly became one. Both Anthony and Hillel would be fired from the band, albeit temporarily, at least once each owing to substance abuse issues.

But through all that—the sparsely attended tours, the deaf-eared journalists, the silent radios, the poor record sales, the lineup changes, the drug issues—some classic records will be made. *Freaky Styley* and *The Uplift Mofo Party Plan* are two of the best alternative rock records of the 1980s—funky, raw, and catchy, expertly played and recorded, with songs that either remained in the band's live rotation for decades or should have, all things considered—and success beyond their wildest dreams arrives shortly into the next decade, though bittersweet in the wake of the death of their friend.

The band that exists today is virtually unrecognizable to the bratty children mugging for the camera on *Thicke of the Night* in March of 1984, not just in the changes that have naturally occurred over four decades of their existence, but in the style of music that they play, and the band's place in popular culture. They are no longer a scrappy,

---

* What Is This released their debut EP *Squeezed* in 1984. After the recording sessions the following year for their self-titled album were completed, Hillel Slovak quit the band and rejoined the Red Hot Chili Peppers. Alain Johannes, Jack Irons, and Chris Hutchinson continued on without him. Later that year they released another EP, *3 out of 5 Live*, but disbanded shortly thereafter; Jack Irons then followed Hillel's lead and returned to the Red Hot Chili Peppers. Throughout the years, Alain Johannes and Jack have continued to play together in a variety of different acts, most notably Eleven, who recorded five albums. Jack Irons joined Pearl Jam, a band he helped form, in 1994, played with them for four years, and is now a solo musician. Alain Johannes is also a celebrated solo musician who has occasionally played with PJ Harvey, Queens of the Stone Age, and Them Crooked Vultures.

obnoxious little act that blends hardcore punk and rhythmic funk, but the seeds planted in their first year together have bloomed into the most successful alternative rock band of all time.

Despite this success—approximately eighty million album sales, countless millions in worldwide touring receipts, entry into the Rock and Roll Hall of Fame in 2012—the band have had setback after setback. While Chad Smith has been a constant presence in the drummer's chair since January 1989, the band loses guitarists at a farcical pace; thirteen different men have filled the spot since 1983. Add two major heroin addictions and a variety of horribly timed injuries that have derailed their progress, and you could be forgiven for thinking they had been cursed in some way, that their success was truly some miracle.

But the longevity that the Red Hot Chili Peppers have enjoyed is thanks to two main reasons. The first is the love between Flea and Anthony Kiedis. The love for each other, for their band, and their desire to keep the journey that they started in December 1982 going, no matter how unlikely success (or future success) might have seemed.

The second reason is because they're *used* to upheaval. Jack Irons and Hillel Slovak leaving the Red Hot Chili Peppers at the end of 1983 meant that the band's earliest days were directed by the need to replace members and keep the (at times sinking) project afloat. Replacing Hillel Slovak with Dix Denney and then Jack Sherman, and replacing Jack Irons with Cliff Martinez was a necessity to ensure their recording contract would go ahead and that the band wouldn't be snuffed out only as it was beginning to flourish. But it was only slightly more than a year later that Jack Sherman himself was ousted. They had done it once, and after that first time, they would do it many more times in the future, with differing levels of grief. Changing members quickly became the norm—not the cataclysmic shift it could have been—and always presented an opportunity for change and growth.

When Hillel Slovak passed away, and Jack Irons left the band in heartbreak, Flea and Anthony knew they would continue. When John Frusciante abruptly quit in 1992, they were playing festival shows in Belgium with a replacement guitarist, Arik Marshall, two months later. They had done it before, and they would do it again. In 1998, when the band hit a wall and realized that there might be brighter avenues to explore after toiling unsuccessfully with Dave Navarro, they weren't afraid to make a drastic change, and have the out-of-practice John Frusciante return to the band. When Frusciante quit *again* in 2009, the question of retirement was never considered once the remaining members reconvened. They had done it before, and they would do it again. Where lesser bands might throw in the towel, when less driven personalities would decide that enough was enough, the Chili Peppers returned to their resilient roots. Their future was extended, exactly when it seemed as if the band had finally run its course. The events of 1983 made this way of thinking possible, because they had not known anything else.

The *Thicke of the Night* performance could be considered the beginning of their story, but it's really the end of their first chapter. Much work led them to this point; as one witnesses them dancing around the KTTV studios stage in their infancy, it's easy to think that *this* is the band, the way it always had been. That this is what emerged fully formed out of the streets of Los Angeles. And if this was the band, it may not have lasted more than a year or two. But much had already happened behind the scenes; the events of 1983 ensured not only that they could get to this spot but also that they would be on top of the world only a decade later. Before December 1982 the Red Hot Chili Peppers did not exist. In many ways, their very existence would have been laughable to those who knew its members. But from a single show, only minutes long, they created something unique in a crowded scene. In the early months of 1983, they were on hold, as two other existing acts, FEAR and What Is This, took precedence.

Twelve months later, those two acts had been largely left behind by Flea and Anthony.

All this in just a year.

In late 2019 John Frusciante unexpectedly returned to the Red Hot Chili Peppers for a third stint, replacing Josh Klinghoffer, who had succeeded him a decade earlier. If it weren't for 1983, that upheaval would mean much more. Instead, it's simply a new chapter, perhaps toward the end of a very long book, but a new chapter nonetheless; the story keeps going. New music is there to be made, more entries into a celebrated repertoire that started with an off-the-cuff rap ditty put together for a one-off show on a cold night in Los Angeles.

The Red Hot Chili Peppers formed as a one-off act in December of 1982, but it's really no surprise that they continued to play together after that first show. They are a band formed around love: a love of music, a love of the spectacle of performance, and a love for each other. They got lucky, in a sense, that their first full year together, 1983, went the way it did. The next thirty-odd years would be far more dramatic, far more widespread, and far more documented, but 1983 is the perfect start to the Red Hot Chili Peppers story, the *only* start that makes sense. The start of something enormous, beloved, and ongoing.

But it's only the start.

ACKNOWLEDGMENTS

IN THIS PROJECT, I have been assisted more than is possible to tell by Leandro Cabo of the Red Hot Chili Peppers Live Archive (www.rhcplivearchive.com). Leni vetted every discovery, assisted with research, did a lot of legwork, and made me feel a little less alone every time I felt like I was putting *way* too much effort into this silly band. I must also thank Mark Minshall, another Chili Peppers fan who has become a close friend and confidant in recent years. I will always enjoy our Sessions chats, and I hope one day that we can actually speak in person.

A big thanks as well to Rebecca Billingham, whose website (www.thechilisource.com) became my first stop every time I needed to track down a half-remembered snippet of an interview or magazine scan. Rebecca is an all-time RHCP fan and one of the best and hardest-working people in our community. Thank you to the Townsend brothers, Sam and Ben, for their support and company (via headphones as I grocery shop) all these years. But I've got to say this: Chocolate Oranges are available at Rawlinson's, that's all. Jack Bratt is the best guitarist in Australia and maybe an even bigger Chili Peppers fan than

I. One day we'll pluck up the courage and call John. Dan Bogosian helped me get this project off the ground, and I am proud to be in the Chili Peppers author club with him. Let's hope this club expands soon. Thank you as well to Skinny from theside.free.fr—the original source for early setlists and fliers.

Jack Sherman was a supreme gentleman we lost far too soon. He will be sorely missed, and I can only hope his sensational work on *The Red Hot Chili Peppers* (and elsewhere) will one day be widely loved. And thank you to Max Elfimov for being Jack's biggest fan.

Thank you to Gary Allen for always being an utter delight. You rock, Gary. And to Fabrice Drouet, Salomon Emquies, Tim Leitch, Pleasant Gehman, Brianna Murphy, Tom Bates, Nicole Bishop, April Tricase, Dan Walkington, Ana Maybury, Grace Bicknell, Emma Vickery, Lockie Clifford, Bec Newing, Jack Markham, Lara Demartino, Skip King, Kevin Moody, David Hughes, Carmaig de Forest, Deanne and Sherri Franklin, Rene Middlekoop, Irena Halder, Steven McDonald, Darrell Vickers, Phil Elverum, Linda Kite, Todd Godson, Rick Cox, Peter Bastone, Jeff Apter, Syndee Coleman, Anna Scott at the Aspen Historical Society, the staff at the Center for Bibliographic Studies and Research at UCR, the California Digital Newspaper Collection, the ONE Archives, and everyone else who answered and fielded my inane questions over the years.

I'm sure I am forgetting some (if not many) people. But who can forget Anthony, Flea, Jack, and Hillel (may he be forever missed) for starting this journey back in December 1982. We wouldn't be here without them. And my endless gratitude to Cliff Martinez, Jack Sherman, John Frusciante, Chad Smith, Dave Navarro, and Josh Klinghoffer for continuing it (and thanks to Dix Denney, Chuck Biscuits, D. H. Peligro, Blackbyrd McKnight, Arik Marshall, and Jesse Tobias for their parts in the story as well).

Thank you to Kara Rota, Benjamin Krapohl, and everyone at Chicago Review Press, for their wonderful help and support.

My eternal love to Oliver Ryan, Josh Riley, Chris Brem, James Robinson, and Mark Clark, who I think is actually responsible for getting me into the band.

To Mum, Dad, Seb, Tory, Willow, Otis, Olly, Hayley, and Hendrix, and to Jae, Hugo, Annie, Dylan, and Ines.

And most of all to Rosa, Boo, Stevie, and Squeaks, for being my home.

APPENDIX: THE 1983 VENUES

1. GRANDIA ROOM, 5657 MELROSE AVENUE, LOS ANGELES.

Dates played: December 16, 1982; December 30, 1982; January 6, 1983; March 31, 1983.

The Grandia Room was rejigged a few times in the 1980s, eventually changing names to the Grandia Palace, before closing in late 1991. The building, which last went by the name the Larchmont, was torn down some time in 2010 and is now a combination apartment block / retail space. This sadly means that to stand in the same room as the first Red Hot Chili Peppers concert is no longer possible.

2. CATHAY DE GRANDE, 1600 NORTH ARGYLE AVENUE, LOS ANGELES.

Dates played: March 4, 1983; March 25, 1983; September 18, 1983.
The Cathay de Grande closed in 1985. The building is now a nightclub that goes under the name the Argyle. Fans looking for the distinctive decrepit roof tiles will be sadly disappointed; the interior has been extensively renovated, much like the rest of the venues on this list.

3. CLUB LINGERIE, 6507 SUNSET BOULEVARD, LOS ANGELES.

Dates played: March 31, 1983; July 18, 1983; November 7, 1983.
Club Lingerie lasted until 1995 before shutting down. Thankfully, the building is still standing and is the subject of another high-end nightclub conversion, this time named the Warwick.

4. HELEN'S PLACE, 4658 MELROSE AVENUE, LOS ANGELES.

Dates played: April 13, 1983; June 4, 1983; June 17, 1983.
Helen's Place was torn down in 2009, and the shopping center that replaced it has also since been torn down. An apartment building is currently being erected in its place.

5. THE PLANT, 12446 VENTURA BOULEVARD, STUDIO CITY.

Dates played: April 29, 1983; August 4, 1983; October 29, 1983.
The Plant closed in late 1983. Returning to its prevenue roots, the building now hosts a salon again.

6. FIESTA HOUSE, 2353 EAST OLYMPIC BOULEVARD, LOS ANGELES.

Date played: May 20, 1983.

Fiesta House operated until early 1984 but remained empty for many years. The building now holds a mechanic shop.

7. CHINA CLUB, 8338 WEST THIRD STREET, LOS ANGELES.

Date played: May 30, 1983.

The China Club restaurant closed in the mid-1980s, and the building has been a variety of different restaurants since.

8. GOLDEN VILLAGE SUPPER CLUB, 6541 HOLLYWOOD BOULEVARD, LOS ANGELES.

Date played: June 5, 1983.

The Golden Village Supper Club moved out of 6541 Hollywood Boulevard in 1983, when it looked like the decrepit building was going to be torn down. But in 1985 the Janes House, Hollywood's oldest, was picked up from its foundations, moved toward the back of the lot, and restored by preservationists. It is now part of a shopping precinct and is home to (what else?) a nightclub.

9. THE VEX, 2580 NORTH SOTO STREET, LOS ANGELES.

Date played: June 11, 1983.

The Vex closed in 1983, and the building it occupied was torn down in the late 1990s to make way for an apartment complex.

10. KIT KAT CLUB, 6550 SANTA MONICA BOULEVARD, LOS ANGELES.

Dates played: July 3, 1983; September 10, 1983.

The Kit Kat closed in 1984 and was rebranded Catz, but shortly afterward the entire building was torn down. Where the building used to stand is now a used-car lot.

11. MUSIC MACHINE, 12220 WEST PICO BOULEVARD, LOS ANGELES.

Dates played: July 4, 1983; July 25, 1983.

The Music Machine managed to survive into the mid-1990s, but the location is now an electrical and lighting store.

12. AL'S BAR, 305 SOUTH HEWITT STREET, LOS ANGELES.

Date played: July 31, 1983.

Al's Bar shut in 2001, but the location still stands and the American Hotel still operates. The ground floor, where the band played, is now a clothing store.

13. POMONA VALLEY AUDITORIUM, 235 WEST THIRD STREET, POMONA.

Date played: August 13, 1983.

The auditorium closed in 1987 and has been used as both a church and a daycare in the years since.

14. UNIVERSAL AMPHITHEATER, 100 UNIVERSAL CITY PLAZA, UNIVERSAL CITY.

Date played: August 17, 1983.

Universal Amphitheater was demolished in 2013 to make way for a Harry Potter attraction.

15. RADIO CITY, 945 SOUTH KNOTT AVENUE, ANAHEIM.

Date played: September 9, 1983.

Radio City fell victim to an arson attack in 1985 and never reopened after its operating permit was revoked. A storage locker complex now occupies the site.

16. E'WU'S PARADISE, 450 SOUTH GALENA STREET, ASPEN.

Dates played: most likely October 10–13, 1983.

E'wu's Paradise closed in 1984, but the Belly Up continues to operate; Chad Smith performed there with Les Claypool in 2015.

17. COUNTRY CLUB, 18419 SHERMAN WAY, RESEDA.

Date played: November 23, 1983.

The Country Club closed in 2000 and is now a church.

NOTES

Before the Beginning: 1982

"Get grant money": Janet Cunningham, in *An Oral/Visual History of the Red Hot Chili Peppers*, ed. Red Hot Chili Peppers and Brendan Mullen (New York: It Books), 82.

"9 p.m. until whenever": Alan Rifkin and Janet Thompson, "L.A. After Hours," *LA Weekly*, April 15, 1982.

"a no-nonsense woman": Flea quote from an undated journal entry published on his Instagram in 2019, since deleted.

Born in Melbourne: Flea, *Acid for the Children* (London: Headline Publishing Group, 2019), 36–44.

"These guys would pick up": Flea, interview by Karl Coryat, *The Bass Player Book* (San Francisco: Backbeat, 1999), 226.

"These guys couldn't really catch a break": Flea, "Bad Influence: Flea on Jazz, Drugs and His Role in 'Low Down,'" interview by Kory Grow, *Rolling Stone*, November 6, 2014, https://www.rollingstone.com/music/music-news/bad-influence-flea-on-jazz-drugs-and-his-role-in-low-down-42923/.

"We needed a bass player": Dave Thompson, *By the Way* (London: Virgin Books, 2004), 20.

"Hillel said, 'Our bass player's a jerk'": Flea, "Flea: The Hottest Chili Pepper," interview by Matt Resnicoff, *Musician*, no. 183 (January 1994), 30.

"Why don't you join our rock band": *Shangri-La*, episode 3, "Wrestling," directed by Jeff Malmberg, aired July 26, 2019, on Showtime.

"He didn't think I was ready": Jack Irons, "Jack Irons: Alt Rock Anti Hero," interview by Patrick Flanary, *Drum Magazine*, 15 May 2007, https://drummagazine.com/jack-irons-alt-rock-anti-hero/.

"I was very shy, I spoke very little English": McDonough Management, "Alain Johannes Talks About Meeting Jack Irons and Hillel Slovak," Youtube video, 1:24, June 26, 2012, https://www.youtube.com/watch?v=xCKNEfUmh_0.

"continues forty-odd years later": Flea, *Acid for the Children*, 162.

"Even though we were starting off": Anthony Kiedis, *Scar Tissue* (London: Sphere, 2004), 57.

"all the loneliest and most unwanted": Kiedis, *Scar Tissue*, 57.

Mexican alter egos: Kiedis, *Scar Tissue*, 73.

"Cal Worthington calls them": Thompson, *By the Way*, 29; Kiedis, *Scar Tissue*, 73. Cal Worthington was a local car salesman known for his cheesy advertisements.

"ringleader and agent provocateur": Steve Roeser, "Stand by Me (And My Friends)," *Goldmine*, August 7, 1992, 48.

Anthony had his first joint: Kiedis, *Scar Tissue*, 26.

Michael had his at roughly: Flea, *Acid for the Children*, 99.

"I liked to smoke weed": Flea, *Acid for the Children*, 165.

"I didn't have that hard-core addict gene": Flea, *Acid for the Children*, 166.

"disturbing the peace": Jeff Spurrier, "L.A. Beat," *Los Angeles Times*, October 18, 1981.

"a great human being": Hillel Slovak, *Behind the Sun*, ed. James Slovak (Hollywood: Slim Skinny Publications, 1999), 25.

"festivities . . . bled out into the parking lot": Flea, *Acid for the Children*, 256.

"amazing man": Flea, *Acid for the Children*, 276.

Queen's "Ogre Battle": Jeff Apter, *Fornication* (London: Omnibus Press, 2004), 32.

"There was a lot of Motown and great R&B": Jack Irons, "A Punk Globe Interview with Musician Jack Irons," interview by Ozgur Cokyuce, *PunkGlobe.com*, October 18, 2010, https://www.punkglobe.com/jackironsinteriew1010.html.

proclaiming that he would one day be a singer: Kiedis, *Scar Tissue*, 25.

stalking of the hotel that Gene Simmons and company were staying at: Apter, *Fornication*, 31.

"We cut our hair and started wearing suits": Tzvi Gluckin, "Forgotten Heroes: Hillel Slovak," *Premier Guitar*, March 17, 2015, https://www.premierguitar.com/artists/forgotten-heroes-hillel-slovak.

"I knew at that moment": Flea, "Jerky, punky, funky," *Guardian*, January 7, 2005, https://www.theguardian.com/music/2005/jan/07/1.

favorite guitarists were Andy Gill, of Gang of Four, and Jimi Hendrix: Koyaanisqatsi, "Hillel Slovak—Interview on Miami (1987)," Youtube video, 2:10, December 3, 2019 (recorded December 6, 1987), https://www.youtube.com/watch?v=6ZgWKxDb5LA.

"An audience watching a modern group": Camel Soundboard, *LA Weekly*, May 12, 1983.

"When I got back": Rick Cox, author interview, December 8, 2021. Who drummed at these shows is long forgotten, but it may have been Read Miller. The Anti Club engagement was most likely just Michael and Rick on stage together.

"Punk rock changed my life": Flea, interview by Mike McCready, *SiriusXM Pearl Jam Radio*, April 24, 2016, https://vimeo.com/167197813.

"Punk deflated the whole bloated rock-star thing": Flea, "Generation Next: Flea of the Red Hot Chili Peppers," interview by Kim Neely, *Rolling Stone*, November 17, 1994, https://www.rollingstone.com/music/music-news/generation-next-flea-of-the-red-hot-chili-peppers-71601/.

"vicious, animal energy": *Punk*, episode 3, directed by Jesse James Miller, aired March 25, 2019, on EPIX.

briefly at their last-ever show: Thompson, *By the Way*, 28.

"There was this girl": Kiedis, *Scar Tissue*, 77.

"I just thought it was disgusting": Thompson, *By the Way*, 27.

"Whatever we thought": Anthony Kiedis, *An Oral/Visual History*, 80. It's unclear if Anthony attended the same performance Michael did, but this seems to imply it.

"pulling his weight": Tim Leitch, "Spit Stix—2004," interview by Mark Prindle, *Prindle Rock and Roll Review Site,* May 2004, http://markprindle.com/stix-i.htm.

Derf himself would counter this: Fred Milner, "Derf Scratch—2004," interview by Mark Prindle, *Prindle Rock and Roll Review Site*, 2004, http://markprindle.com/scratch-i.htm.

"crazy-looking dingy storage shed": Flea, *Acid for the Children*, 331.

"I think he thought we were junkies": Apter, *Fornication*, 52.

"Man, were my reference points": Flea, *Acid for the Children*, 332.

Flea related to Stix's friend: Apter, *Fornication*, 51.

"They were all really good players": Flea, *Oral/Visual History*, 23.

"What Is This got some good deep grooves going": Flea, *Acid for the Children*, 331.

"FEAR was no kiddie punk rock band": Anthony Kiedis, *Oral/Visual History*, 23.

"He was confiding to friends": Anthony Kiedis, *Oral/Visual History*, 23.

"Hillel turned ashen": Flea, *Acid for the Children*, 334.

"Hillel softened his resentment": Flea, *Acid for the Children*, 368.

"The rhythm section was neatly polished off": Phil Heiple, "Punk Rock Triumph in Goleta," *Daily Nexus*, October 28, 1982.

The rest of the night was pure chaos: Richard Gibbs, Facebook message to author, May 13, 2020.

more pressing issue for Lee Ving: All filming dates provided by the American Film Institute, https://www.afi.com/.

Hillel and new bassist Reumschüssel clashed: Thompson, *By the Way*, 53.

Anthony implies it was in 1982: Kiedis, *Scar Tissue*, 101.

Anthony who gave him the name: Flea, "I'm Flea, ASK ME ANYTHING," Reddit, accessed September 25, 2021. https://www.reddit.com/r/IAmA/comments/2ktu98/im_flea_ask_me_anything/.

"I'd been called Flea here and there": Flea, *Acid for the Children*, 332.

"Why you wanna call yourself something": Gary Allen, *Oral/Visual History*, 19.

"He was Michael when I met him": Janet Cunningham, *Oral/Visual History*, 83.

"He was the first kid I met": Flea, "Flea Starts from Scratch," interview by Scott Malandrone, *Bass Player*, February 1996, 50.

"I was kind of a bastard": Kiedis, *Scar Tissue*, 58.

"It created a profound shift": Anthony Kiedis, *Oral/Visual History*, 24.

"The moment I set eyes on him": Penelope Spheeris, "Penelope Spheeris on Suburbia and the Little Rascals," interview by Simon Abrams, Roger Ebert, January 30, 2019, https://www.rogerebert.com/interviews/penelope-spheeris-on-suburbia-and-the-little-rascals.

"Lee introduced me as his new bass player": Flea, *Oral/Visual History*, 24.

"I was fucked up on MDA": Flea, "Close-Ups," interview by Bruce Kalberg, *NOMAG*, April–May, 1983.

"I was 20 when we were filming": Syndee Coleman, Facebook message to author, November 17, 2021.

it peaked at no. 62: Robert Hilburn, "Top 10 Singles Dance to Another Tune," *Los Angeles Times*, December 28, 1982.

"It was mind-blowing": Anthony Kiedis, "Icons," interview by Kate Sullivan, *Spin*, August 2002, 64.

"It started dawning on me": Kiedis, *Scar Tissue*, 103.

"He'd never been in a band before": Flea, "Funk Brothers," interview by Alan Di Perna, *Guitar World*, July 2006, 70.

"I had never noticed musical aspiration": Flea, *Acid for the Children*, 372.

"came into the kitchen": Flea, *Acid for the Children*, 371–372.

Show #1: December 16, 1982

dance "battles" between rival crews: Thomas Guzman-Sanchez, *Underground Dance Masters: Final History of a Forgotten Era* (Santa Barbara: Praeger, 2012), 83.

"no-strings-attached evening": Robert Hilburn, "Hollywood Showcase," *Los Angeles Times*, December 5, 1970.

The first Rhythm Lounge session: Salomon Emquies, email message to author, May 26, 2019.

"We'd hang out at the Rhythm Lounge": Flea, *Oral/Visual History*, 16.

"fashion-influenced": Gary Allen, *Oral/Visual History*, 16.

the way the story is normally told: see Thompson, *By the Way*, 50; Kiedis, *Scar Tissue*, 104; Apter, *Fornication*, 58, among many others.

"a chap named Gary Allen": Anthony Kiedis, "Rock and Roll Hall of Fame Induction Ceremony," Rock and Roll Hall of Fame, Cleveland, Ohio, filmed April 14, 2012, video of speech, https://www.youtube.com/watch?v=dEui0E4cXG0.

"Flea and Hillel were living in an apartment": Gary Allen, email message to author, punctation lightly edited for clarity, February 21, 2019.

very next day started writing his own raps: Flea, *Acid for the Children*, 372.

forgiven Flea for leaving: Flea, *Oral/Visual History*, 16.

"the unplanned, unexpected, and organic": Flea, *Acid for the Children*, 369.

"We had no idea": *Behind the Music*, "Red Hot Chili Peppers," season 2, episode 32, directed by Yann Debonne, aired May 30, 1999, on VH1.

even met the band's guitarist, Kelvyn Bell: Kiedis, *Scar Tissue*, 85; during the same trip, they caught a show by the avant-garde jazz group the Lounge Lizards, led by saxophonist John Lurie. Lurie and the band, especially Flea, would become close friends a few years later.

"make people feel the way": Kiedis, *Scar Tissue*, 86.

entirely made up in the few days: Kiedis, *Scar Tissue*, 105.

"was just a guitar riff": Jack Irons, *Oral/Visual History*, 16.

Anthony already had the lyrics: Thompson, *By the Way*, 50; Apter, *Fornication*, 58. An article in the street magazine *BAM* in 1991 even suggested it was written on the night of the gig, which is untrue.

"translating poems he had written": Flea, "Chili Con Carnage," interview by Scott Cohen, *Details for Men*, October 1991, 12.

attempt to mimic "Defunkt": Flea, "Funkin'Hell," interview by Lisa Johnson, *Raw*, January 22, 1992, 20; Flea, "Red Hot Chili Peppers," interview by Sylvie Simmons, *Mojo*, July 2004, 72.

"the very first song that we ever wrote": Flea, "Fleamail," Red Hot Chili Peppers, April 27, 2006, https://web.archive.org/web/20060504021637/http://www.redhotchilipeppers.com/news/journal.php?uid=208.

"He was still in Fear at the time": Syndee Coleman, Facebook message to author, November 16, 2021.

running through the song in the apartment: Fabrice Drouet, email message to author, September 15, 2018.

Flea repeated the same: Flea, *Acid for the Children*, 373.

Flea states it was never *rehearsed*: Flea, "The Red Hot Chili Peppers' Spicy Funk," interview by Jeff Silberman, *BAM*, June 1, 1984.

"hummed it to each other": Flea, "Born to Be Wired," interview by Cary Darling, *BAM*, August 9, 1985, 28.

quick a capella run-through: Kiedis, *Scar Tissue*, 105.

thirty people in the club: Kiedis, *Scar Tissue*, 105.

specific figure of twenty-seven: Flea, *Acid for the Children*, 374.

"the boom box up on one shoulder": Gary Allen, Facebook message to author, August 8, 2019.

dance at the opening show: Flea, *Oral/Visual History*, 16; Flea, *Acid for the Children*, 374.

first show and *at a later show*: Salomon Emquies, email message to author, May 26, 2019; Salomon Emquies, *Oral/Visual History*, 19.

under the name Tony Flow: Keidis, *Scar Tissue*, 105; Thompson, *By the Way*, 50; Dimitri Erhlich, "The Red Hot Chili Peppers," *Interview*, August 1991, 106; just three of its many appearances over the years.

made up to be farcically alliterative: Flea, *Acid for the Children*, 372.

"There was a time when Hillel and I": Anthony Kiedis, interview with fans, *99x*, June 8, 2000, https://soundcloud.com/user-121858192/rhcp-6800-99x-studio. "I used to shout across the room to you, and you'd come dancing like a fool."

"so much fun": *Behind the Music*, "Red Hot Chili Peppers," season 2, episode 32, directed by Yann Debonne, aired May 30, 1999, on VH1.

"days and days": Anthony Kiedis, *Fandemonium*, 14.

"everybody who was in that room": Kiedis, *Scar Tissue*, 106.

"BAM! From the first note": Flea, *Oral/Visual History*, 16.

"They were so good": Gary Allen, email message to author, February 21, 2019.

he was stunned: Salomon Emquies, email message to author, May 26, 2019.

conflicting, incorrect details: Thompson, *By the Way*, 50; Apter, *Fornication*, 58; Jeff Thompson, *True Men Don't Kill Coyotes* (London: Virgin, 1993), 57.

members themselves are prone to misremembering: Kiedis, *Scar Tissue*, 104; Flea, *Acid for the Children*, 374.

"It's hard to actually remember the exact date": amdation1, "Red Hot Chili Peppers MTV 2006 documentary part1," YouTube video, 9:43, September 25, 2009, https://www.youtube.com/watch?v=ziP_Oh52gRs. By "became a band," Anthony might also be referring not to the first-ever performance but to a later decision to keep the new project going.

"Way, way back in": Bram van Splunteren, "The Red Hot Chili Peppers—A Dutch Connection," Vimeo video, 1:24:10, February 10, 2019, https://vimeo.com/316406105.

February was mentioned as early as June 1984: Jeff Silberman, "The Red Hot Chili Peppers' Spicy Funk," *BAM*, June 1, 1984.

The later January 6, 1983, show: *Oral/Visual History*, 238.

newspaper advertisements for the same date: Nightclubbing, *Los Angeles Reader*, December 17, 1982.

Show #2: December 30, 1982

"performances by The Flow": Scoring the Clubs, *LA Weekly*, January 6, 1983. It's unclear if the use of the plural *performances* means the band played more than once, but it's unlikely.

Show #3: January 6, 1983

"indeed fast and hard": BigRobFR, "1983 Punk Rock Series on KTTV Channel 11 – Pt. 4," Youtube video, 3:33, April 27, 2009 (originally aired February 1983 on KTTV), https://www.youtube.com/watch?v=Df4qYYTqz7A.

Show #4: March 4, 1983

Matt Dike recalls the uncertainty: Matt Dike, *Oral/Visual History*, 19.

drawing upon jazz groups: Kiedis, *Scar Tissue*, 108.

Red Hot Peppers being another offered up: Apter, *Fornication*, 61.

Moses and his burning bush as the source: Thompson, *By the Way*, 51.

suggesting the name the Red Hots: Gary Allen, email message to author, February 21, 2019.

some of their possible selections: David Hughes, email message to author, March 2, 2020. These songs weren't necessarily played on the night, but they were in Hughes's and Callahan's collections and in heavy rotation at the time. John Callahan passed away in February 2013.

backed by the CIA: Gary Webb, "America's 'Crack' Plague Has Roots in Nicaragua War," *San Jose Mercury*, August 18, 1996.

site of a drug bust in July 1983: "58 Arrested in Hollywood Drug Raid," *Los Angeles Times*, July 25, 1983.

"Growing up in Hollywood": Anthony Kiedis, "The Red Hot Chili Peppers Eat It Raw," interview by Roy Trakin, *Musician*, December 1989, 127.

"they went down really well": Thompson, *By the Way*, 51.

Hillel who introduced the song: Kiedis, *Scar Tissue*, 109–110.

"She'll Be Coming" performance: Dave Thompson, *By the Way*, 51; though it's not clear where this information comes from. This may have also been an off-the-cuff cover of Funkadelic's "Comin' Round the Mountain," but judging from the band's later claims of ignorance toward George Clinton's music at this stage in their careers, this is unlikely.

"So fun, no thought involved": Flea, *Oral/Visual History*, 143.

"I couldn't conceive of someone": Kiedis, *Scar Tissue*, 110.

"A four piece funk combo": Craig Lee, Bruce D. Rhodewalt, Pleasant Gehman, and Marci Marks, L.A.-Dee-Da, *LA Weekly*, March 17, 1983.

"Hollywood scenesters are there": Flea, *Oral/Visual History*, 143.

Show #5: March 25, 1983

Funk to Death scrawled up top: *Oral/Visual History*, 153.

"There was absolutely no shame in our game": Kiedis, *Fandemonium*, 14.

Show #6: March 31, 1983

"My friend Kevin that I went with": Linda Kite, Facebook message to author, June 10, 2020. "I do recall telling Kevin after their set 'these guys are on to something…'"

"Local rock bands that couldn't get bookings": Cindy Jourdan, "Getting There," *LA Weekly*, December 21, 1978.

"when Brendan started the Masque": Flea, "L.A.'s Punk Magnet," *Los Angeles Times*, October 14, 2009.

"After our first record": Kiedis, *Scar Tissue*, 169.

"we checked him out": Anthony Kiedis, "Born to Be Wired," interview by Cary Darling, *BAM*, August 9, 1985, 26.

"didn't know very much about that stuff yet": Flea, *Oral/Visual History*, 29.

Bob Forrest also takes credit for introducing: Bob Forrest, *Running with Monsters* (New York: Crown Archetype, 2013), loc. 702 of 2946, Kindle.

Show #8: April 13, 1983

"place for me and my friends": Jeff Spurrier, L.A. Beat, *Los Angeles Times*, February 20, 1983.

"If someone said": Jeff Spurrier, L.A. Beat, *Los Angeles Times*, February 20, 1983.

"she's the only one": Pleasant Gehman, "Thoroughly Modern Helen: A Tribute to the Anti Club," *Pleasant Gehman: Confessions of a Postmodern Showgirl* (blog), May 4, 2014, http://pleasantgehman.blogspot.com/2014/05/thoroughly-modern-helen-tribute-to-anti.html.

"working class psychedelia": Craig Lee, "Checking out the 'Paisley Underground'," *Los Angeles Times*, December 18, 1983.

spray-painting Anthony's face: Dan Stuart, email message to author, March 29, 2020.

"peanuts and beer he was consuming": Apter, *Fornication*, 53.

Show #9: April 29, 1983

"Everyone else": Anthony Kiedis, interview by Howard Stern, *The Howard Stern Show*, WXRK, July 10, 2004.

"strange bar in LA": Thompson, *By the Way*, 57; he most likely means the Plant, even though it had been a live venue under a different name for many years. But it *was* undeniably an unusual room to see a band in.

"knew a thing or two": Blackie Dammett, *Lords of the Sunset Strip* (Beverly Hills: The Three Marketeers, 2013), loc 4986 of 9684, Kindle.

Recording Session: Early May, 1983

"For me, this whole process was": Kiedis, *Scar Tissue*, 115.

"I was just happy": Tim Leitch, email message to author, September 10, 2021.

three-hour long session was bankrolled: Kiedis, *Scar Tissue*, 194; Flea also refers to the session being three hours long in *Oral/Visual History*, 148.

Fabrice Drouet chipping in: Flea, *Acid for the Children*, 317.

Drouet attended the session: Fabrice Drouet, email message to author, May 30, 2019.

utilizing some of the tricks: Tim Leitch, email message to author, November 21, 2019.

"Himi Limi": Such as at the band's first ever performance outside the United States on August 17, 1985, in Sankt Goarshausen, Germany. Or more recently on *The Late Late Show with James Corden*, "Carpool Karaoke: Red Hot Chili Peppers," season 2, episode 129, directed by Glenn Clements, aired June 13, 2016, on CBS.

Dammett claims Thursday, May 5: Dammett, *Lords of the Sunset Strip*, loc 4986 of 5684.

"sounds about right": Tim Leitch, email message to author, November 21, 2019.

"by far the most productive": Kiedis, *Scar Tissue*, 115.

picked up a copy of the demo tape: Nate Pottker, "In Conversation with Pete Weiss," *Bob Forrest Music* (blog), December 2013, https://

bobforrestmusic.files.wordpress.com/2013/12/peteweiss_inconversation.pdf.

bundle of China White: Kiedis, *Scar Tissue*, 116.

"We weren't quite clear": Anthony Kiedis, *Oral/Visual History*, 90.

"scornful looks": Kiedis, *Scar Tissue*, 117.

"pooped all over": Flea, Liner Notes for Red Hot Chili Peppers, *The Red Hot Chili Peppers*, Red Hot Chili Peppers, recorded 1984, EMI Records, 72435-40380-2, CD.

Forrest was DJ'ing at the Cathay de Grande: Brendan Mullen, "Bob Forrest Tells All," *LA Weekly*, November 24, 1999.

"better times": Kiedis, *Scar Tissue*, 118. It should be noted that in the 2011 documentary *Bob and the Monster* (dir. Keirda Bahruth), Forrest himself seems quite unsure that this story is actually true. Anthony, on the other hand, is quite sure that it is. Neither has a world-class memory.

"It was then that I noticed Anthony": Forrest, *Running with Monsters: A Memoir*, loc 667 of 2946.

"Growing up": Kiedis, *Fandemonium*, 12; he makes several understandable and obvious exceptions, such as Jimi Hendrix.

"For six months": Forrest, *Running with Monsters: A Memoir*, loc 682 of 2946.

Show #10: May 20, 1983

"Two songs": Peter Bastone, Facebook message to author, November 21, 2019. They most likely played more than two songs, but the band's repertoire of six or seven songs only lasted about fifteen minutes anyway.

What Is This played a show: Camel Soundboard, *LA Weekly*, May 26, 1983.

"There were definitely some bizarre feelings": Thompson, *By the Way*, 53.

a vengeful and jealous bouncer: Kiedis, *Scar Tissue*, 114.

"the most recent 86'd Zero patron": Donald Adams, Red Baron, Shari Famous, Marci Marks, and Craig Lee, L.A.-Dee-Da, *LA Weekly*, June 2, 1983.

"The thing I like about the Chili Peppers": Flea, "Close-Ups," interview by Bruce Kalberg, *NOMAG*, April–May, 1983.

"We saw playing our songs": Kiedis, *Scar Tissue*, 113.

"Cliff Martinez is a great drummer": Flea, "Close-Ups."

Show #11: May 30, 1983

"bone-crunching mayhem funk": rhcpfreak2006, "Red Hot Chili Peppers—MTV Cutting Edge 1984," YouTube video, 4:59, December 19, 2007 (originally aired August 1984 on MTV), https://www.youtube.com/watch?v=Y121u9_wkpA.

"bone-crunching mayhem": DeeAnne Rodeen, "Red Hot Chili Peppers Beat It to Death," *Daily Nexus Arts and Entertainment*, April 7, 1988.

the cover was done at Hillel's request: Kiedis, *Scar Tissue*, 120.

"Any time there was an opportunity": Flea, *Oral/Visual History*, 100.

"Appearing in print or in photo in Scratch": Pleasant Gehman, "Boswelling the Scene," *LA Weekly*, September 8, 1983.

"a reaction against in-crowd snobbishness": Ruben MacBlue, in *Whores: An Oral Biography of Perry Farrell and Jane's Addiction*, ed. Brendan Mullen (Boston: Da Capo Press, 2005), loc 574 of 6120, Kindle.

Show #12: June 4, 1983

"I was just getting my feet wet": All quotes from Carmaig de Forest, author interview, February 26, 2021.

Show #13: June 5, 1983

"Everyone came in their clothes from the night before": Pleasant Gehman, "Princess of Hollywood," in *More Fun in the New World: The Unmaking and Legacy of L.A. Punk*, ed. John Doe and Tom DeSavia (Boston: Da Capo Press), 195.

"the boulevard was a gravel road": Dan Morain, "Owner Dies; Home's Future Uncertain," *Los Angeles Times*, January 20, 1983.

Horseheads show definitely happened: Steven McDonald, email message to author, January 10, 2020; Craig Lee, "Triple Bill of 'Exciting' Bands," *Los Angeles Times*, June 7, 1983.

Show #14: June 11, 1983

"Good bands seen this week": Pleasant Gehman, Shari Famous, Donald Adams, and Craig Lee, L.A.-Dee-Da, *LA Weekly*, June 23, 1983, 43.

Show #15: June 17, 1983

asking the band to open for him: Randy Stodola, Facebook message to author, March 2, 2020.

"His bowler cap": Dammett, *Lords of the Sunset Strip*, loc 5009 of 9684.

"Anthony, how long has your band": Ruben MacBlue, "Interview with the Red Hot Chili Peppers," *Scratch* #2, June 1983.

Flea made a great impression on Steven: Steven McDonald, email message to author, May 8, 2020.

meet Grandmaster Flash himself, even performing: Halloween Night, Shari Famous, Donald Adams, and Craig Lee, L.A.-Dee-Da, *LA Weekly*, July 7, 1983, 45.

"I first encountered Flea and Anthony": Brendan Mullen, introduction to *Oral/Visual History*.

"Damn, better really have our shit together": Kiedis, *Oral/Visual History*, 144.

Show #16: July 3, 1983

"It wasn't like playing for sleazy old guys": Flea, "Funk Brothers," interview by Alan Di Perna, *Guitar World*, July 2006, 72.

"Kit Kat Club is fast becoming": Pleasant Gehman, Bruce D. Rhodewalt, Craig Lee, and Marci Marks, L.A.-Dee-Da, *LA Weekly*, July 29, 1982. A few weeks later the paper would publish a photo of film star Elliot Gould arm in arm with the club's promoter, Suzanne Schott.

"too much coffee": Cliff Martinez, *Oral/Visual History*, 140.

"underwear rock": Scoring the Clubs, *LA Weekly*, March 3, 1983.

played with Flea in the group: Cliff Martinez, *Oral/Visual History*, 29.

"I went for a run": Kiedis, *Scar Tissue*, 120.

"levitating with nervous energy": Thompson, *By the Way*, 61.

"audibly gasped": Kiedis, *Scar Tissue*, 121.

"It felt great": *Behind the Music*, "Red Hot Chili Peppers," season 2, episode 32, directed by Yann Debonne, aired May 30, 1999, on VH1.

decision made *on the night*: Robin Smith, "Fighting Talk," *Record Mirror*, February 1988, 38.

"spontaneous thing to do": Apter, *Fornication*, 66.

"Since we were playing": Kiedis, *Scar Tissue*, 120.

"It might have been Hillel's": Flea, "Funk Brothers," interview by Alan Di Perna, *Guitar World*, July 2006, 72. The most recent "socks on cocks" display was in Wantagh, New York, on August 12, 2000.

"So, as a razz": Anthony Kiedis, "Anthony Kiedis," interview by Lawrence Grobel, *Penthouse*, January 2002, 123.

"People would come over": Flea, "Get a Grip: Red Hot Chili Peppers Exposed," interview by Pete Stanton, *Smash Hits*, March 1994, 36.

"It was so funny": Thompson, *By the Way*, 61.

recalled that the show was recorded: Thompson, *By the Way*, 61.

"giving the bare breasted dancers": Shari Famous, Donald Adams, and Craig Lee, L.A.-Dee-Da, *LA Weekly*, July 14, 1983.

"No pubes!": Thompson, *By the Way*, 61.

"painted green": Apter, *Fornication*, 66.

"I thought they were black": Laurie Kammerzelt, "Red Hot Chili Peppers," *Artist Magazine*, 1984, http://www.artistwd.com/joyzine/music/rh_chili_peppers/peppers.php.

Show #17: July 4, 1983

thoughts about the band's name and Anthony's lyrics: Brian Kild, email message to author, May 16, 2020.

"Southern California's badest": "Nite Life," *In Touch*, issue 85, November 1983.

Show #18: July 18, 1983

"I was psyched sitting there": Flea, *Oral/Visual History*, 144.

"wise soul": Kiedis, *Scar Tissue*, 273.

"wanted it nice and clean": Flea (@flea333), Twitter, May 8, 2021, 3:28 a.m., https://twitter.com/flea333/status/1390720207082037248. "It is Karl. I originally did it but they took off my bass and replaced it with his. He played what I had originally recorded but 'professionally' I think they replaced jack and Hillel too I can't remember. Produced by Keith Forsey. He wanted it nice and clean."

"when they were playing their hot": Richard Cromelin, "Red Hot Chili Peppers and Bad Brains," *Los Angeles Times*, July 20, 1983.

from a previous concert listing: "The Red Hot Chili Peppers, Four White Boys That Sound Like Captain Beefheart Playing James Brown" Camel Soundboard, *LA Weekly*, July 21, 1983.

"I met a guy at the Lingerie": Kiedis, *Oral/Visual History*, 26; Anthony never mentions Richardson by name, but he was a tall man who played bass and hailed from Atlanta.

"That afternoon we smoked some pot": Kiedis, *Scar Tissue*, 122.

"actually really liked Lindy": Flea, Liner Notes for Red Hot Chili Peppers, *The Red Hot Chili Peppers*, 1984. EMI Records 72435-40380-2-0, 2003.

"We got moo shu pork": Kiedis, *Scar Tissue*, 122.

Show #20: July 31, 1983

"Fast and Furious": John Danger, "Black's Paradise," *Los Angeles Record*, July 3, 1914. American Hotel history sourced from "POSTcards from the Past," Tales of the American, 2018, https://talesoftheamerican.com/history/.

"created by artists for artists": Laurie Pike, "Raise a Glass for Al's Bar—It's Last Call," *Los Angeles Times*, August 16, 2001.

"gay guy": Rachel Kreisel, "Finding Aid for American Hotel and Al's Bar Project Records," UCLA, last modified September 30, 2020, https://oac.cdlib.org/findaid/ark:/13030/c87m0dnc/entire_text/.

"hostile disco": David Velasquez, comment on "Necropolis of Love—The Hope, 1984," *Bimble's Windy Weather* (blog), January 2, 2009, http://windyweather-bimble.blogspot.com/2008/10/necropolis-of-love-hope-1984.html.

"We kept going over it": David Velasquez, Facebook message to author, April 24, 2020.

"very friendly guys": David Velasquez, Facebook message to author, April 24, 2020.

"We kept putting it off": Skip King, Facebook message to author, April 28, 2020.

showing his fresh ink off: Rick Cox, author interview, December 8, 2021.

Show #21: August 4, 1983

Hagen lip-synched to a couple: Miss Cari, Miss Shari Famous, Miss Marci Marks, Donald Adams, and C. Lee, L.A.-Dee-Da, *LA Weekly*, August 25,

1983, 41. Inside this report were the first signs that the *LA Weekly* writing staff were growing tired of the Chili Peppers' omnipresent shenanigans: "Do we have to mention *them* again?"

teaming up with brothers John and Dix Denney: Halloween Knight, Shari Famous, Marci Marks, and C. Lee, L.A.-Dee-Da, *LA Weekly*, August 11, 1983, 41.

"went north with the band": Dammett, *Lords of the Sunset Strip*, loc 5024 of 9684.

"I remember the first time": Flea (@flea333), Instagram photo, January 17, 2019, https://www.instagram.com/p/Bstzb0-B9Kq/.

Show #22: August 13, 1983

Flea's relationship with Oingo Boingo's: Richard Gibbs, Facebook message to author, May 13, 2020.

"That ought to be a": Halloween Knight, Shari Famous, Marci Marks, and C. Lee, L.A.-Dee-Da, *LA Weekly*, August 11, 1983, 41.

"a cruel new wave audience": Jeff Spurrier, "The Chili Peppers Remain Red Hot," *Los Angeles Times*, February 12, 1984.

Show #23: August 17, 1983

"Here we were with no record deal": Kiedis, *Scar Tissue*, 125. The Universal Amphitheater's capacity was six thousand, so the band may have been playing to much more. Likewise, two hundred is probably too high an estimate of an audience for many of their earlier shows around the clubs of Los Angeles.

"running amok": Dammett, *Lords of the Sunset Strip*, loc 5045 of 9684. Whether the expression "running amok" is a watered-down reference to some other racier act can only be speculated.

"weirdest clothes": Kiedis, *Scar Tissue*, 125; Jason Lloyd, January 30, 2019, comment on Emilio Loza, https://www.facebook.com/groups/179734645377051/posts/2514874038529755/.

"lobby concessions applauded": Dammett, *Lords of the Sunset Strip*, loc 5045 of 9684.

"a bathrobe and with a face full": Kiedis, *Scar Tissue*, 125; considering Elfman's sense of humor, the shaving cream may have been a visual gag.

"exploded on to the stage jumping around": Emilio Loza, May 6, 2020, comment on Duncan, https://www.facebook.com/groups/179734645377051/posts/3485683098115506/.

"acting all big-time and shit": Pete Weiss, *Oral/Visual History*, 143.

"gift for all he had accomplished": Dammett, *Lords of the Sunset Strip*, loc 5045 of 9684. By his own admission, he was also there trying to get Anthony representation for acting work, so perhaps he wasn't as confident in this new career as he was implying.

"After all the negative commotion": Dammett, *Lords of the Sunset Strip*, loc 5024 of 9684.

Show #25: September 10, 1983

"triumphant return": Kiedis, *Scar Tissue*, 126.

executives from record labels: Halloween Knight, Shari Famous, Marci Marks, Craig Lee, and Donald Adams, L.A.-Dee-Da, *LA Weekly*, September 22, 1983.

"cool and exciting thing": Kiedis, *Scar Tissue*, 122.

meetings that he and Flea would have: Kiedis, *Scar Tissue*, 122.

"whereby the two labels": "Enigma Records," *New on the Charts*, August 1984, 17.

"recording demos for an interested label": Halloween Knight, Shari Famous, Donald Adams, and C. Lee, L.A.-Dee-Da, *LA Weekly*, August 18, 1983. If the band did record another set of demos in later 1983 prior to Hillel and Jack leaving, they have not been referenced by any member of the band in the years since, and have not surfaced unofficially.

"particularly aggressive": Kiedis, *Scar Tissue*, 126.

"If we were going to try": Kiedis, *Scar Tissue*, 122.

Show #26: September 18, 1983

"I was still excited": Kiedis, *Scar Tissue*, 126; his retelling is almost certainly a condensed version of events.

"It wasn't like these were incidental guys": Kiedis, *Scar Tissue*, 126.

"emotionally devastated": Apter, *By the Way*, 65.

retold in band biographies and interviews: Apter's *Fornication* implies the Chili Peppers got their deal first (71); Thompson's *By the Way* refers to a "simultaneous" offer (64). Linda Laban gets it right ("Red Hot Chili Peppers," *Record Collector*, August 1990, 64).

considered by MCA in early September: Halloween Knight, Shari Famous, Marci Marks, Craig Lee, and Donald Adams, L.A.-Dee-Da, *LA Weekly*, September 22, 1983.

"Hillel and Jack told me": Lindy Goetz, *Oral/Visual History*, 28.

"would never have worked out": Thompson, *By the Way*, 64.

"We'd been with this group": Thompson, *By the Way*, 64.

"Once I started thinking": Kiedis, *Scar Tissue*, 127.

"immediately suggested": Kiedis, *Scar Tissue*, 127.

"I not only wanted to be a musician": Cliff Martinez, "Interview: Cliff Martinez," interview by Mister French, *The Offline People*, February 19, 2011, http://theofflinepeople.blogspot.com/2011/02/interview-cliff-martinez.html.

"ungodly racket": Apter, *Fornication*, 73.

could play every rhythm track: Jerry Kishbaugh, "Captain Beefheart Preparing 'Ice Cream for Crow'," *Citizen's Voice*, March 26, 1982.

"wacky one-room apartment": Kiedis, *Scar Tissue*, 127.

"I'd seen the Chili Peppers several times": Cliff Martinez, *Oral/Visual History*, 29.

"It was a style": Apter, *Fornication*, 74.

they decided to play anyway: Chris Ziegler, "The Weirdos: We Were Toxic," *Los Angeles Record*, December 13, 2013, https://larecord.com/interviews/2013/12/13/the-weirdos-we-were-toxic.

"loveable fellow": Kiedis, *Scar Tissue*, 127.

"Things were shaky enough": Goetz, *Oral/Visual History*, 28.

"new Chili Peppers": Halloween Knight, Marci Marks, and Craig Lee, L.A.-Dee-Da, *LA Weekly*, October 13, 1983.

whole band would be traveling: Halloween Knight, Shari Famous, Marci Marks, Craig Lee, and Donald Adams, L.A.-Dee-Da, *LA Weekly*, September 22, 1983.

visited London, Paris, and Amsterdam: Kiedis, *Scar Tissue*, 127.

acid, and imbibing it in the cemetery: Flea (@flea333), Twitter, March 26, 2020, 2:42 a.m., https://twitter.com/flea333/status/1242839350246690817. "Just to be clear, the majority of my first ever trip to London was spent in Catford. I took acid in the Catford cemetery. Summer of '83." "Taking acid in a graveyard" is a lyric in the 2016 Red Hot Chili Peppers song "Dreams of a Samurai," which may or may not be related to this formative period. Of course, graveyards and cemeteries are two different things . . .

chalked up either to a fight: Kiedis, *Oral/Visual History*, 92.

"ditched": Kiedis, *Scar Tissue*, 128.

"it made a gonglike noise": Kiedis, *Oral/Visual History*, 95.

lost the jacket and the cups: Kiedis, *Scar Tissue*, 7.

L.A.-Dee-Da mention of the trip: Halloween Knight, Shari Famous, Marci Marks, Craig Lee, and Donald Adams, L.A.-Dee-Da, *LA Weekly*, September 22, 1983.

The next mention of it: Halloween Knight, Marci Marks, and Craig Lee, L.A.-Dee-Da, *LA Weekly*, October 13, 1983.

"funky bass player": Classified, *LA Weekly*, October 6, 1983.

"in particular thanks": "Club Lingerie," *LA Weekly*, October 6, 1983.

absconded with the rent money: Forrest, *Running with Monsters*, loc 716 of 2946.

"they posted notices": Kiedis, *Scar Tissue*, 128. A late rent notice, dated November 1, 1983, is reproduced on page 85 of *Oral/Visual History*. This date implies they might have actually been evicted a few weeks *after* returning from Europe.

Show #27: Circa October 10–13, 1983

"on their way to Aspen": Shari Famous, Donald Adams, and Craig Lee, L.A.-Dee-Da, *LA Weekly*, July 14, 1983.

"truly going to be the next big thing": Deanne Franklin, email message to author, April 9, 2020. Ironically, years later, Fair worked at EMI with the band, executive producing 1989's "Show Me Your Soul" for the *Pretty Woman* soundtrack.

"make it big": David Moss, March 1, 2016, comment on Moss, https://www.facebook.com/groups/aspenusa/posts/616117951868500/. The connection between Bono, his wife, Cher, and the Kiedis family can be explored further in *Lords of the Sunset Strip* and *Scar Tissue*.

band being asked to leave by Moss: Sherri Franklin, email message to author, April 9, 2020.

rendition of the Beverly Hillbillies theme song: Gary Allen, email message to author, February 21, 2019.

"They told us to take": Gilbert Garcia, "The Chili Peppers' Flea discusses 'Magic' inspirations," *Daily Texan*, March 9, 1989. David Moss said in an April 9, 2020 Facebook message to the author that there was "much more to the story" and that it "involved a physical altercation," perhaps with an audience member, but he was not forthcoming on any details. Sadly, Moss passed away in December 2020.

"so pissed": Sherri Franklin, email message to author, April 9, 2020.

"prepared a beautiful organic dinner": Gary Allen, email message to author, August 30, 2020.

"We all got high": Sherri Franklin, email message to author, April 9, 2020.

"We left and will never play there again": Thompson, *By the Way*, 56.

the year's first heavy snow: Nolan J. Doesken and Thomas B. McKee, *Colorado Climate Summary, Water-Year Series, October 1983–September 1984, Climatology Report* (Fort Collins, CO: Colorado Climate Center, February 1985).

"their onstage patter": Kiedis, *An Oral Visual History of the Red Hot Chili Peppers*, 24.

"I learned how to talk": Flea, *Acid for the Children*, 335.

one catalyst for him leaving: Flea, *Acid for the Children*, 361.

Show #28: October 29, 1983

"There is a deep-rooted": Pleasant Gehman, Marci Marks, and Craig Lee, L.A.-Dee-Da, *LA Weekly*, December 22, 1983.

Show #29: November 7, 1983

"some in-crowders were claiming": Halloween Knight, Carri and Craig Lee, L.A.-Dee-Da, *LA Weekly*, November 17, 1983.

Flea's head-banging antics: Rosie Flores, email message to author, October 19, 2020.

"wasn't cutting it": Kiedis, *Scar Tissue*, 130.

"We thought we would always be": Kiedis, *Scar Tissue*, 131.

"RED HOT CHILI PEPPERS Need": Classified, *LA Weekly*, November 17, 1983.

managed to meet Hugh Hefner: Halloween Knight, Miss Carri, Marci Marks, and Craig Lee, L.A.-Dee-Da, *LA Weekly*, November 24, 1983.

Show #30: November 23, 1983

"the cream of country music talent": Charles A. Barrett, "Lavish Country Music Nitery to Open by Owner of Roxy," *Hollywood Reporter*, November 19, 1979.

"Chili Peppers was something": Jeff Spurrier, "Slap in the Ear by What Is This," *Los Angeles Times*, March 18, 1984.

no memories of the Chili Peppers: Peter Case, email message to author, September 17, 2020.

also did not recall anything: Tony Marsico, Facebook message to author, September 17, 2020.

"he was a great kid": Tony Marsico, *Late Nights with Bob Dylan* (Los Angeles: Swingomatic, 2008), n.p.

"vibe . . . was growing stale": Flea, *Acid for the Children*, 360.

the band rehearsed Flea's original material: Tim Leitch, "Spit Stix—2004," interview by Mark Prindle, *Prindle Rock and Roll Review Site,* May 2004, http://markprindle.com/stix-i.htm.

"I just said straight up": Rick Cox, author interview, December 8, 2021.

"a lot of people": Kiedis, *Scar Tissue*, 131. No other names besides Rick Cox, Jack Sherman or Mark 9 have ever been mentioned, but Jack Sherman stated in a 2014 interview with *The Five Count* that "many, many, many people" auditioned for the spot, and a 1984 interview with the whole band in *BAM* magazine (Jeff Silberman, "The Red Hot Chili Peppers' Spicy Funk," *BAM*, June 1, 1984) gives the figure of thirty.

"air raid siren": Jack Sherman, "Interview with Jack Sherman," interview by RealInspectorShane, Michael Steele, July 2010, https://web.archive.org/web/20130702122639/http://www.mickisteele.net/jack_sherman.html.

"We were starting to spin our wheels": Sherman, "Interview with Jack Sherman," interview by RealInspectorShane.

"She said a couple of guys": Jack Sherman, "Interview with Jack Morris Sherman," interview by Max Elfimov, February 2018, http://rhrsandse.tilda.ws/.

"It was a pleasant conversation": Sherman, "Interview with Jack Morris Sherman," interview by Elfimov.

"I remember seeing this guy": Sherman, "Interview with Jack Morris Sherman," interview by Elfimov.

band's lead singer was absent: Kiedis, *Scar Tissue*, 133–136.

"Shaking his head from side to side violently": Apter, *Fornication*, 74.

"I always liked to play funk music": Jeff Silberman, "The Red Hot Chili Peppers' Spicy Funk," *BAM*, June 1, 1984.

"old-hat": Jack Sherman, "An Evening with the Red Hot Chili Peppers' Jack Sherman," interview by Dustin Wilmes and Justin Cline, *The Five Count*, July 2014, http://thefivecount.com/interviews/an-evening-with-the-red-hot-chili-peppers-jack-sherman/.

"huge incentive": Apter, *Fornication*, 75.

"to make it": Sherman, "Evening with Jack Sherman," interview by Wilmes and Cline.

"He's drumming away": Sherman, "Evening with Jack Sherman," interview by Wilmes and Cline.

"hip avant-garde art school refugee": Kiedis, *Scar Tissue*, 132.

"I heard about them from him": John Frusciante, *Oral/Visual History*, 30.

"roof-raising": Apter, *Fornication*, 74.

"How in the world": Apter, *Fornication*, 74.

"Almost like this resentful acceptance": Sherman, "Evening with Jack Sherman," interview by Wilmes and Cline.

"We played some of our songs": Kiedis, *Scar Tissue*, 132.

"He wasn't the raw": Kiedis, *Scar Tissue*, 133.

"really good player" and "amazing guitar player": Flea & Lindy Goetz, *Oral/Visual History*, 29.

"embracing": Kiedis, *Scar Tissue*, 132.

"cascading harmony": Sherman, "Interview with Jack Morris Sherman," interview by Max Elfimov, February 2018, http://rhrsandse.tilda.ws/.

"Something in me wanted the acceptance": Jack Sherman, "An Evening with the Red Hot Chili Peppers' Jack Sherman," interview by Dustin Wilmes and Justin Cline, *The Five Count*, July 2014, http://thefivecount.com/interviews/an-evening-with-the-red-hot-chili-peppers-jack-sherman/.

"We were on stage": Jack Sherman, "Interview with Jack Morris Sherman," interview by Elfimov.

other agreement was a four-part split: Apter, *Fornication*, 89.

Epilogue: March 9, 10, or 11, 1984

Viewership wasn't the only issue: David Leboitz, "Talk Show Graveyard: Thicke of the Night," *Deadshirt*, July 2, 2014, http://deadshirt.net/2014/07/02/talk-show-graveyard-thicke-of-the-night/; and Darrell Vickers, former staff member on the show, email message to author, December 12, 2020.

INDEX

Page numbers in *italics* refer to photographs.